KU-216-597

SHORTLIST

London
2010

WHAT'S NEW | WHAT'S ON | WHAT'S BEST

www.timeout.com/london

London

Contents

London by Area

Essentials

Published by Time Out Guides Ltd
Universal House
251 Tottenham Court Road
London W1T 7AB
Tel: + 44 (0)20 7813 3000
Fax: + 44 (0)20 7813 6001
Email: guides@timeout.com
www.timeout.com

Managing Director Peter Fiennes
Editorial Director Ruth Jarvis
Business Manager Dan Allen
Editorial Manager Holly Pick
Assistant Management Accountant Ija Krasnikova

Time Out Guides is a wholly owned subsidiary of Time Out Group Ltd.

© Time Out Group Ltd
Chairman Tony Elliott
Chief Executive Officer David King
Group General Manager/Director Nichola Coulthard
Time Out Communications Ltd MD David Pepper
Time Out International Ltd MD Cathy Runciman
Time Out Magazine Ltd Publisher/Managing Director Mark Elliott
Production Director Mark Lamond
Group IT Director Simon Chappell
Marketing & Circulation Director Catherine Demajo

Time Out and the Time Out logo are trademarks of Time Out Group Ltd.

This edition first published in Great Britain in 2009 by Ebury Publishing
A Random House Group Company
Company information can be found on www.randomhouse.co.uk
Random House UK Limited Reg. No. 954009
10 9 8 7 6 5 4 3 2 1

Distributed in the US by Publishers Group West
Distributed in Canada by Publishers Group Canada

For further distribution details, see www.timeout.com

ISBN: 978-1-84670-131-3

A CIP catalogue record for this book is available from the British Library.

Printed and bound in Germany by Appl.

The Random House Group Limited supports The Forest Stewardship Council (FSC), the leading international forest certification organisation. All our titles that are printed on Greenpeace approved FSC certified paper carry the FSC logo. Our paper procurement policy can be found at www.rbooks.co.uk/environment.

Time Out carbon-offsets all its flights with Trees for Cities (www.treesforcities.org).

London Shortlist

The **Time Out London Shortlist 2010** is one of a series of annual guides that draws on Time Out's background as a magazine publisher to keep you current with everything that's going on in town. As well as London's key sights and the best of its eating, drinking and leisure options, it picks out the most exciting venues to have opened in the last year and gives a full calendar of events from September 2009 to December 2010. It also includes features on the important news, trends and openings, all compiled by local editors and writers. Whether you're visiting for the first time in your life or the first time this year, you'll find the *Time Out London Shortlist* contains all you need to know, in a portable and easy-to-use format.

The guide divides central London into five areas, each containing listings for Sights & Museums, Eating & Drinking, Shopping, Nightlife and Arts & Leisure, and maps pinpointing their locations. At the front of the book are chapters rounding up these scenes city-wide, and giving a shortlist of our overall picks. We also include itineraries for days out, plus essentials such as transport information and hotels.

Our listings give phone numbers as dialled within London. To dial them from elsewhere in the UK, preface them with 020; from abroad, use your country's exit code followed by 44 (the country code for the UK), 20 and the number given.

We have noted price categories by using one to four pound signs (£-££££), representing budget, moderate, expensive and luxury. Major credit cards are accepted unless otherwise stated. We also indicate when a venue is NEW and give **Event highlights**.

All our listings are double-checked, but places do sometimes close or change their hours or prices, so it's a good idea to call a venue before visiting. While every effort has been made to ensure accuracy, the publishers cannot accept responsibility for any errors that this guide may contain.

Venues are marked on the maps using symbols numbered according to their order within the chapter and colour-coded as follows:

❶ Sights & Museums
❶ Eating & Drinking
❶ Shopping
❶ Nightlife
❶ Arts & Leisure

Map key	
Major sight or landmark	
Railway station	
Underground station	⊖
Park	
Hospital	
Casualty unit	✚
Church	✚
Synagogue	✿
Congestion Zone	Ⓒ
District	MAYFAIR
Theatre	●

Time Out **London** Shortlist 2010

About **Time Out**

Founded in 1968, Time Out has expanded from humble London beginnings into the leading resource for those wanting to know what's happening in the world's greatest cities. As well as our influential what's-on weeklies in London, New York and Chicago, we publish nearly 30 other listings magazines in cities as varied as Beijing and Mumbai. The magazines established Time Out's trademark style: sharp writing, informed reviews and bang up-to-date inside knowledge of every scene.

Time Out made the natural leap into travel guides in the 1980s with the City Guide series, which now extends to over 50 destinations around the world. Written and researched by expert local writers and generously illustrated with original photography, the full-size guides cover a larger area than our Shortlist guides and include many more venue reviews, along with additional background features and a full set of maps.

Throughout this rapid growth, the company has remained proudly independent, still owned by Tony Elliott over four decades after he started Time Out London as a single fold-out sheet of A5 paper. This independence extends to the editorial content of all our publications, this Shortlist included. No establishment has been featured because it has advertised, and no payment has influenced any of our reviews. As for our critics, there's definitely no such thing as a free lunch: all restaurants and bars are visited and reviewed anonymously, and Time Out always picks up the bill.

For more about the company, see www.timeout.com.

Don't Miss 2010

Saatchi Gallery

WHAT'S BEST
Sights & Museums

One effect of London winning the 2012 Olympics has been that the year tends now to occupy the minds of planners as the ultimate deadline for new openings and improvements: witness two blockbuster expansions – huge extensions for two of the city's world-class attractions, Tate Modern (p65) and the British Museum (p120) – both of them due for, yes, 2012. But even in the shadow of the great sporting jamboree (and you can see progress on the main stadium in east London from the tube or DLR near Stratford), there has been plenty of action.

The South Bank remains London's key tourist destination. The principal attractions are well established – Tate Modern, Shakespeare's Globe (p63) and Borough Market (p69); the County Hall triumvirate (p58) and the

London Eye (p63); the Southbank Centre (p73) – but in the last year the Aquarium has received a major refurb, the Garden Museum (p59) has been given a terrific redesign and the eccentric mural of the Topolski Century (p65) has finally reopened in the railway arches behind the Royal Festival Hall.

Across the river, the City authorities have been making a concerted effort to alter the reputation of the most ancient part of London as a place for bankers rather than pleasure-seekers. It should be an easy sell, given the number of wonderful historic attractions here – the Tower of London (p163) and St Paul's (p162) are only the best known – and easy access from the South Bank over the Millennium Bridge. St Paul's and the Monument (p162) have

SHORTLIST

Best new
- British Music Experience (p185)
- Saatchi Gallery (p94)

Most welcome returns
- Garden Museum (p59)
- Monument (p162)
- Museum of London (p108)
- Royal Institution & Faraday Museum (p108)
- Whitechapel Art Gallery (p179)

Best views
- London Eye (p63)
- St Paul's Cathedral (p162)
- Top deck of a Heritage Routemaster bus (p76)
- Westminster Cathedral (p79)

Best free attractions
- British Museum (p120)
- Natural History Museum (p85)
- Sir John Soane's Museum (p153)
- Tate Britain (p78)
- Victoria & Albert Museum (p88)
- Wellcome Collection (p126)

Best unsung attractions
- Old Operating Theatre (p63)
- Petrie Museum (p121)
- Wallace Collection (p101)

Best late events
- British Museum (p120)
- Tate Britain (p78)
- Victoria & Albert Museum (p88)

Best outdoor
- Swimming in the Hampstead Heath ponds (p170)
- Thames Clipper back from the O2 Arena (p188)
- Watching the herons in Regent's Park (p98)

been splendidly refurbished (for a guided walk around various Wren buildings, see pp51-53). Don't neglect the often disregarded Museum of London (p108), which should gain a more central place in visitors' affections when the £20.5m of improvements are completed in spring 2010. There will be four impressive new galleries and inviting street-level windows, through which you'll be able to peer in at the Lord Mayor's golden coach. Also in 2010, starchitect Jean Nouvel's new shopping centre, One New Change, will open (see box p167).

Fans of art are especially well catered for in London these days. As well as superstars Tate Modern, Tate Britain (p78) and the National Gallery (p76), visitors can now check out the new homes of the Saatchi Gallery (p94) and Haunch of Venison (p107). Quirkier delights are the 20th-century classics at the creaky old Courtauld (p149) and Trafalgar Square's controversial Fourth Plinth (see box p77). East

The biggest and the best Sunday Market in England. Bargains galore, acres of parking, fantastic food court delights.
Wembley Market open Sundays.

WEMBLEY SUNDAY MARKET

Directions: Wembley Park tube or follow brown signs to Wembley Stadium
wembleymarket.co.uk   01895 632221
Closed for major stadium events check for details

WENDY FAIR MARKETS

Victoria & Albert Museum

London's Whitechapel Art Gallery (p179) has also received a terrific refurbishment, at once improving the gallery's ability to display challenging work, and preserving the character of the early 20th-century buildings it inhabits.

The always rewarding Science Museum (p88) has now been joined by a number of scientific and medical museums – the Wellcome Collection (p126) and reborn Royal Institution & Faraday Museum (p108) are notable – while literature gets a boost with the reopening of Keats House (p171) in Hampstead – in good time for the release of Jane Campion's *Bright Star* biopic – and pop music has its first interactive museum in the shape of the British Music Experience (p185).

Brilliant though these all are, first-time and return visitors alike are inevitably going to spend most time at the headline attractions. The 'Moctezuma' blockbuster show (see box p123) and five new galleries at the British Museum should be a big success, and millions will enjoy the wing of new galleries (we're loving the Buddhas) at the V&A (p88) and the Darwin Centre at the NHM (p85).

Doing the geography

This book is divided by area. The **South Bank** primarily covers riverside Bankside, home of Tate Modern, and the revamped Southbank Centre. Over the river, **Westminster & St James's** cover the centre of UK politics, while the impressive Victorian museums of **South Kensington**, the Knightsbridge department stores, and the boutiques and eateries of **Chelsea** lie to the west.

The **West End** includes most of what is now central London. We start north of unlovely Oxford Street, in the elegant, slightly raffish shopping district of **Marylebone**. South, between Marylebone and St James's, is **Mayfair**, as expensive as its reputation but less daunting, with fine mews and pubs. Eastward are **Fitzrovia**, its elegant streets

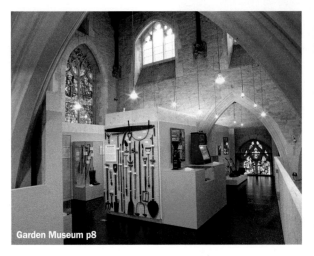

Garden Museum p8

speckled with inviting shops and restaurants; the squares and Georgian terraces of literary **Bloomsbury**, home of academia and the British Museum; and up-and-coming area **King's Cross**. Head south for **Covent Garden**, so popular with tourists that locals often forget about the charms of its boutique shopping, and **Soho**, notorious centre of filth and fun.

The **City** comprises the once-walled Square Mile of the original city, now adjoined by the focal area for bars and clubs, Shoreditch; **Holborn & Clerkenwell** have wonderful food.

Around these central districts **neighbourhood London** has clusters of fine restaurants, bars and clubs, servicing what are mainly residential zones, but also some of London's must-sees: Greenwich, Kew and Hampton Court Palace.

Making the most of it

Some tips for getting the best out of London in 2010. Don't be scared of the transport system: invest in an Oyster travel smartcard (p213) and travel cashless through the city by bus and tube. Buses are best for getting a handle on the topography. Some good sightseeing routes are RV1 (riverside), 7, 8 and 12, along with the Routemaster Heritage Routes (p76). Crime in central London is low, so walking is often the best way to appreciate its many character changes. No one thinks any the less of someone consulting a map – so long as they dive out of the stream of pedestrian traffic. And, despite our reputation, most Londoners will be happy to help with directions.

To avoid the worst of the crowds, avoid the big draws at weekends and on late-opening nights, and aim to hit exhibitions in the middle of their run. Last entry can be up to an hour before closing time (we specify where last entry is more than an hour before closing), so don't turn up just before a place closes. Some sights close at Christmas and Easter – ring ahead to confirm openings.

Albion

WHAT'S BEST
Eating & Drinking

Last year was an especially hard one for London's restaurateurs. The crumbling economy has meant there's hardly been a shortage of restaurant-related casualties: Tom Aikens' eco-friendly chippy Tom's Place, nominated for *Time Out* magazine's best sustainable restaurant award, was nonetheless forced to shut after just six months of operation; another promising eaterie, Aaya (owned by Gary Yau, brother of acclaimed restaurateur Alan Yau) only survived for a similar period.

Even so, London has been showing true British 'chin up and carry on' spirit, with figures for the latter half of 2008 indicating a record number of restaurant openings, many of them still surprisingly high-profile ventures. A single luxury hotel – the

wonderfully traditional Connaught (p202) – welcomed two restaurants from Hélène Darroze, grand dame of French cuisine, as well as a great pair of excellent, stylish bars – the Coburg and the coolly sophisticated Connaught Bar (p108). Indeed, London's top-end cocktail venues are drawing the capital's drinking scene ever closer to New York or Sydney, and there are now stellar bars all over town: for starters, try Player (p135) in Soho, Calloo Callay (p165) in Shoreditch or Westbourne House (p191) in Notting Hill.

Angela Hartnett, Darroze's predecessor at the Connaught, bolstered her position as one of the country's top female chefs with the understated rustic Italian food at her new Mayfair restaurant Murano and a posh 'gastropub' and deli operation in grand historic premises: York & Albany (p209) up in north London.

A far more modest opening was Paul Merrony's Giaconda Dining Room (p142), amid the guitar shops of London's 'Tin Pan Alley'. A top chef in his native Sydney, Merrony's restaurant arrived without fanfare, but quickly gained a loyal following with its brilliantly conceived modern international menu. The return of Anna Hansen – one of the original co-owners of the Providores & Tapa Room (p103) – to the dining scene with Clerkenwell's Modern Pantry (p156) was also handled quietly, but soon jolted the tired concept of 'fusion food' out of its torpor. In Chelsea, Sushinho (p96) has also given fusion a kick-start, bringing together an exciting mix of Brazilian bar culture and neat Japanese food.

Despite such global shenanigans, flying the flag for Brit bites has never been more fashionable. St Pancras Grand (p127), with British chef Billy Reid at the reins, was one of many openings to highlight the glory of modern and traditional British cooking. Meanwhile, young chef Tristan Welch brought British cooking further into the limelight with his witty interpretations of British classics at the relaunched Launceston Place (p89) – his 'Cornish cream tea' with raspberry foam and Earl Grey tea ice-cream is not to be missed. Likewise, Sir Terence Conran's dedication to pure Brit flavour was epitomised in his Boundary Project – Albion (p164), the casual caff set on the ground floor serves unpretentious, nostalgic dishes from kedgeree to welsh rarebit. And the Michelin men finally crowned British stalwart St John (p157) with a star in January 2009 – a move that was long overdue. A third outpost of this

SHORTLIST

Best new eats
- Ba Shan (p129)
- Bocca di Lupo (p132)
- Corrigan's Mayfair (p108)
- Giaconda Dining Room (p142)
- Trishna (p105)
- York & Albany (p209)

Best of British
- Albion (p164)
- Launceston Place (p89)
- St John (p157)
- St Pancras Grand (p127)

Best global scoff
- Hakkasan (p115)
- Modern Pantry (p156)
- Moro (p157)
- Providores & Tapa Room (p103)
- Sushinho (p96)

Best for vegetarians
- Beatroot (p129)
- Ottolenghi (p172)
- Saf (p166)
- Tibits (p111)

Best drop-in nosh
- Cha Cha Moon (p133)
- Hummus Bros (p122)
- Lantana (p115)
- Princi (p135)

Best gastropubs
- Anchor & Hope (p66)
- Eagle (p156)
- Harwood Arms (p94)

Best traditional pubs
- French House (p134)
- Lamb & Flag (p143)
- Ye Olde Mitre (p159)

Best for cocktails & wine
- Calloo Callay (p165)
- Connaught Bar (p108)
- Terroirs (p144)

wagamama

uk ı ireland ı holland ı australia ı uae ı belgium ı new zeal

Modern Pantry p15

modern British pioneer – simple, classic combinations of gutsy, carefully sourced ingredients – is due to open in the West End in late 2009. We can't wait.

Gastropubs have also been contributing to the revolution in modern British dining, and have become an enduring feature of the London culinary repertoire, with star openings including Mike Robinson's Harwood Arms (p94) in Fulham and the Bull & Last (p171) in Highgate. Don't neglect the old favourites: Anchor & Hope (p66) and, daddy of them all, the Eagle (p156) still turn out top nosh in relaxed surroundings.

Against the backdrop of all this Britishness, it comes as some relief that ethnic eateries continue to flourish so widely. The world's food is well represented by the quality of restaurants such as the Snazz Sichuan (p127), home-style Thai from Brick Lane's caff-style Rosa's (p181), and stellar dim sum destination Yum Cha (p172) in Camden. And longer-established foreign cuisines – those of Spain

and Italy – are still very much in favour, as proven by the expansion of the Brindisa group to include two new tapas restaurants: Soho's Tierra Brindisa and Casa Brindisa (p89) in South Kensington. Alan Yau, in a surprise break from his Chinese roots, teamed up with expert Italian baker Rocco Princi to set up Princi (p135) and wow the denizens of Soho with freshly baked breads, as well as excellent pizzas, pastas and pastries; he has also expanded his existing Chinese noodle bars, with a new Whiteleys shopping centre branch being added in early 2009 to the original Soho Cha Cha Moon (p133).

Indian food is another strong presence, with a new branch of the haute cuisine Cinnamon Club, Cinnamon Kitchen (p165), having opened in the City; Mumbai's world-renowned Trishna seafood restaurant (p105) arriving in Marylebone; and new, cheaper options like Chaat (p180) springing up. Ba Shan (p129), the third opening from the team behind Chinese restaurants Bar Shu and

Baozi Inn (p129), opened with little fanfare in spring 2009 but quickly gained some considerable critical acclaim; the 'tapas'-style serving of Sichuanese and north-eastern Chinese dishes proved a delight.

Terroirs (p144) and Bocca di Lupo (p132) took the top two spots in *Time Out* magazine's annual top 50 restaurants feature, despite having only just opened. The winning formula at the former was an exceptional 'natural' wine list and inspired artisanal nibbles, while the latter wowed diners with ex-Moro chef Jacob Kenedy's rustic and regional Italian fare.

Some of the old hands were keen to show they still hadn't lost their touch: on the day Richard Corrigan announced he would be closing long-standing favourite Lindsay House, he also launched Corrigan's Mayfair (p108) to much applause; J Sheekey launched a spanking-new oyster bar next door to the original seafood restaurant; and the River Café reopened – better than ever – in September 2008 after months of refurbishment following fire damage. Another talented chef due to reappear on the scene as we go to press is Maria Elia, who will head up the brand-new Dining Room in the magnificently refurbished Whitechapel Art Gallery (p179). We're also still waiting eagerly for David Thompson's Long Chim – a casual Thai eaterie from the man whose supreme mastery of Thai cooking can for now only be sampled in the very expensive surroundings of Belgravia's Nahm. Pastries are also likely to be big news in the capital – Ladurée is to open a City branch, and rumours are flying that master pâtissier-chocolatier Pierre Hermé will open a London venture. On the London dining scene, the only difficulty is keeping up.

Neighbourhood watch

The **South Bank**, close to foodie-magnet Borough Market (p69), offers plenty of quality chain options on the riverside – check out Skylon for a drink with fantastic views – but **Soho**, in the West End just across the river, is probably the best place in London for both cheap and chic bites: canteen-style Busaba Eathai (p132), Hummus Bros (p122) and Princi do a brisk trade near upmarket neighbours such as Bocca di Lupo, Arbutus (p128) and Dehesa (p133). Also in the West End, **Covent Garden** remains a busy tourist trap, but some very decent options have emerged, from ice-cream at Scoop (p144) to Mexican at Wahaca (p145) or Indian at Masala Zone (p142). Expense-account eats are concentrated in **Mayfair**: top-name chefs here include Claude Bosi at Hibiscus (p109) and Jason Atherton at Maze (p110). Further west, **Marylebone** is another foodie enclave, replete with top-notch delis, cafés and – on Sundays – a farmers' market. Superb options here include the formidable L'Autre Pied (p101) and La Fromagerie (p101). Both **South Kensington** and **Chelsea** do expensive, special-occasion destinations, such as Zuma (p92), but the arrival of the likes of Casa Brindisa and the Botanist (p95) has brought in more affordable fare. The **City** still isn't great for evening eats, though some places – among them L'Anima (p164) – now open at weekends. **Clerkenwell** next door is famously a culinary hotspot: from the Modern Pantry to the Clerkenwell Kitchen (p155), via the Eagle, St John and Moro (p157), most London restaurant trends are or have been represented here. **Shoreditch**, just north-east of the City, is still the place for a top night out – and the bars are being joined by some interesting restaurants.

Store Rooms p23

Shopping

Londoners are unstoppable
shoppers. Yes, they've been
battered by the recession, but the
economic downturn has also
underlined their tenacity: unable
to resist a bargain, they're still
trawling the city's street markets
and superluxe department stores
and sniffing out the snips in
flagship fashion outlets, world-
class boutiques and tradition-
soaked arcades on a shopping tour
of duty that will surely never end.

In the past year, London's
shopkeepers have fallen back on
their creative instincts, thinking
up increasingly wily ways to tempt
customers in. High-concept pop-up
shops, packed with limited edition
products, appear and disappear
across the capital; high-street
outlets stock young design talent
at budget prices; and department

stores are refreshed and renewed.
At Europe's largest urban shopping
mall, the new Westfield London
(p192), international luxury labels
are still making a noise.

Fashionable young things

London's design strength has long
been its young upstarts: recent
graduates firmly entrenched in
the youth scene that they design
for. Man-of-the-moment Henry
Holland garnered feverish attention
at London Fashion Week with his
loopy, colour-drenched styles, but
it's Gareth Pugh savvy Londoners
have pinned their hopes on. The
recent *Time Out* magazine guest
editor's dark, fetish-like creations
can sell for £1,105 a pop, and his
presence on the local fashion scene
pushed street style – that genre of

ART FOR LESS

£7.95
WINSOR & NEWTON
WINTON OIL 200ML
TITANIUM WHITE
DOUBLE PACK
RRP £20.60

LESS THAN HALF PRICE

£4.95
WINSOR & NEWTON
COTMAN WATERCOLOUR
POCKETS SKETCHERS BOX
RRP £10.50

LESS THAN HALF PRICE

LESS THAN HALF PRICE

SPECIAL OFFER

£9.95
MOLESKINE
SKETCHBOOK
13X21CM
100 PAGES
RRP £12.95

£9.95
MOLESKINE
WATERCOLOUR
NOTEBOOK
9X14CM 200GSM
RRP £12.95

CASS VALUE

£9.95
CASS ART
HOG BRUSH PACK
SET OF 6
RRP £18.95

£6.50
FABER CASTELL
9000 8B-2H
12 DRAWING PENCILS
RRP £13.50

LESS THAN HALF PRICE

SPECIAL OFFER

HALF PRICE

£6.95
SEAWHITE
A5 CONCERTINA
SKETCHBOOK
70 PAGES 140GSM

£4.95
LETRASET
PROMARKER 5 SETS
RRP £9.95

£3.95
DALER-ROWNEY
OIL PASTEL
SET OF 24
RRP £10.25

LESS THAN HALF PRICE

£8.50
REEVES 16x12
TRIPLE PACK CANVAS
RRP £23.97

£9.95
WINSOR & NEWTON HENRY & WILLIAM
COLLECTION INK SET OF 8X14ML
RRP £20.55

LESS THAN HALF PRICE

**FLAGSHIP STORE: 66-67 COLEBROOKE ROW
ISLINGTON N1, 5 MINS FROM ANGEL TUBE, 020 7354 2999**

ALSO AT: 13 CHARING CROSS RD WC2 (NEXT TO THE NATIONAL GALLERY),
24 BERWICK STREET W1, 220 KENSINGTON HIGH STREET W8.
ALL STORES OPEN 7 DAYS WWW.CASSART.CO.UK

ALL OFFERS SUBJECT TO AVAILABILITY AND PRICE CHANGE. PRICES VALID 05.05.09. CASS PROMISE, ASK INSTORE FOR DETAILS.

mismatched personal dressing for which London is famous – in a more sombre, punky and generally gothic direction.

Most young Londoners mix vintage with high street, shopping in chain stores full of high-profile design collaborations at rock-bottom prices. Japanese chain Uniqlo (p113) has *Dazed & Confused* magazine's creative director Nicola Formacetti on its books, for example. Vintage outfitters Beyond Retro (p182) are still the biggest and the best, and both Brick Lane (p182) and Camden Market (p173) reward careful rummaging.

To find something a little more unusual, get the low-down on sample sales, pop-up shops and one-off shopping events in *Time Out* magazine's weekly Shopping & Style section, or turn off the high street to indulge Londoners' obsession with the boutique. Try men's emporiums A Butcher of Distinction (p183) and the Library (p89), new avant-garde design at Savile Row's b store (p113), KJ's Laundry (p105) or Koh Samui (p145). Noteworthy newcomers are A Child of the Jago (p166), high-concept streetwear store Goodhood (p183), lingerie boudoir Apartment C (p105) and rock-star bespoke tailoring courtesy of Sir Tom Baker (p137).

When money is no object, Mayfair's hallowed Dover Street Market (p111), brainchild of Comme des Garçons' Rei Kawakubo, is London's most revered concept store. It's also worth checking out the well-established department stores: Harvey Nichols (p92) is still nicely curated, Selfridges (p106) shows no signs of age as it celebrates its centenary, and Liberty (p136) has enjoyed a recent revamp at the hands of fashion consultant Yasmin Sewell.

SHORTLIST

Best new
- Apartment C (p105)
- A Child of the Jago (p166)
- Ben Pentreath Ltd (p124)
- Store Rooms (p184)

Cutting-edge concepts
- Dover Street Market (p111)
- Goodhood (p183)

Best boutiques
- A Butcher of Distinction (p183)
- KJ's Laundry (p105)

Best markets
- Brick Lane (p182)
- Portobello Market (p191)

Best sensory experience
- Borough Market (p69)
- Columbia Road Market (p182)
- Miller Harris (p112)

Best shoes
- Black Truffle (p182)
- Tracey Neuls (p107)

Best of British
- A Gold (p182)
- James Smith & Sons (p145)

Best retro clothing
- Brick Lane Thrift Store (p182)
- Rellik (p192)

Most eccentric
- Dog & Wardrobe (p182)
- Playlounge (p137)

Best books & music
- Foyles (p136)
- Rough Trade East (p183)

Best shopping streets
- Broadway Market (p182)
- Exmouth Market (p159)
- Lamb's Conduit Street (p124)
- Mount Street (p112)

In spring 2009, three new luxury labels opened flagship stores on Mount Street (p112), the historic pink-brick Mayfair road that is fast replacing Sloane Street as the 'in' place to shop: here gunsmiths, antique galleries and a traditional butcher now rub shoulders with goth-rock designer Rick Owens, a five-floor Lanvin flagship and a new, budget-friendly Marc by Marc Jacobs, alongside existing luxe residents Christian Louboutin and Balenciaga.

Get cultural

In a city bursting with history, the steady closure of London's independent bookshops seems sad, even incongruous. Still, you can browse the travel literature in the the wonderfully grimy Edwardian conservatory of Daunt Books on Marylebone High Street (p106), or the never-ending selection of new titles at Foyles (p136), where you can try before you buy in the great café. Persephone Books on Lamb's Conduit Street (p124) and the London Review Bookshop are new city classics, while Cecil Court (p145) is an unbeatable old stager. Magma (p159) and the bookstore at the Photographers' Gallery (p128) have a wonderful range of contemporary art titles. Don't neglect the museum stores, either: the London Transport Museum (p141) and Southbank Centre (p73) are full of strikingly designed gifts.

Record and CD shops have also taken a beating in recent times, with the second-hand vinyl shops along Berwick Street seeing several closures, high-street monster Zavvi falling to the recession and the wonderful Fopp chain dwindling to one minor outlet. Indie temple Rough Trade East (p183), however, has settled nicely into its 5,000sq ft of the Old Truman Brewery site.

Westfield London p21

Markets valued

Neighbourhood markets remain the lifeblood of London shopping, but few are still the domain of salt-of-the-earth Cockney costermongers. Instead, you'll find fashion kids showing off their new vintage sunglasses over a soy latte and a bag of heirloom tomatoes. Borough Market (p69) is superb for foodies, but canalside Broadway Market (p182) is well worth the trek into Hackney. Lush flower market Columbia Road (p182) is a lovely Sunday morning outing; try to get there before 11am, then follow Brick Lane down to Old Spitalfields Market (p183) and the nearby

Sunday (Up)Market, which is great for fashion, crafts and vintage clobber. You'll be an expert in East End street-style by early afternoon.

London's most famous markets are also both going strong: despite a huge fire in 2008 and ongoing major redevelopment, Camden's markets (p173) remain a major tourist attraction, and – if you can stomach the crowds – Portobello Road Market (p191) is terrific for antiques, bric-a-brac and star-spotting. Alfie's (p173), also in the vicinity, is more laid-back and full of odd characters.

Neighbourhood watch

With more than 40,000 shops and 80 markets, shopping in London can be exhausting. So limit the territory you cover in each outing, sticking to one or two earmarked areas at a time. **Regent Street** is home to the flagships of many mid-range high-street clothing ranges. For a taste of retail past, **St James's Street** is full of anachronistic specialists, including London's oldest hatter and the royal shoemaker. **Savile Row** has been given a shake-up in recent years by a handful of tailoring upstarts, concept fashion emporium b store and even an Abercrombie & Fitch. **Mayfair** – especially Conduit Street and Bond Streets Old and New – remains the domain of major catwalk names such as British big guns Mulberry, Burberry and Vivienne Westwood, and newcomers Georgina Goodman and Luella Bartley.

To the north, it's best to hurry across heaving **Oxford Street** with its department stores, budget fashion outlets and language schools and duck instead into pedestrianised Gees Court and **St Christopher's Place** – pretty, interconnecting alleyways lined

with cafés and shops that lead to the bottom of Marylebone. Curving **Marylebone High Street** has excellent fashion, perfumeries, gourmet food shops and chic design stores.

A couple of London's most celebrated streets have recently been lifted out of the chain-dominated doldrums. **Carnaby Street** has been salvaged by an influx of quality youth clothing brands and the Kingly Court centre; the decline of the **King's Road** has halted, with some hip stores taking their cue from the Shop at Bluebird.

Nor should **Covent Garden** be written off as a tourist trap. New flagships have opened up in the piazza, while, to the north-west, cobbled Floral Street and the offshoots from Seven Dials remain fertile boutique-browsing ground. Don't miss sweet little Neal's Yard, with its wholefood cafés and organic herbalist. A little further north, **Lamb's Conduit Street** is a quiet retreat crammed with appealing indie shops.

Unless you're looking to work the platinum AmEx card among the global designer salons of Sloane Street or marvel at the art nouveau food halls of Harrods, there's little reason to swing by **Knightsbridge**. But do drop in on pretty Ortigia, on a corner of Sloane Square, and the cute shops of Elizabeth Street.

For luxe designer labels without the crush, **Notting Hill** (especially where Westbourne Grove meets Ledbury Road) overflows with feminine boutiques. On the other side of town, **Brick Lane** (mostly around the Old Truman Brewery and on its offshoot Cheshire Street) has a dynamic collection of offbeat clothing and homeware shops. The boutiques of **Islington** are also usually worth having a nose around, along Upper Street, and especially down Camden Passage.

Matter

WHAT'S BEST
Nightlife

Just when you thought you'd got your disco head around London's clubland, it goes and rejigs itself again. Legendary venues Turnmills and the End have closed, hot on the heels of Canvas, the Cross and the Key in King's Cross.

Don't fret: the owners are all off doing new, amazing things. Fabric (p160), still doing a roaring trade in leftfield electronic wiggery, opened Matter in the O2 (p188) – and made a stonking success of it. People from the End shimmied over to the London Bridge area (see box p72) and nights previously at the Cross made for venues like Fire (p188) in 'Vauxhall Village' – formerly old-school gay turf, now day-and-night partying for everyone.

Pioneering T Bar (p169) upped sticks from Shoreditch High Street to a new location near Liverpool Street, which is very close to not having moved at all. In any case,

the High Street is hardly dying a death: the Last Days of Decadence (p168) is a glamorous new opening. A few blocks away, retro promoters Lady Luck have settled into City strip-club Platinum (p169), while on nearby Curtain Road the Queen of Hoxton (no.1, www.thequeenof hoxton.co.uk) has added its name to the 'superpub' revolution that's spread across the capital. Other notable boozer/clubs include Star of Bethnal Green (p184), Paradise by Way of Kensal Green (p192) and the Old Queen's Head (p172) – all of them evidence that London nightlife is edging closer to where people actually live.

The closures have forced promoters to get more creative when trying to find a home for their night. Any space is up for grabs: witness the excitement about Dalston. Edgier than increasingly gentrified Shoreditch, the top end of Kingsland Road has this year teemed with hip young things searching for the next party. Licensing and/or opening hours for these surreal bars beneath Turkish cafés and video shops are erratic, but established Kingsland Road faves include Visions Video (no.588) and Bar 512 (no.512), while Dalston Superstore (117 Kingsland High Street, 7254 2273, www.dalston superstore.com) was a huge hit immediately on opening in 2009.

Musically, it's currently all about disco: watch out for the immensely talented Disco Bloodbath boys – their Dalston parties are always roadblocked – and producer and DJ Serge Santiago.

Take it off!

Burlesque continues to cover the mainstream in kitsch and feathers, with many a regular club night adding a stripper, but to get on trend mention 'boylesque' – yep, burlesque done by blokes. Big on the gay scene, straight boys are now also discovering the joys of stripping to a screaming crowd. Magic and cabaret are also currently hip – not the end-of-pier stuff your grandparents might have enjoyed, but very young Londoners doing twisted, surreal things on stage. The best are found at sweet supper club Volupté (p160), RVT (p188) and the Bethnal Green Working Men's Club (p184).

Bistrotheque (p180) remains the centre of the alt/drag/performance art world, and you'll find edgy drag queens and raw young performers cutting their teeth here. People are flocking to the West End for La Clique at the Hippodrome (p139) – the run was supposed to end this summer, but we hear it's coming back in autumn – or to the ace basement performance space at the Leicester Square Theatre (p138).

SHORTLIST

Best new venues
- Last Days of Decadence (p168)
- Matter (p188)
- T Bar (p169)

Best indie mash-ups
- Proud (p177)
- Punk (p138)

Best for bands
- Bardens Boudoir (p184)
- Luminaire (p175)
- Shepherd's Bush Empire (p192)

Best for cutting-edge jazz
- Vortex Jazz Club (p184)

Best leftfield dance action
- Arches (p70)
- Fabric (p160)

Rockin' pub-clubs
- Notting Hill Arts Club (p192)
- Paradise by Way of Kensal Green (p192)
- Star of Bethnal Green (p184)

Best out-clubs
- Circus at Last Days Of Decadence (p168)
- Fire/Lightbox (p188)

Best for retro dress-up
- Bethnal Green Working Men's Club (p184)
- Lady Luck at Platinum (p169)

Best cabaret & drag
- Bistrotheque (p180)
- Basement at Leicester Square Theatre (p138)
- London Hippodrome (p139)

Best comedy
- Comedy Store (p138)
- Lowdown at the Albany (p119)
- Soho Theatre (p140)

*Kitsch
Cabaret*

Madame
Jojo's

THE HEART OF SOHO'S DARKNESS

www.madamejojos.com

Live music, dead venues

Clubs weren't the only aspect of London nightlife to see significant change this past year. The loss of the End was matched by closure of the historic 2,000-capacity Astoria to make way for a major new transport link. Apart from rock sentimentalists who could overlook the place's unimpressive sound and lack of atmosphere because they'd seen Nirvana there in 1989, few mourned its passing. But it was symbolic of the death of so many mid-sized rock venues.

Don't be fooled. There's plenty of life on the London music scene: it's just downsized. Camden indie types, for example, received a completely remodelled Proud (p177) – get there early to score one of the stables, full of tables and chairs, and perfect for lounging and hipster-spotting. Our monthly free On The Up shows (click the 'On the Up' link under music at www.time out.com) are also in Camden, at the Barfly (p175); recent tips for stellar success have included Joe Gideon and the Shark (who supported Nick Cave after drummer Jim Sclavunos saw them at an On the Up); Drums of Death, who jumped on tour with Peaches and helped produce her new album; and Frankmusik, who had his own T4 programme and supported the Pet Shop Boys.

Indie types shouldn't stick to Camden: in the east, Shoreditch is home to endless rough-and-ready gig spaces like Old Blue Last (p168), where the punters are as young and riotous as the bands, and Dalston again shines bright with Bardens Boudoir (p184) and the Vortex Jazz Club (p184); in north London, the Luminaire (p175) is superb.

Nor is it all gloom in the larger venues. The O2 entertainment complex (p188) has pretty much cornered the market for classic rock

Vortex Jazz Club

DON'T MISS: 2010

gigs (from Led Zeppelin to, last year, AC/DC), as well as booking pop stars like Britney and Michael Jackson, and KOKO (p175) and the Scala (p127) continue to do good work with mid-range bands.

The key point is that London's music scene is defined by rampant diversity. The trend for all things rockabilly, say, with Teddy boys and psychobillies gathering at Ye Olde Axe (69 Hackney Road, 7729 5137) on Saturday or showing off their hot rods at the Ace Café, a fixture on the North Circular since 1938. On any night, you'll find death metal, folk whimsy and plangent griots on one or other of the city's many stages.

Gay disco

Despite the influx of straight ravers to some club nights, 'Vauxhall Village' remains the main hub of all things gay and out. RVT (p188) is the key venue, a friendly, historic gay boozer that hosts comedy nights, arty performance parties and bear-fondling discos. Fire (p188) and its rave-tastic Lightbox room remains the key party place, opening very, very late. The Ghetto (p168), formerly Soho's beloved dingy dive, was forced to relocate by the Astoria's closure: Old Street now gets a weekly dose of Meat Whiplash, courtesy Jonny Slut. The arrival of Ghetto in an already burlesqued Shoreditch opens up a third gay scene to add to Vauxhall and, of course, the daddy: Soho.

Just for laughs

Stand-up comedy has gone stadium-sized: Russell Brand, Michael McIntyre and TV's Mighty Boosh all played sold-out runs at the O2 (p188) last year. It's not all supernova shows, though: check out the Comedy Store (p138), still the one that all the comedians want to play, and the Soho Theatre (p140), great for interesting new performers. Line-ups at Lowdown at the Albany (p119) remain strong.

While London's nightlife is lively all year, anyone who's after comedy in late July or August is likely to be disappointed. Most performers go to the Edinburgh Festival and many venues are dark. Come in June or October instead: comedians are either trying out fresh shows or touring their Edinburgh triumph.

Making the most of it

Whatever you're doing, check the transport before you go: festivals, repairs and engineering tinkerage throw spanners in the works all year, notably on public holidays, but also many weekends. Regularly updated information can be found at www.tfl.gov.uk. Public transport isn't as daunting as you might think. The tube is self-evident, but doesn't run after midnight (New Year's Eve is the sole exception). Black cabs are pricey and hard to find at night, but safe. There are also licensed minicabs (some bigger nightclubs run their own service); on never take an illegal minicab, touted outside every club. Far better to research the slow, but comprehensive night bus system (p214) before leaving your hotel (see www.tfl.gov.uk's Journey Planner). A few minutes working out which bus gets you safe to bed can can save hours of blurry-visioned confusion later.

You'll also kick yourself if you came all this way to see an event, only to arrive the one weekend it isn't on – or to find dates have changed. We've done our best to ensure the information in this guide is correct, but things change with little warning: www.timeout.com has the latest details or, if you're already here, buy *Time Out* magazine for comprehensive weekly listings; www.dontstayin. com is excellent for on-the-ground clubbing news and indie fans should check www.irlondon.co.uk. Record shops are invaluable for flyers and advice – try the friendly folk at Rough Trade East (p183).

If the dates won't quite work out, don't despair. There's something going on here, no matter the day, no matter the hour. So if a useless mate forgets to get tickets, it isn't the end of the world. Even long-in-the-tooth Londoners fall across brand new happenings just by taking the wrong street, and the best way to get a taste of 'real London' – instead of the city every postcard-collecting tourist sees – is to go with the flow. Someone tells you about a party? Check it out. Read about a new band? Get a ticket. Sure, you've some 'essentials' in mind but if you miss them this time… hell, come back next year.

Everyman Hampstead p34

WHAT'S BEST
Arts & Leisure

London isn't just the political hub of Britain – it's the cultural and sporting capital too. Classical music of all types is studied and performed here, ambitious and inventive actors, directors and dancers learn their chops, films are premiered and shot, but you also find two of the nation's top four football teams, national stadiums for football and rugby, international centres of tennis and cricket. In the run-up to the 2012 Olympics there has been a distinct change in priorities, with public funding previously earmarked for the arts redirected to improving sports venues and training – at a time when money is already tight because of the recession. But those with creative ambitions still flood to the city, and the opening of Kings Place (p127) suggests the culturati aren't going to twiddle their thumbs for the next two years.

Classical music & opera

The completion of Kings Place (p127) was the biggest news in classical music of the last year. An office block-cum-auditorium, it provides a permanent home for the very different Orchestra of the Age of Enlightenment (www.oae.co.uk) and London Sinfonietta (www. londonsinfonietta.org.uk), as well as sculpture galleries and two concert halls with fine acoustics. There's a bustling programme all year, but the annual Kings Place Festival in early September – 100 concerts across all genres in three days – looks set to become a major fixture on the cultural calendar.

Not that London was short of headline venues before Kings Place arrived. At the Barbican (p169), the London Symphony Orchestra (http://lso.co.uk) plays 90 concerts

a year, while the Royal Festival Hall at the Southbank Centre (p73) will host Esa-Pekka Salonen's Philharmonia Orchestra (www.philharmonia.co.uk) for a semi-staged performance of Berg's *Wozzeck* in October 2009 and the London Philharmonic Orchestra (www.lpo.org.uk) for a world premiere of Górecki's Symphony No.4 in April 2010, plus Haitink's Chicago Symphony Orchestra in September 2009 and Barenboim's Berlin Staatskapelle in January 2010 for the impressive Shell Classic International 2009/10 season.

Opera buffs can choose between acclaimed theatre directors Rupert Goold (*Turandot*) and Deborah Warner (Handel's *Messiah*) at the Coliseum (p146) in late 2009, or Franz Liszt's *Mayerling* in October 2009 at the Royal Opera House (p148), with Carlos Acosta and Lauren Cuthbertson (see box p147) among those dancing the lead.

Much of the city's classical music action happens in superb venues on an intimate scale. The exemplary Wigmore Hall (p107), Cadogan Hall (p93) and LSO St Luke's (p169) are all terrific, atmospheric venues, and a number of London's churches host fine concerts: try the reborn St Martin-in-the-Fields (p78) and St John's Smith Square (p80).

Dance

London offers an unmatched range of dance styles and performers, way beyond the usual choice of classical or contemporary, and – apart from the quieter summer months – there's something worth seeing every night of the week. Sadler's Wells (p177) lives up to its self-billing as 'London's Dance House' with a packed programme of top-quality work from native talent and big international names. It also hosts must-see festivals: the

DON'T MISS: 2010

S H O R T L I S T

Best new venue
- Kings Place (p127)

Best venues
- Cadogan Hall (p97)
- Coliseum (p146)
- National Theatre (p71)
- Sadler's Wells (p177)
- Siobhan Davies Studios (p73)

Best cinemas
- BFI Southbank (p71)
- Curzon Soho (p139)

Best festivals
- Breakin' Convention (p43)
- London Film Festival (p37)
- The Proms (p45)

Best bargains
- Place (p127)
- Prince Charles (p140)
- Standing tickets at Shakespeare's Globe (p63)
- Standing tickets at the Coliseum (p146)
- £10 Monday at the Royal Court Theatre (p97)

Most innovative work
- London Sinfonietta at Kings Place (p127)
- Royal Ballet's Wayne McGregor at the Royal Opera House (p148)
- Royal Court Theatre (p97)

Best off-West End theatres
- BAC (Battersea Arts Centre) (p188)
- Donmar Warehouse (p148)

Best of the West End
- *La Cage aux Folles* at Playhouse Theatre (p148)
- *La Clique* at the London Hippodrome (p139)
- *Sister Act* at the London Palladium (p139)

hip hop of Breakin' Convention (p43) is a highlight. Autumn sees Dance Umbrella (p36) unfold with cutting-edge work from around the world performed across the city.

One of the year's biggest shows, at the Barbican in late October 2009, is a new commission from rebel choreographer Michael Clark, based on the music of David Bowie, Lou Reed and Iggy Pop. Another must-see is the long-awaited return of Mark Morris's masterpiece 'L'Allegro, Il Penseroso ed Il Moderato' in the 2010 Spring Dance season at the Coliseum.

If you're interested in emerging talent, head to the Place (p127), home of the Place Prize in early autumn, and Siobhan Davies Dance Studios (p73) – worth visiting to just to ogle the beautiful Sarah Wigglesworth-designed building. For full-on ballet, the world-class Royal Ballet dances at the Royal Opera House. New works by resident choreographer Wayne McGregor, whose mercurial, frenetic movement is nothing like ballet as most people know it, are always worth checking out.

Film

Like much of the London arts scene, the 2009 'credit crunch' made a profound dent on the film and cinema landscape. With more mainstream titles creeping on to the playbills of even such arthouse stalwarts as the Curzon Soho (p139) or, should you venture up to north London, the revamped Everyman Hampstead (5 Hollybush Vale, 0870 066 4777, www.everyman cinema.com), smaller films are finding it hard to breathe in the capital. The problem is exacerbated by the sheer number of films being released, which gets bigger every week. The cinemas committed to programming foreign and

alternative films amount to few more than the redoubtable BFI Southbank (p71) and the ICA (p83).

Don't fret. As the multiplexes stuff their screens with bloated blockbusters (many presented in the seemingly obligatory 3D or IMAX alternative formats), smaller, less formal venues have begun to pick up the slack: Close-up (www.close-upvideos.com/film-program), run by enthusiasts behind the Brick Lane DVD rental shop, is just one of many regular film nights, and major venues such as Tate Modern (p65) and the British Museum (p120) include film screenings on their packed rosters. Keep an eye on *Time Out* magazine or www.timeout.com for details of the city's diverse film festivals too: Palestinian, Human Rights Watch, Italian, Sci Fi and Frightfest are just a flavour of what's going on.

Theatre

After a bumper 2007 at the box office and a record-breaking 2008 (even after the 'credit crunch' had become a reality), theatreland is looking healthy and surprisingly wealthy. Economic hard times, so far, seem to have sent people to the theatre in search of distraction, rather than chasing them away. Nonetheless, West End producers are likely to be cautious: 2009/2010 will certainly see the usual crop of celebrity-led productions and musicals piggy-backing on popular movies – Matthew Warchus directs *Ghost*, the musical, in 2010 (see box p141) and *Priscilla Queen of the Desert*, designed by the Oscar-winning team from the orginal, is already shaking its tassels at the Palace Theatre (p139).

In musicals, Broadway exports are strong right now, despite a handful of long-running Lloyd Webber musicals (*Phantom* is the

Donmar Warehouse

biggest, while *Joseph* has been resurrected through a TV talent show) and the continued success of the fine Brit-musical *Billy Elliot* (at the Victoria Palace Theatre, p80). Acclaimed transatlantic travellers include *Hairspray* (Shaftesbury Theatre, p148) and jukebox musical *Jersey Boys* (Prince Edward Theatre, p140), but the Tony-winning *Spring Awakening*, whose London version transferred from the off-West End Lyric Hammersmith (p192) to the Novello (p148), may herald a more adventurous era: this teenage angst musical is based on Wedekind's bleak German fin-de-siècle drama.

Theatrical subsidies are set to decrease, but the Royal Court (p97) and National Theatre (p71) remain very safe bets for high-quality theatre. And even that previously endangered species the commercial straight play has revived, although producers barely deviate from the formula of well-known actor plus excellent director plus classic text. Despite a recent crop of celebrity Hamlets (*Doctor Who*'s David Tennant in 2008, Jude Law in 2009), the critics are really looking forward

to Rory Kinnear's version at the National in 2010. Also at the National, Donmar Warehouse (p148) director Michael Grandage – whose star is high after running a West End season for which he persuaded the likes of Kenneth Branagh and Judi Dench to perform in quality, straight plays at very affordable prices – is going to do Büchner's *Danton's Death*.

At the younger, cultier end of the scale, watch out for the masters of immersive theatre, Punchdrunk (www.punchdrunk.org.uk), whose masked revels send the audience through many-roomed venues in search of the action, which erupts spectacularly all over the place.

What's on

We've included long-running musicals we think are likely to survive into 2010. However, a new crop will inevitably open through the year, along with seasons at individual venues. *Time Out* magazine and www. timeout.com have the most informed and up-to-date listings.

WHAT'S ON
Calendar

Great River Race

The following is our selection of annual events, plus the best one-offs confirmed when this guide went to press. To stay current with what's happening, buy the weekly *Time Out* magazine and check www.timeout.com/london; always confirm dates before making any travel plans. The dates of public holidays are given in **bold**.

September 2009

5 **Great River Race**
Thames, Richmond to Greenwich
www.greatriverrace.co.uk

12-13 **Mayor's Thames Festival**
Westminster & Tower Bridges
www.thamesfestival.org

19 **Tour of Britain**
Tower of London to Westminster
www.britishcycling.org.uk
Last stage of the eight-day cycle race.

19-20 **Open House London**
Various locations

www.openhouselondon.org
Free access to over 600 buildings.

20 **Freewheel**
Various locations
www.londonfreewheel.com
50,000 cyclists on a traffic-free route.

23 Sept-31 Jan 2010
Turner and the Masters
Tate Britain, p78
www.tate.org.uk/britain

24 Sept-24 Jan 2010
Moctezuma: Aztec Ruler
British Museum, p120
www.britishmuseum.org

26 **Great Gorilla Run**
Mincing Lane, the City
www.greatgorillas.org/london
Fund-raising 7km run, in gorilla suits.

late Sept-early Nov
Dance Umbrella
Various locations
www.danceumbrella.co.uk
The city's headline dance festival.

October 2009

Ongoing Dance Umbrella (see Sept); Turner and the Masters (see Sept); Moctezuma (see Sept)

4 **Pearly Kings & Queens Harvest Festival**
St Martin-in-the-Fields, p78
www.pearlysociety.co.uk
A 3pm service for the professional Cockneys, in traditional outfits.

14-29 Oct **London Film Festival**
BFI Southbank, p71
www.bfi.org.uk/lff

15-18 **Frieze Art Fair**
Regent's Park, p98
www.friezeartfair.com

17 **Diwali**
Trafalgar Square, p79
www.london.gov.uk
Celebrated by Hindus, Jains and Sikhs.

20-21 **Spandau Ballet**
O2 Arena, p188
www.theo2.co.uk

late Oct-late Apr 2010 **Shell Wildlife Photographer of the Year**
Natural History Museum, p85
www.nhm.ac.uk/wildphoto

28 Oct-7 Nov **Michael Clark**
Barbican Centre, p169
www.barbican.org.uk
Return of the rebel choreographer.

November 2009

Ongoing Dance Umbrella (see Sept); Turner and the Masters (see Sept); Moctezuma (see Sept); Shell Wildlife Photographer of the Year (see Oct); Michael Clark (see Oct)

5 **Bonfire Night**

8 **London to Brighton Veteran Car Run**
Serpentine Road in Hyde Park, p90
www.lbvcr.com

8 **Remembrance Sunday Ceremony**
Cenotaph, Whitehall

13-22 **London Jazz Festival**
Various locations
www.serious.org.uk

14 **Lord Mayor's Show**
Various locations in the City
www.lordmayorsshow.org
A grand inauguration procession for the new Lord Mayor.

mid Nov
State Opening of Parliament
House of Lords, p76
www.parliament.uk

Nov-Dec **Christmas Tree & Lights**
Covent Garden, Regent Street & Trafalgar Square
www.london.gov.uk
See box p39.

December 2009

Ongoing Turner and the Masters (see Sept); Moctezuma (see Sept); Shell Wildlife Photographer of the Year (see Oct); Christmas Tree & Lights (see Nov)

3-7 **Eddie Izzard**
O2 Arena & Wembley Arena
www.theo2.co.uk, www.whatson wembley.com
Immensely popular, surreal comedian.

mid Dec
Bankside Winter Festival
Tate Modern & the Globe, pp63-65
www.visitsouthwark.com

mid Dec **Spitalfields Festival**
Various locations
www.spitalfieldsfestival.org.uk
Classical music, walks and talks.

25 **Christmas Day**

28 **Boxing Day Bank Holiday**

31 **New Year's Eve Celebrations**
Trafalgar Square & the South Bank
See box p39.

Do something out of the ordinary...

Escape to Ham House and Garden in Richmond – a green oasis of calm and tranquillity.

Outstanding and unique treasure house offering a glimpse of life in the 17th century.

Properly festive

Getting the best out of Christmas and New Year.

London never used to be much fun at the turn of the year. With no public transport on Christmas Day, the centre of the capital feels eerily deserted – a magical transformation for a city usually teeming with people, but not one that's easy to enjoy unless you've got a designated driver who's happy to forgo the egg nog. And New Year's Eve seemed to involve cramming as many idiots as possible into Trafalgar Square (p79), without so much as a drink to keep them warm.

Things have changed. Us Brits might have a reputation for not thinking much of Johnny Foreigner, but we know a good thing when we see it: the explosion of middle European Christmas markets across London is a case in point. Each has its own style – from the traditional market on the South Bank to the fairground of Winter Wonderland (www.hydeparkwinter wonderland.com) – but mulled wine, spiced German cakes and, increasingly, ice rinks are usual. For pretty Christmas lights, skip the commercialised ones on Oxford and Regent's Streets and head instead for St Christopher's Place, Marylebone High Street and Covent Garden, while the best window displays are the enchantingly old-fashioned ones at Fortnum & Mason (p82) and the annual show-stoppers at Harvey Nichols (p92).

More interested in partying than present-buying? The week after Christmas is when the locals go nuts, and the best advice is to do as they do: forget paying inflated prices for a disappointing New Year's Eve bash and go out instead on New Year's Day. Parties kick off from 5am and attract a cooler crowd, happy in the knowledge they're paying a third of the price for exactly the same DJs as were playing at midnight – check *Time Out* magazine to find out what's happening. If you do want to join the mob for the traditional New Year's Eve bash, head to the South Bank, where a full-on fireworks display is launched from the London Eye and rafts on the Thames.

London Marathon p43

January 2010

Ongoing Turner and the Masters (see Sept); Moctezuma (see Sept); Shell Wildlife Photographer of the Year (see Oct)

1 New Year's Day

13-17 London Art Fair
Business Design Centre, Islington
www.londonartfair.co.uk

16-31 London International Mime Festival
Various locations
www.mimefest.co.uk

February 2010

Ongoing Shell Wildlife Photographer of the Year (see Oct)

6, 27 Feb Six Nations
Twickenham Stadium
www.rfu.com
The annual rugby union tournament.

14 Chinese New Year Festival
Chinatown & Trafalgar Square
www.chinatownchinese.co.uk

mid Feb **Imagine**
Southbank Centre, p73
www.southbankcentre.co.uk

Children's literature festival.

16 Poulters Pancake Day Race
Guildhall Yard, p161
www.poulters.org.uk
City livery companies race – tossing pancakes as they go – in full regalia.

March 2010

Ongoing Shell Wildlife Photographer of the Year (see Oct)

early Mar-late Apr **Kew Spring Festival**
Royal Botanic Gardens, Kew (p186)
www.kew.org.

early-late Mar **Word Festival**
Various East End locations
www.londonwordfestival.com
Hip annual literature festival takes over various East End venues.

late Mar-early Apr **London Lesbian & Gay Film Festival**
BFI Southbank, p71
www.llgff.org.uk

April 2010

Ongoing Shell Wildlife Photographer of the Year (see Oct); Kew Spring Festival (see Mar); Lesbian & Gay Film Festival (see Mar)

Camden Crawl

2 Good Friday

3 Oxford & Cambridge Boat Race
On the Thames, Putney to Mortlake
www.theboatrace.org

5 Easter Monday

early Apr-mid May **Spring Loaded**
Place, p127
www.theplace.org.uk
Seven-week dance festival.

14-17 **Mark Morris**
Coliseum, p146
www.eno.org
The choreographer's masterpiece
'L'Allegro, Il Penseroso ed Il Moderato'.

17 **London Philharmonic
Orchestra**
Southbank Centre, p73
www.southbankcentre.co.uk
Premiere of Górecki's Symphony No.4.

19-21 **London Book Fair**
Earls Court Exhibition Centre
www.londonbookfair.co.uk

late Apr **Camden Crawl**
Various locations in Camden
www.thecamdencrawl.com
Splurge of new musical talent, usually
favouring busy indie guitars.

25 **London Marathon**
Greenwich Park to the Mall
www.virginlondonmarathon.com

May 2010

Ongoing Spring Loaded (see Apr).

early May **Breakin' Convention**
Sadler's Wells, p177
www.breakinconvention.com
Jonzi D's terrific festival brings street
and contemporary dance together.

3 Early May Bank Holiday

25-29 **Chelsea Flower Show**
Royal Hospital Chelsea, p94
www.rhs.org.uk

31 Spring Bank Holiday

June 2010

early June **Beating Retreat**
Horse Guards Parade, Whitehall
www.army.mod.uk
A pageant of military music and preci-
sion marching, beginning at 7pm.

early June **Hampton Court
Palace Festival**
www.hamptoncourtfestival.com
Two weeks of concerts.

Rockers reborn

Elvis lives! Or rather – live at the O2 Arena.

The O2 Arena (p188) has already managed some pretty special rock regenerations in its few years of operation. There was the triumphant return of rock dinosaurs Led Zeppelin, as well as huge residencies: first, the massive, 21-date residency by Prince, then this year no fewer than 50 sold-out nights of Michael Jackson – 'King of Pop!', as the adverts put it. But in 2010, the O2 will excel itself: they're going to bring Elvis back from the dead.

The 'Elvis Presley in Concert' show (28 February) combines a live band with film recordings of the great man in action. Given the King never played outside North America (his five 'foreign' shows were all in Canada), this is as close as British fans can ever got to the real thing. The band is impressive: many of the musicians that backed Elvis in life reprise the role here (from the classic Vegas shows you get guitarist James Burton, bassist Jerry Scheff, drummer Ronnie Tutt and musical director/conductor Joe Guercio; backing vocals come from the Imperials, Stamps and Sweet Inspirations), a 16-piece orchestra will be on hand to pluck the heartstrings.

But all eyes will be on the huge projections of Elvis himself: vocals and visuals are drawn from the MGM concert film *Elvis on Tour* (1972) and the 1973 TV special *Elvis: Aloha from Hawaii*. You'll feel like the King is right there in front of you.

early June **Epsom Derby**
Epsom Racecourse
www.epsomderby.co.uk

early June **Royal Ascot**
Ascot Racecourse
www.ascot.co.uk

early June-mid Aug
Opera Holland Park
www.operahollandpark.com

early June **Spitalfields Festival**
Various locations
www.spitalfieldsfestival.org.uk
Classical music, walks and talks.

mid June
Open Garden Squares Weekend
Various locations
www.opensquares.org
Private gardens opened to the public.

mid June **Meltdown**
Southbank Centre, p73
www.southbank.co.uk
A fortnight of contemporary music and culture, curated each year by different musicians – Ornette Coleman in 2009.

mid June **LIFT**
Various locations
www.liftfest.org.uk
A week of international theatre.

mid June **Wireless Festival**
Hyde Park, p90
www.o2wirelessfestival.co.uk

mid June **Trooping the Colour**
Horse Guards Parade, St James's
www.trooping-the-colour.co.uk
The Queen's official birthday parade.

21 June-4 July **Wimbledon Lawn Tennis Championships**
www.wimbledon.org

late June-late July **London Festival of Architecture**
Various locations
www.newlondonarchitecture.org

late June-early July
City of London Festival

Various locations around the City
www.colf.org
A festival of mostly free music and art.

late June-late Aug
English Heritage Picnic Concerts
Hampstead Heath, p170
www.picnicconcerts.com
Evening concerts of grown-up pop/rock
and light classical at Kenwood House.

July 2010

Ongoing Opera Holland Park
(see June); Wimbledon (see June);
London Festival of Architecture
(see June); City of London Festival
(see June); English Heritage Picnic
Concerts (see June)

early July **Pride London**
Oxford Street to Victoria
Embankment
www.pridelondon.org
A huge annual gay and lesbian parade.

early July-late Sept
Watch This Space
National Theatre, p71
www.nationaltheatre.org.uk
Alfresco theatre beside the Thames.

mid July **Lovebox Weekender**
Victoria Park, Hackney
www.lovebox.net
Top-quality weekend music festival.

mid July **Chap Olympiad**
Bedford Square Gardens,
Bloomsbury
www.thechap.net
The likes of the Hop, Skip and G&T are
fiercely contested – in Victorian attire.

mid July
Somerset House Summer Series
Somerset House, p153
www.somerset-house.org.uk/music
Nine concerts in the fountain court.

mid July-mid Sept
**The Proms (BBC Sir Henry Wood
Promenade Concerts)**
Royal Albert Hall, p89
www.bbc.co.uk/proms

late July **Greenwich & Docklands
International Festival**
Various locations
www.festival.org
Four days of outdoor theatricals, usu-
ally on an impressively large scale.

August 2010

Ongoing Opera Holland Park
(see June); English Heritage
Picnic Concerts (see June);
Watch This Space (see July);
the Proms (see July)

early Aug
Great British Beer Festival
Earl's Court Exhibition Centre
www.camra.org.uk
A great chance to sample British beer.

early Aug **Underage Festival**
Victoria Park, Hackney
www.underagefestivals.com
A hip and immensely popular music
festival for 14- to 18-year-olds.

London Festival of Architecture

early-late Aug
Portobello Film Festival
Various locations in west London
www.portobellofilmfestival.com

28-29 Notting Hill Carnival
Various locations in Notting Hill
www.nottinghillcarnival.biz
Europe's biggest street party.

30 Summer Bank Holiday

September 2010

Ongoing Watch This Space (see July); the Proms (see July)

early Sept Great River Race
See above Sept 2009.

mid Sept Mayor's Thames Festival
See above Sept 2009.

mid Sept Tour of Britain
See above Sept 2009.

mid Sept Open House London
See above Sept 2009.

late Sept Freewheel
See above Sept 2009.

late Sept Great Gorilla Run
See above Sept 2009.

late Sept-early Nov
Dance Umbrella
See above Sept 2009.

October 2010

Ongoing Dance Umbrella (see Sept)

early Oct Pearly Kings & Queens Harvest Festival
See above Oct 2009.

mid Oct-early Nov
London Film Festival
See above Oct 2009.

mid Oct Frieze Art Fair
See above Oct 2009.

from late Oct Shell Wildlife Photographer of the Year
See above Oct 2009.

November 2010

Ongoing Dance Umbrella (see Sept); London Film Festival (see Oct); Shell Wildlife Photographer of the Year (see Oct)

5 Diwali
See above Oct 2009.

5 Bonfire Night

7 Remembrance Sunday Ceremony
See above Nov 2009.

early Nov London to Brighton Veteran Car Run
See above Nov 2009.

early Nov Lord Mayor's Show
See above Nov 2009.

mid Nov London Jazz Festival
See above Nov 2009.

mid Nov State Opening of Parliament
See above Nov 2009.

Nov-Dec Christmas Tree & Lights
See above Nov 2009.

December 2010

Ongoing Shell Wildlife Photographer of the Year (see Oct); Christmas Tree & Lights (see Nov)

mid Dec Bankside Winter Festival
See above Dec 2009.

mid Dec Spitalfields Festival
See above Dec 2009.

24 Christmas Day Bank Holiday

27 Boxing Day Bank Holiday

31 New Year's Eve Celebrations
See above Dec 2009.

Itineraries

National Theatre p50

London by Night

Funny things go on in London after dark. Civil servants duck out of Westminster and sneak into secret S&M clubs, and city gents swap their suits for Kanye West sunglasses and dance till sun-up in a hail of drum 'n' bass. The night is when London lets its hair down, and that makes it the best time to catch Londoners without their famous 'reserve'. The following itinerary takes in the best of the bright lights: on foot, by boat and on the tube. Arm yourself with a charged Oyster smartcard (p213) and you're ready to set off.

There's a lot to fit in, so get an early start with a sunset ride on the Thames Clipper (p214) from **Tower Millennium Pier** (close to Tower Hill tube) to the Queen Elizabeth II Pier. You'll get a prime view of three iconic towers – the Tower of London (p163), Tower Bridge (p163) and One Canada Square (p178), the less-catchy name for Canary Wharf tower – just as

the lights come on. Disembark at the former Millennium Dome. Once London's biggest white elephant, it has been reinvented as the surprisingly successful **O2** entertainment complex (p188). Depending on your tastes and timing, you might be able to take in a WWE wrestling bout or the Spandau Ballet comeback tour before you move on.

From the O2, take the steps down to North Greenwich tube and ride the Jubilee Line one stop west to Canary Wharf. Climb through the bowels of the rocketship tower at **One Canada Square** and change to a Docklands Light Railway (DLR) train bound for Bank. Surreally empty after dark, the DLR whispers around the knees of the tallest buildings in Britain. Rising to the stratosphere, the illuminated windows of London's banking houses blast unimaginable amounts of candlepower into the night sky.

The Thames and the City

Leave Bank station by Exit 4 and sit on the steps of the Parthenon-like **Royal Exchange**, one-time home of the London stock exchange. From this vantage point, you have a view over one of the most valuable intersections in the world. To the right is the fortress that is the Bank of England (p166) and to the left is Mansion House, the grand pied-à-terre of the Lord Mayor of London. Cross Cornhill to Lombard Street, then bear right on King William Street to reach the river.

As you amble over **London Bridge**, pause to admire one of London's best evening vistas (Ivan Luckin may have sold the previous London Bridge to America, but he couldn't sell this view). To the east, the bows of the HMS *Belfast* (p62) strike a military pose in front of the spotlit turrets of Tower Bridge, with the circuit-board towers of Canary Wharf protruding behind. While you're here, it would be a pity not to stop for a pint in one of London's oldest coaching inns, the George Inn (77 Borough High Street, 7407 2056), a charmingly creaky vessel from 1676 (the courtyard opens up from the east side of Borough High Street).

It's now time to begin one of London's great night-time walks. Returning to London Bridge, pick up the riverside **Thames Path** by Southwark Cathedral (p65). Walk west along Montague Street, Clink Street and Bankside to Shakespeare's Globe (p63), which manages to capture some of the turnip-throwing thrill of Elizabethan theatre despite being the brainchild of US movie-actor Sam Wanamaker. A few doors down is one of London's triumphs, the Tate Modern (p65), which keeps its doors open until 10pm on Friday and Saturday. Stretching north from this powerhouse of modern art, the Millennium Bridge leads the eye inexorably to the dome of St Paul's (p162).

Continue west along the riverfront past a tacky collection of plazas and arcades around the Oxo Tower to emerge among the brutalist concrete blocks of the **Southbank Centre** (p73). As this is London's premier artistic enclave, you'll almost certainly find something here to entertain you: there are plenty of buskers and free events at Royal Festival Hall, and we rate the movie programme at the BFI Southbank (p71), particularly if there's a *Wizard of Oz* theme night, and the more-hit-than-miss summer performances in front of the National Theatre (p71). Alternatively, you can enjoy some free entertainment watching the fairly grown-up skateboarders performing ollies and kickflips in the concrete catacombs under the Queen Elizabeth Hall.

If you'd rather enjoy the views, skip these worthy institutions and take a turn on the space-age Ferris wheel known as the **London Eye** (p63). The wheel only spins until 8pm (9pm in summer) so you'll have to hurry to get here in time, but the top of the arc offers an eagle-eye view over London, from the red beacon atop Canary Wharf in the east to the white chimney stacks of Battersea Power Station to the west. Those lights in the Houses of Parliament (p76) across the Thames are probably MPs staying up late to file their expenses claims.

Take a last breath of Thames air, then duck across Jubilee Gardens and York Road to Waterloo tube. Go three stops northbound on the Northern line to Leicester Square. Emerging from the Underground (p128), scoot quickly east through the awfulness (easier said than done during a movie premier) and turn north along Wardour Street to Shaftesbury Avenue, the gateway to London's theatreland. *Les Mis* has been showing in London for 23 years, so there's no rush to take in a performance at the Queen's Theatre – instead, walk a block north to **Old Compton Street** to soak up the carnival atmosphere of London's longest-established gay and lesbian quarter. The street-side cabaret rages through the night on Friday and Saturday – ask for a street seat at Balans (60 Old Compton Street, 7437 5212, www.balans.co.uk) for a prime view of the beautiful and outrageous people.

Alternatively, hail a rickshaw and demand to be taken to one of Soho's finest eateries. Locals are sceptical of London's rickshaws (and black-cab drivers can't stand them), but rolling through the West End at street-level certainly offers a different vantage point over London. Unless you reserved six months ago, you probably won't get a table at the Ivy (1 West Street, 7836 4751, www.the-ivy.co.uk), but it's only five minutes' pedal to Anthony Demetre's **Arbutus** (p128), hugely popular but blessed with a counter that can usually accommodate diners without bookings.

After night falls, to paraphrase Was Not Was, out come the freaks. And where do they go? Yep, Camden. Digest your dinner on the short walk to Tottenham Court Road tube, then ride the rails north to Camden Town. Although the bovver boot rebellion of punk has been replaced by a Goth version of Cosplay, this hasn't diminished the spectacle. There are even a few decent bars to relax in. From the station, walk north along Chalk Farm Road beneath the railway arches to enjoy a late drink and arty photos of AC/DC and PJ Harvey at **Proud** (p177). You're also perfectly placed to tap into London's exciting live music scene. Tomorrow's headliners at Glastonbury can be found gathering momentum at venues like **Barfly** (p175), conveniently close on Chalk Farm Road. When you finally emerge, engage in a time-hallowed London tradition – trying to hail a black cab to take you home to bed.

Old Royal Naval College p53

The Wren Route

St Paul's Cathedral is a City landmark with real staying power: in 2010 it will be 300 years since Sir Christopher Wren's masterpiece was opened as the centrepiece of the post-Great Fire rebuilding of London. Like some 17th-century Rogers or Foster, Wren and his associates peppered the skyline with towers, and even though many disappeared through demolition or as a result of brutal carpet-bombing during the Blitz, many can still be visited.

Do the route on a weekday – most of the churches are closed (except for services) at weekends, and you'll have to choose either St Mary Aldermary (open Mon, Wed, Thur) or St Mary Abchurch (open Tue) – and expect to start by about 9am. This route is as much about walking as gawping.

Jump off the tube at dingy Farringdon station, turn right out of the exit, then immediately left

down Farringdon Road until you reach Ludgate Circus. Stand on the west side and admire the view up Ludgate Hill to St Paul's to get an impression of what the cathedral must have looked like when it was first built, rising above the huddle of rooftops and the spires of the lesser Wren churches – the black spire situated to the left of the dome belongs to one of them, **St Martin Ludgate**.

Hidden behind you off Fleet Street is **St Bride's** (p153). Its steeple is the tallest of any Wren church and was supposedly the model for the tiered wedding cake. Take the first left off Fleet Street for a closer look. The church burnt out during the Blitz, so the interior is a reconstruction, albeit a lovely one. Visit the crypt museum to find out about the construction of the church (several generations of wall are exposed, along with various artefacts) and the life and death of Fleet Street – a facsimile of the *Evening News* from 30 December 1940 gives a graphic description of the devastation wreaked by one particular wartime raid.

Retrace your steps to Ludgate Circus and climb Ludgate Hill, braving the crowds on the cathedral steps to enter **St Paul's** (p162). You could easily spend a couple of hours here, sufficient for a climb up to the famous Whispering Gallery to look down within the cathedral, then on up and outside for the giddying views of the City from the Gold Gallery (more than 500 steps from the ground), and finally back down into the crypt (check out the skull and crossbones on the lintel). Here Nelson's grand monument is right beneath the central dome, while Wren's tomb is tucked modestly away at the east end in the south aisle.

Emerging from the cathedral, turn right and pass through **Temple Bar**, another Wren creation. This gateway originally stood at the western end of Fleet Street to mark the boundary between the City of London and Westminster, but impeded the traffic and was removed by the Victorians. It then stood for many years on a country estate in Hertfordshire, returning in 2004 to become the entrance to the new Paternoster Square, home to the London Stock Exchange.

Grab a coffee and cross the square to emerge on Newgate Street. Opposite is **Christ Church**, which was almost destroyed during World War II. The ruined nave is now a rose garden; take a seat and sip your coffee. The surviving tower is a spectacular private home, its ten storeys linked by lift.

Head east along Angel Street, across Aldersgate Street, to Gresham Street. First you'll see **St Anne & St Agnes**, with a

St Paul's Cathedral

leafy churchyard and regular classical recitals. Further along Gresham Street, catch a glimpse of the tower of **St Alban Wood Street**, like Christ Church now a private house. Continue past **St Lawrence Jewry** – the church of the Corporation of London – to Moorgate, crossing into Lothbury to enter **St Margaret Lothbury** (7606 8330, www.stml.org.uk). This has one of the loveliest interiors of any Wren church, with an impressive wood screen by the great man himself.

Retrace your steps to Moorgate and turn left down Prince's Street to enter Bank tube. Take the Mansion House exit, following the path around to **St Stephen Walbrook** (39 Walbrook, 7606 3998, www.ststephenwalbrook.net), the most grandiose Wren church, a mass of creamy stone with a soaring dome, fabulously bulbous pulpit and incongruous modern altar by Henry Moore.

Turn left out of the church and left again into Cannon Street. Just past Cannon Street station, take another left on to St Swithin's Lane and head downstairs into the brick-vaulted cellar bistro of the **Don** (the Courtyard, 20 St Swithin's Lane, 7626 2606, www.thedonrestaurant.com), where hearty, meaty lunches are served until 3pm on weekdays. Turn left back on to Cannon Street, then duck left into Abchurch Lane. **St Mary Abchurch** (7626 0306) is a real gem, with a shallow, painted dome and a beautiful reredos by Grinling Gibbons. It was shattered into 2,000 pieces by a wartime bomb and painstakingly pieced back together.

Back on Cannon Street, head east to reach the top end of London Bridge. Cross the street using the underpass, turning left off King William Street into Monument Street. Recently reopened, the **Monument** (p162) is the world's tallest isolated stone column, built to commemorate the Great Fire. It was designed by Wren and his associate Robert Hooke. Climb the 311 steps to be rewarded with great views over the City and river.

Get back on to Cannon Street and head west to Bow Lane, topped and tailed by two churches from Wren's office: at the southern end, **St Mary Aldermary** (7248 4906, www.stmaryaldermary.co.uk) is obscure but beautiful, with flamboyant Gothic vaulting; at the northern end, **St Mary-le-Bow** is famous for its bells, but it's a post-war reconstruction inside.

Retrace your steps down Bow Lane, this time turning right into Queen Victoria Street to reach Peter's Hill and the Millennium Bridge. Cross the river, turning east off the bridge for Shakespeare's Globe. Overshadowed by the

theatre at **49 Bankside** is the house commonly – probably incorrectly – said to be the one from which Wren watched St Paul's rise across the river. Whatever the truth, the views of the cathedral are superb. Buy an ice-cream from one of the vans to munch while waiting for the riverbus at Bankside Pier.

Take the Thames Clipper east to Masthouse Pier, from which it's a ten-minute walk along the river path to Island Gardens. Stock up on fluids from the kiosk, soak up the views of the **Old Royal Naval College** (p186) then cross under the river using the Greenwich Foot Tunnel. Emerging from the tunnel, pass the *Cutty Sark* (still under refurbishment) and turn left into College Approach. The College is straight ahead. It's one of the most extensive groups of baroque public buildings in England and survives much as Wren planned it. Don't miss the Painted Hall, built to his designs between 1696 and 1704; the name is apt as most of the rich decoration is *trompe l'oeil*.

Continue through the college to the eastern gate, turn right into Park Row and enter Greenwich Park. Crowning the hilltop is the Royal Observatory, where crowds wait their turn to stand astride the Prime Meridian Line. Carry on to enter **Flamsteed's House**, the only bit of the complex by Wren. Built for the first Astronomer Royal, it's a dainty contrast to the Royal Naval College, the living quarters cosily domestic, with only the Octagon room at the top hinting at Wren's baroque flair. You emerge through the 'Time & Greenwich' gallery.

It's been a long day: treat yourself to a pint. As you head back to the *Cutty Sark*, the **Gipsy Moth** (60 Greenwich Church Street, SE10 9BL, 8858 0786) is conveniently close to the DLR station.

ITINERARIES

Wellcome Collection

CSI: London

Forget Vegas, Miami and New York: London is the true home of forensics. And with a couple of Sherlock Holmes movies in the works, deerstalkers on the capital's fashion pages and the centenary of the infamous Crippen case, there's never been a better time to sniff out the city's detective history. You'll need a sharp pair of eyes to keep track of every clue and, if you want to see justice in action, travel light: real sleuths don't carry bags, cameras or mobile phones.

Start around 10am at Baker Street station, where the silhouettes on the walls hint at why you're here. Exit on to Marylebone Road (north) and check out the larger-than-life statue to your left, before turning right on to **Baker Street**. When Sir Arthur Conan Doyle introduced the world to Sherlock Holmes in 1887, Baker Street ended much further south, and the address of the world's greatest

detective at 221B didn't exist. It does now: it's the location of the **Sherlock Holmes Museum** (7935 4430, www.sherlock-holmes. co.uk), a popular and quirky homage to the man and his exploits. Buy your ticket from the chintzy souvenir shop before asking the 'bobby' on the doorstep to let you up to the first-floor study. If you're lucky, Holmes or Watson may greet you. Even if you're not, you can sit in their chairs, rifle through their bedside belongings and test your Holmes knowledge on the waxwork dioramas upstairs.

Return to the tube and turn left on to Marylebone Road for bus Stop P. Hop on a no.8, 30 or 205 for the ten-minute ride to Euston Square. You'll pass Devonshire Place, on the right, where Conan Doyle had an ophthalmic practice in 1891. He claims never to have seen a patient there, spending his time churning out over 50 Holmes

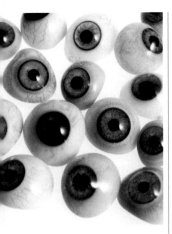

Leave the cases of gruesome medical instruments for another day and move on, exiting left on to Euston Road, then left again for Gower Street and **University College London**. The university's collection of instruments that belonged to Victorian polymath and fingerprint pioneer Sir Francis Galton can be seen by appointment (Galton Collection, 7679 2647, www.ucl.ac.uk/museums/galton); Galton's classification of the different fingerprint patterns is still in use today.

At bus Stop N, catch a no.24 to Whitehall, taking a seat on the left. As you pass the Biological Sciences building, spare a thought for the great forensic science lecturer Sir Bernard Spilsbury. Brilliant, handsome and usually seen sporting a red carnation in his Savile Row suit, Spilsbury's star quality transformed the beastly science of the dead into a quite glamorous, media-friendly pursuit. He became a household name after his identification of Dr Hawley H Crippen's wife from the mutilated, headless remains found in their coal cellar secured Crippen's conviction. Back then, his methods were sometimes questioned, with Conan Doyle himself joining protests when Spilsbury's reputation swayed a jury on slender evidence. In 1947, having conducted more than 25,000 post mortems and testified in 200 murder trials, Spilsbury took his own life, poisoning himself with coal-gas in his laboratory. Recent DNA tests on the Crippen remains wouldn't have cheered him up: they've shown the body parts probably weren't the wife.

Five minutes later, the bus crosses New Oxford Street, where Crippen bought five grains of hyoscin poison from a pharmacist shortly before his wife disappeared.

adventures for *Strand* magazine. Get off at Euston Square, cross Euston Road by the traffic lights and head for the stern neo-classical columns of the racy **Wellcome Collection** (p126).

In the first-floor 'Medicine Now' exhibition, scan your fingerprint to generate a unique biometric profile and try out a basic face recognition system. The 'similar' people you are compared to might make you question your looks. If you're happy answering a few personal questions, you can also contribute to research trying to link facial characteristics with behaviour. Across the room, browse the 110 volumes of the human genome, the genetic instructions that provide the foundation for DNA profiling. Before you leave, nip into the 'Medicine Man' exhibition in the next room and seek out the scraggy clump of King George III's hair, which modern forensic analysis has found to contain high levels of arsenic. It seems the drugs administered by his physicians may have heightened rather than relieved poor 'mad' George's symptoms.

At **Cambridge Circus**, look out for the red neon signs of St Martin's Theatre (West Street, www.the-mousetrap.co.uk), where Agatha Christie's *The Mousetrap* – the quintessential country house murder mystery – remains the world's longest-running play. Not far ahead, it was on **Cecil Court** that a murder in an antiques shop prompted the first use of identikit pictures to catch a suspect.

Just after Trafalgar Square (p79), disembark on Whitehall and take the second left into Whitehall Place. Here Sir Robert Peel founded the London Metropolitan Police in 1829. Cut under the bridge on the left and turn right into **Great Scotland Yard**. Originally the public entrance to the police station, the street name is forever synonymous with the Met, even at their new home near St James's Park tube. Cross over Northumberland Avenue ahead of you and enter the pub. The **Sherlock Holmes** (10-11 Northumberland Street, 7930 2644, www.sherlockholmespub.com) was previously known as the Northumberland Hotel, in which

Sir Henry Baskerville met Holmes and Watson in *The Hound of the Baskervilles*. The entire building is now a Holmes shrine. Recharge downstairs with a pint, a Basil Rathbone film and a nod to the stuffed Hound itself. Or dine on Holmes and Watson's favourite meals (sirloin and Cumberland sausages) upstairs, beside another intricate reproduction of their study.

Fortified, turn right out of the pub and right again on to the Strand. Cross the street for bus Stop F and catch a no.11, 15 or 23 bus to Ludgate Hill. Once again, the interesting sights are on the left. Watch out for the **Royal Courts of Justice** (7947 6000, www.hmcourts-service.gov.uk) – where new DNA evidence recently overturned Sean Hodgson's conviction for murder after he had spent 30 years in prison – and Burleigh Street, once home to *Strand* magazine.

Leave the bus at Ludgate Hill, opposite City Thameslink, and track back before turning right down Old Bailey. At the crossroads, sneak a peek at the Georgian splendour of St Bart's hospital (site of Holmes and Watson's first meeting in *A Study in Scarlet*), before turning around to admire the Edwardian baroque of the Central Criminal Court, better known as the **Old Bailey** (7248 3277). Built on the site of Newgate Prison, these 18 courts were the last taste of freedom for Crippen, 'brides in the bath' murderer George Joseph Smith, Ruth Ellis and the Kray twins – the Krays even hatched an elaborate plot to murder a witness as he walked to take the stand here. If you want to see the legals at work, ring the bell by the door on Newgate Street and ask the frosty security guards if there is space in any of the courts' public galleries. But don't expect proceedings to be as exciting as they are on the telly.

Old Bailey

London by Area

County Hall

The South Bank

LONDON BY AREA

The South Bank has been drawing in tourists for centuries, but the entertainments on offer have changed somewhat. Sure, **Shakespeare's Globe** has risen again, but if you're after the prostitutes, gamblers and bear-baiting that traditionally occupied visitors here, you'll be needing a time machine. Instead, enjoy the wonderfully refurbished **Southbank Centre**, **BFI Southbank** cinema complex and **Hayward** gallery, a cluster of national cultural institutions on which logic has finally been imposed. Or join the multitude strolling along the broad riverside walkway that takes you from Tower Bridge to Westminster Bridge and beyond. This strings together fine views and must-see attractions like **Tate Modern**, the **London Eye** and the Millennium and Hungerford Bridges. Cheeky new venues keep cropping up, but

it's still-fab **Borough Market**, foodie central, that typifies the South Bank's appeal: visitors find it charming, but locals love it too.

Sights & museums

City Hall

Queen's Walk, Bankside, SE1 2AA (www.london.gov.uk). London Bridge tube/rail. **Open** 8.30am-6pm Mon-Thur; 8.30am-5.30pm Fri. **Admission** free. **Map** p61 F2 ❶

Designed by Lord Foster, this eco-friendly rotund glass structure leans squiffily away from the river. Home to London's metropolitan government, the building has the Photomat (a huge aerial photo of the city you can walk on), a café and an information desk. Outside, the Scoop amphitheatre offers free entertainments in summer.

County Hall

County Hall, Riverside Building, Queen's Walk, SE1 7PB (www.londoncounty

hall.com). Westminster tube/Waterloo tube/rail. **Map** p60 A3 ❷

The magnificent County Hall, opened in 1922 and former seat (until 1989) of London's metropolitan government, is now home to three very different attractions. Dalí Universe (7620 2720, www.daliuniverse.com; £12, £10 reductions) places trademark attractions such as the Mae West Lips sofa and the Spellbound painting alongside sculptures, watercolours (including his flamboyant tarot cards), rare etchings and lithographs. A new café serves organic fare. The recently thoroughly refurbished London Aquarium (7967 8000, www.londonaquarium.co.uk; £13.25, free-£11.50 reductions) is one of Europe's largest. There are tanks of bright fish from the coral reefs and the Indian Ocean and temperate freshwater fish from the rivers of Europe and North America, as well as jellyfish, sharks, piranhas, octopuses and a touch pool with giant rays. Finally, the Moviem (7202 7040, www.the-moviem.com; £15, £9 reductions) is dedicated to films made in Britain and by Britons since the 1950s. The 30,000sq ft space is focused more on fun (plenty of Star Wars stuff) than painstaking historical reconstruction – although the story of Pinewood Studios is told. The Chamber at the Moviem, once a magnificent debating chamber, is now a fine performance space, while downstairs there's the Horror Promenade.

Design Museum

Shad Thames, SE1 2YD (7403 6933/ www.designmuseum.org). Tower Hill tube/London Bridge tube/rail. **Open** 10am-5.45pm daily. **Admission** £8.50; free-£6.50 reductions. **Map** p61 F3 ❸

The temporary exhibitions in this white 1930s building (previously a banana warehouse) focus on modern and contemporary industrial and fashion design, architecture, graphics and multimedia developments. The smart Blueprint Café has a fine balcony overlooking the river, and you can buy designer books and items relating to the current exhibition in the shop.

Event highlights Architect David Chipperfield (from Sept 2009).

Fashion & Textile Museum

83 Bermondsey Street, Borough, SE1 3XF (7407 8664/www.ftmlondon.org). London Bridge tube/rail. **Open** 11am-6pm Wed-Sun. **Admission** £5; free-£3 reductions. **Map** p61 F4 ❹

Flamboyant as its founder, fashion designer Zandra Rhodes, this pink and orange museum reopened in 2008. It holds 3,000 of Rhodes' garments, some on permanent display, along with her archive of paper designs, sketchbooks, silk screens and show videos. A quirky shop sells ware by new designers, there's a little café and temporary exhibitions cover such delights as Swedish fashion and underwear.

Garden Museum

NEW *Lambeth Palace Road, SE1 7LB (7401 8865/www.gardenmuseum.org. uk). Lambeth North tube/Waterloo tube/rail.* **Open** 10.30am-5pm Tue-Sun. **Admission** £6; free-£5 reductions. **Map** p60 A4 ❺

Renamed and splendidly refurbished, the world's first horticulture museum looks better than ever. Topiaries, old roses, herbaceous perennials and bulbs give all-year interest in the small garden at the back, and most plants are labelled with their country of origin and year of introduction to these islands. The replica of a 17th-century knot garden was created in honour of John Tradescant, buried here after a life of intrepid plant hunting and gardening for Charles I.

Golden Hinde

St Mary Overie Dock, Cathedral Street, SE1 9DE (0870 011 700/www.golden hinde.org). Monument tube/London Bridge tube/rail. **Open** 10am-5.30pm daily. **Admission** £6; £4.50 reductions; £18 family. **Map** p61 E2 ❻

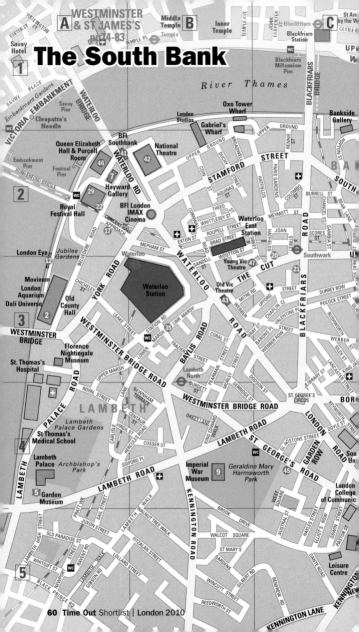

The South Bank

River Thames

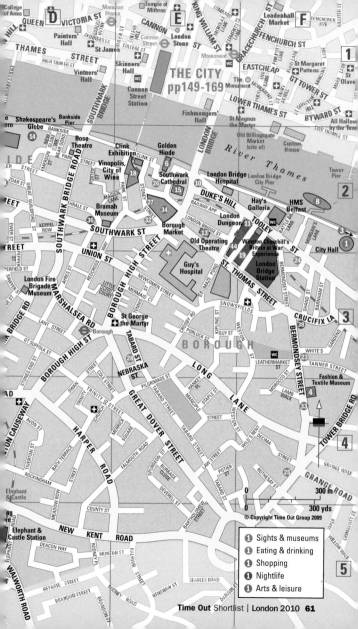

THE CITY pp149-169

River Thames

Time Out Shortlist | London 2010 **61**

① Sights & museums
① Eating & drinking
① Shopping
① Nightlife
① Arts & leisure

This replica of Sir Francis Drake's 16th-century flagship is so meticulous it was able to reprise the privateer's circumnavigatory voyage. On weekends, it swarms with children dressed up as pirates, while 'Living History Experiences' allow participants to dress in period clothes, eat Tudor fare and learn the skills of the Elizabethan seafarer; book well in advance.

Hayward

Belvedere Road, SE1 8XX (7921 0813/box office 0870 169 1000/www.hayward.org.uk). Embankment tube/Waterloo tube/rail. **Open** 10am-6pm Mon-Thur, Sat, Sun; 10am-10pm Fri. **Admission** varies. **Map** p60 A2 **7**

For more than four decades, this brutalist concrete building has proved itself a versatile host for contemporary exhibitions of art loaned from around the world. Casual visitors can hang out in the new industrial-look café (which becomes a bar at night), before visiting the free contemporary exhibitions at the inspired Hayward Project Space – take the stairs to the first floor from the glass foyer extension.

HMS Belfast

Morgan's Lane, Tooley Street, SE1 2JH (7940 6300/www.iwm.org.uk). London Bridge tube/rail. **Open** Mar-Oct 10am-6pm daily. *Nov-Feb* 10am-5pm daily. **Admission** £9.95; free-£6.15 reductions. **Map** p61 F2 **8**

This large light cruiser is the last surviving big gun World War II warship in Europe. Built in 1938, the *Belfast* provided cover for convoys to Russia, and was instrumental in the Normandy Landings. It now makes an unlikely playground for children, who tear easily around its cramped complex of gun turrets, bridge, decks and engine room. **Event highlights** 'Shipbuilding through the Ages' (until 31 Dec 2010).

Imperial War Museum

Lambeth Road, Lambeth, SE1 6HZ (7416 5320/www.iwm.org.uk). Lambeth

North tube/Elephant & Castle tube/rail. **Open** 10am-6pm daily. **Admission** free. *Special exhibitions* prices vary. **Map** p60 B4 **9**

Antique guns, tanks, aircraft and artillery are parked up in the main hall of this imposing edifice, which illustrates the history of armed conflict from World War I to the present day. The tone of the museum darkens as you ascend: the third-floor Holocaust Exhibition is not recommended for under-14s; Crimes against Humanity – a minimalist space in which a film exploring contemporary genocide and ethnic violence rolls relentlessly – is unsuitable for under-16s. Attemping to survive the 'Terrible Trenches', complete with 'splat the rat' interactivities and assorted mud-related grisliness, is more family-friendly.

Event highlights 'The Children's War' (until Jan 2010); 'Breakthrough: 20th-century War Art' (until 31 Dec 2010).

London Bridge Experience

2-4 Tooley Street, Bankside, SE1 2PF (0800 043 4666/www.thelondonbridge experience.com). London Bridge tube/rail. **Open** 10am-6pm daily. **Admission** £19.95; £14.95-£15.95 reductions. **Map** p61 E2 **10**

Old London Bridge, finished in 1209, was the first Thames crossing made of stone – and London's only Thames bridge until Westminster Bridge was finished in 1750. This kitsch, family-focused exhibition is a costumed tour of the crossing's past, as well as a scary adventure into the haunted foundations of the bridge: dank, pestilential catacombs peopled by crazed zombies and animatronic torture victims.

London Dungeon

28-34 Tooley Street, SE1 2SZ (7403 7221/www.thedungeons.com). London Bridge tube/rail. **Open** *Jan* 10.30am-5pm daily. *Feb, Mar* 9.30am-6.30pm daily. *Apr, Aug* 9.30am-7pm daily. *May-July, Sept, Oct* 10am-5.30pm daily. *Nov, Dec* 10am-5pm daily. **Admission**

Shakespeare's Globe

five years: it has proved so popular that no one wants it to come down, and it's now scheduled to keep spinning for another two decades. A 'flight' takes half an hour, allowing plenty of time to ogle the Queen's back garden and follow the snake of the Thames. Some people book in advance (taking a gamble with the weather), but it's possible to turn up and queue for a ticket on the day. There can be long queues in summer, and security is tight. Book a ride after dark on one of the Eye's 'Night flights' for a twinkly view of London.

Old Operating Theatre, Museum & Herb Garret

9A St Thomas's Street, SE1 9RY (7188 2679/www.thegarret.org.uk). London Bridge tube/rail. **Open** 10.30am-5pm daily. **Admission** £5.45; free-£4.45 reductions; £13.25 family. No credit cards. **Map** p61 E2 ⑬
The atmospheric tower that houses this salutary reminder of antique surgical practice used to be part of the chapel of St Thomas's Hospital. Visitors enter by a vertiginous wooden spiral staircase to view an operating theatre dating from 1822 (before the advent of anaesthetics), with tiered viewing seats for students. As fascinatingly gruesome are the operating tools, which look like torture implements.

Shakespeare's Globe

21 New Globe Walk, SE1 9DT (7902 1400/box office 7401 9919/www. shakespeares-globe.org). Mansion House or Southwark tube/London Bridge tube/rail. **Open** *Exhibition & tours* 10am-5pm daily. Tours every 15mins. **Admission** £9; £6.50-£7.50 reductions; £20 family. **Map** p61 D2 ⑭
The original Globe Theatre, where many of William Shakespeare's plays were first staged and which he co-owned, burned to the ground in 1613 during a performance of *Henry VIII*. Nearly 400 years later, it was rebuilt not far from its original site, using construction methods and materials as

£20.95; £15.95-£18.95 reductions. **Map** p61 F2 ⑪
Enter the Victorian railway arches beneath London Bridge station for this jokey celebration of torture, death and disease. Visitors are led through a dry-ice fog past gravestones and hideous rotting corpses to experience nasty symptoms in the Great Plague exhibition: an actor-led medley of corpses, boils, projectile vomiting and worm-filled skulls. The Great Fire and Judgement Day also get the treatment.

London Eye

Riverside Building, next to County Hall, Westminster Bridge Road, SE1 7PB (0870 500 0600/www.londoneye.com). Westminster tube/Waterloo tube/rail. **Open** *Oct-May* 10am-8pm daily. *June-Sept* 10am-9pm daily. **Admission** £15.50; free-£12 reductions. **Map** p60 A3 ⑫
Hard to believe that this giant wheel was originally intended to turn for only

LONDON BY AREA

THE ALL NEW
LONDON
SEA·LIFE.
AQUARIUM
GET CLOSER THAN EVER BEFORE

sealifelondon.co.uk

close to the originals as possible. It's a fully operational theatre, with historically authentic (and often very good) performances from April to October. In the UnderGlobe is a fine exhibition on the history of the reconstruction and Shakespeare's London. Guided tours, lasting 90mins, run all year.

Event highlights 'As You Like It' (until 10 Oct 2009).

Southwark Cathedral

London Bridge, SE1 9DA (7367 6700/ tours 7367 6734/www.dswark.org/ cathedral). London Bridge tube/rail. **Open** 8am-6pm daily (varies on religious holidays). **Admission** free. *Suggested donation £4.* **Map** p61 E2 ⑮
The oldest bits of this building date back more than 800 years, and the retro-choir was the setting for several Protestant martyr trials under Mary Tudor. There are memorials to Shakespeare and Sam Wanamaker (the force behind Shakespeare's Globe), while Chaucer features in the stained glass. The courtyard is one of the area's prettiest places for a rest, especially during the summer.

Tate Modern

Bankside, SE1 9TG (7401 5120/7887 8888/www.tate.org.uk). Southwark tube or London Bridge tube/rail. **Open** 10am-6pm Mon-Thur, Sun; 10am-10pm Fri, Sat. *Tours* 11am, noon, 2pm, 3pm daily. **Admission** free. *Special exhibitions* prices vary. **Map** p61 D2 ⑯
This powerhouse of modern art is awe-inspiring even before you enter, thanks to its industrial architecture. Built as Bankside Power Station, it was shut down in 1981, but opened as a spectacularly popular museum in 2000. The gallery now attracts five million visitors a year to a building intended for half that number – a projected £165 million extension, the pyramid-like TM2 annexe, has recently received planning permission. Inside, the original cavernous turbine hall houses the Unilever Series of temporary, large-

Tate Modern

scale installations, while the permanent collection draws from the Tate organisation's magnificent collection of modern art (international works from 1900) to display Matisse, Rothko, Bacon, Twombly and Beuys. The Tate-to-Tate boat service (7887 8888, £4.30 adult) – decor courtesy of Damien Hirst, bar on board – links with Tate Britain (p78) every 20 minutes.

Event highlights 'Sold Out: Pop Art' (1 Oct 2009-17 Jan 2010); 'John Baldessari: Pure Beauty' (13 Oct 2009-10 Jan 2010); 'Unilever Series: Miroslaw Balka' (13 Oct 2009-5 Apr 2010).

Topolski Century

NEW *150-152 Hungerford Bridge, Concert Hall Approach, SE1 8XU (www.topolskicentury.org.uk). Waterloo tube/rail.* **Open** 11am-7pm Mon-Sat; noon-6pm Sun. **Admission** free. **Map** p60 A2 ⑰
This extensive, recently restored mural, underneath the railway arches, depicts the extraordinary jumble of 20th-century events through the faces of Bob Dylan, Winston Churchill and

LONDON BY AREA

ROYAL FESTIVAL HALL

many, many others. It's the work of Polish-born Feliks Topolski, who made his name as a war artist in World War II – he was one of the first to depict the horrors of the concentration camps.

Vinopolis

1 Bank End, SE1 9BU (0870 241 4040/www.vinopolis.co.uk). London Bridge tube/rail. **Open** *Jan-Nov* noon-10pm Mon, Thur, Fri; 11am-9pm Sat; noon-6pm Sun. *Dec* noon-6pm daily. Last entry 2hrs before closing. **Admission** £19.50-£32.50; free under-16s. **Map** p61 E2 🔞
Vinopolis is more of an introduction to wine-tasting than a resource for cognoscenti, but you do need to have some prior interest to get a kick out of it. Participants are furnished with a wine glass and an audio guide. Exhibits are set out by country, with five opportunities to taste wine or bubbly from different regions – as well as microbrewed beer.

Winston Churchill's Britain at War Experience

64-66 Tooley Street, SE1 2TF (7403 3171/www.britainatwar.co.uk). London Bridge tube/rail. **Open** *Apr-Oct* 10am-6pm daily. *Nov-Mar* 10am-5pm daily.

Admission £10.45; free-£5.95 reductions; £26 family. **Map** p61 F3 🔞
This old-fashioned exhibition recalls the privations endured by the British during World War II. Visitors descend from street level in an ancient lift to a reconstructed tube station shelter. The experience continues with displays about London during the Blitz, including real bombs, rare documents, photos and reconstructed shopfronts. The displays on rationing and food production are fascinating, the set-piece walk-through bombsite quite disturbing.

Eating & drinking

Borough Market (p69) is great for gourmet snackers – and also has the top-quality **Tapas Brindisa** (the newest outpost is in South Ken, p88). Under the Royal Festival Hall there are outposts of quality chains: **Feng Sushi**, **Giraffe**, **Pain Quotidien**, **Ping Pong**, **Wagamama** (p122) and **Strada**, with our pick still **Canteen** (below).

Anchor & Hope

36 The Cut, SE1 8LP (7928 9898). Southwark or Waterloo tube/rail.

Open 5-11pm Mon; 11am-11pm Tue-Sat; 12.30-5pm Sun. **££. Gastropub. Map** p60 C3 ⓴

An offshoot of modern British pioneer St John (p157), this gastropub serves the likes of brawn or cold roast beef on dripping toast to pensioners and style-mag mavens alike, the former recognising good-value, top-quality food when they see it, the latter ensuring they stay bang on the current retro British trend. At lunch, half the room is laid for diners, with several tables free even after 1pm on a recent visit; you're unlikely to be as lucky post-work.

Baltic

74 Blackfriars Road, SE1 8HA (7928 1111/www.balticrestaurant.co.uk). Southwark tube/rail. **Open** noon-3pm, 6-11pm Mon-Sat; noon-3pm, 6-10.30pm Sun. **£££. Eastern European. Map** p60 C3 ㉑

London's only East European 'destination' restaurant, Baltic has wow factor. Make your way through the lively bar to the high-ceilinged main room, its stark whiteness punctuated by exposed beams, bare red brickwork and a chandelier of gleaming amber shards. Add a great cocktail list, a wide choice of vodkas, an eclectic wine list and proper, friendly service, and you have Baltic bliss.

Canteen

Royal Festival Hall, Belvedere Road, SE1 8XX (0845 686 1122/www.canteen.co.uk). Waterloo tube/rail. **Open** 8am-11pm Mon-Fri; 9am-11pm Sat, Sun. **££. British. Map** p60 A2 ㉒

Furnished with utilitarian but warm plain oak tables and benches, Canteen is tucked into the back of the Royal Festival Hall. Dishes range from a bacon sandwich and afternoon jam scones to full roasts. Classic breakfasts (eggs benedict, welsh rarebit) are served all day, joined by the likes of macaroni cheese or sausage and mash with onion gravy from lunchtime. Unpretentious and often busy.

Garrison

99-101 Bermondsey Street, SE1 3XB (7089 9355/www.thegarrison.co.uk). London Bridge tube/rail. **Open** 8am-11pm Mon-Fri; 9am-11pm Sat; 9am-10.30pm Sun. **££. Gastropub. Map** p61 F3 ㉓

An attractive attempt to strike out from gastropub clichés. Behind the lovely bright green exterior tiling, the dominant colours are light greys and whites, and the style of the rickety furniture cramming the bar could be called 'distressed rustic rococo'. Staff are attentive and friendly, and there's a lively buzz of chat from tablefuls enjoying gutsy combinations like Orkney calf's liver with smoked bacon.

Magdalen

152 Tooley Street, SE1 2TU (7403 1342/www.magdalenrestaurant.co.uk). London Bridge tube/rail. **Open** noon-2.30pm, 6.30-10.30pm Mon-Fri; 6.30-10.30pm Sat. **£££. British. Map** p61 F3 ㉔

The Magdalen is very comfortable, with discreetly elegant, understated decor and a slightly hushed atmosphere in its ground- and first-floor dining rooms. The frequently changing, seasonal menus are imaginative and notably refined (duck ham with peas and mint, warm squid and saffron salad, tender roast Middle White pork loin with sage and potato gratin), showing admirable ambition. Service is charming, and presentation very pretty. All rather surprising in an area full of tacky tourist attractions.

M Manze

87 Tower Bridge Road, SE1 4TW (7407 2985/www.manze.co.uk). Borough or Bermondsey tube. **Open** 11am-2pm Mon; 10.30am-2pm Tue-Thur; 10am-2.15pm Fri; 10am-2.45pm Sat. **£. No credit cards. Pie & mash. Map** p61 F4 ㉕

The finest remaining purveyor of the dirt-cheap traditional foodstuff of London's working classes. It is not only

LONDON BY AREA

the oldest pie shop, established in 1902, but the most beautiful, with marble-top tables, tiles and worn wood benches. Expect mashed potato, minced beef pies and liquor (a parsley sauce); braver souls should try the stewed eels.

Rake

Winchester Walk, SE1 9AG (7407 0557). London Bridge tube/rail. **Open** noon-11pm Mon-Fri; 10am-11pm Sat. **Pub. Map** p61 E2 ㉖

The streets around Borough Market have never been short of places to drink, but this pub has a few characteristics that help it stand out. For one thing, it's tiny, with a canopied, heated patio adjunct. For another, it's run by the folks behind the Utobeer stall in the market: expect the list of brews to be varied and enticing.

Roast

Floral Hall, Borough Market, Stoney Street, SE1 1TL (7940 1300/www. roast-restaurant.com). London Bridge tube/rail. **Open** 7-9.30am, noon-2.30pm, 5.30-10.30pm Mon-Fri; 8-10.30am, 11.30am-3.30pm, 6-10.30pm Sat; noon-3.30pm Sun. **£££. British. Map** p61 E2 ㉗

Perched above the market, Roast celebrates its marvellous location with a menu inspired by British produce, much of it sourced from the stallholders below. Seasonality and freshness are the buzzwords and there's no doubting the quality of the ingredients.

Royal Oak

44 Tabard Street, SE1 4JU (7357 7173). Borough tube. **Open** 11am-11pm Mon-Fri; noon-11pm Sat; noon-6pm Sun. **Pub. Map** p61 E3 ㉘

A pub for luvvies and lovers of Lewes brewery Harveys, the Royal Oak seems wonderfully trapped in time. Its ales from the Sussex stable – Mild, Pale, Old, Best and Armada – are all under £3, while a felt-tipped menu boasts classics such as game pie, rabbit casserole and Lancashire hotpot. Music hall

stars Flanagan & Allen, celebrated in framed, hand-bill form, would have tucked into the same decades ago; these days, there's wine too.

Skylon

Royal Festival Hall, Belvedere Road, SE1 8XX (7654 7800/www.dandd london.com). Waterloo tube/rail. **Open** *Bar* 11am-1am daily. *Brasserie* noon-11.45pm daily. *Restaurant* noon-2.30pm, 5.30-10.45pm daily. **£££. Bar-brasserie. Map** p60 A2 ㉙

There can't be many better transport views than this in London. Sit near the bar (between the two restaurant areas) to watch trains, cars and red buses trundle across two bridges, as well as boats pootling along the Thames. In spite of its aircraft-hangar proportions, the space feels surprisingly intimate: plenty of bronze, walnut and slate. For drinks, choose from ten bellinis, nine martinis and a list of 1950s classics, or the good wine list; the food, on our last visit, was rather less impressive.

Table

83 Southwark Street, SE1 0HX (7401 2760/www.thetablecafe.com). Southwark tube/London Bridge tube/rail. **Open** 7.30am-5pm Mon-Fri; 7.30am-11pm Fri; 9am-3pm Sat, Sun. **£. Café. Map** p61 D2 ㉚

Based in the ground floor of a Bankside architecture company, the Table is a cut above your regular office canteen. Mix and match a salad or choose from hot meals that include flans, a daily risotto and sardines, then hope to find a seat at the shared solid wood tables. Multifunctional, cheap and stylish.

Tsuru

NEW *4 Canvey Street, SE1 8AN (7928 2228/www.tsuru-sushi.co.uk). Southwark tube/London Bridge tube/rail.* **Open** 11am-6pm Mon-Wed; 11am-9pm Thur, Fri. **£. Japanese. Map** p61 D2 ㉛

A tiny yet remarkable canteen, to which media honeys from the Blue Fin

Bermondsey Street

Building slip away every lunch hour to deplete the supply of silky, umami-rich katsu curries. On Thursdays and Fridays, the welcoming space becomes a trendy nightspot where ippin ryori (Japanese 'tapas') can be enjoyed along with sake and shochu cocktails.

Wine Wharf

Stoney Street, Borough Market, SE1 9AD (7940 8335/www.winewharf.com). London Bridge tube/rail. **Open** noon-11pm Mon-Sat. **Wine bar**. Map p61 E2 ❸❷

Leather sofas are stuffed in among wood beams at this temple to the grape, with plenty of wood tables on which to rest dishes such as potted salt beef while drinking. The sheer number of by-the-glass options is commendable and the list is given a big going-over twice a year. For beer-lovers, Brew Wharf (7378 6601, www.brew wharf.com) and its microbrewery are tucked just behind the Wine Wharf.

Shopping

London's very own *bouquinistes* sell second-hand books, maps and old prints from long tables in front of BFI Southbank.

Bermondsey Street

London Bridge tube/rail.
Map p61 F4 ❸❸

Bermondsey Street has become decidedly cool over the last few years, through you'd hardly believe it on the approach from the north under a grimy railway bridge. There's a brand-new boutique hotel (p195) at the southern end of the street, and Zandra Rhodes's Fashion & Textile Museum (p59) is complemented by such slick shops as bermondsey167 (no.167, 7407 3137, www.bermondsey167.com), a concept store that marries impeccable interior design with highbrow fashion, Cockfighter (no.96, 7357 6482) for T-shirts and sweaters, eco-footwear at Terra Plana (no.124, 7407 3758, www. terraplana.com) and posh pet accessories at Holly & Lil (no.103, 07836 592415, www.hollyandlil.com). Rhodes is fond of lovely Igloo Flowers (no.88, 7403 7774, www.iglooflowers.com), and there are pubs and lots of caffs.

Borough Market

Southwark Street, Borough, SE1 1TL (7407 1002/www.boroughmarket.org. uk). London Bridge tube/rail. **Open** 11am-5pm Thur; noon-6pm Fri; 9am-4pm Sat. **Map** p61 E2 ❸❹

The foodie's favourite market occupies a sprawling site near London Bridge. Gourmet goodies – rare-breed meats, fruit and veg, cakes and preserves, oils and teas – run the gamut from Flour Power City Bakery's organic loaves to chorizo and rocket rolls from Spanish specialist Brindisa via Neal's Yard Dairy's speciality British cheeses. The market is now open on Thursdays, when it tends to be quieter than at always-mobbed weekends. Leave your hotel hungry to take full advantage of numerous free samples.

Lower Marsh

Waterloo tube/rail. **Map** p60 B3 **35**
Lower Marsh Market (7926 2530, www.lower-marsh.co.uk), a street market since Victorian times, still has some veg stalls and more unusual treats, but visitors will also want to explore the quirky independent shops and cafés: Scooterworks (no. 132, 7620 1421, www.scooterworks-uk.com) provides spare scooter parts, mellow vibes and very good coffee, while Radio Days (no.87, 7928 0800, www.radiodayvintage.co.uk) sells interesting vintage clothes and accessories. For books, get them new at Crockatt & Powell (nos.119-120, 7928 0234, www.crockattandpowell.co.uk) or second-hand at Jane Gibberd (no.20, 7633 9562).

Nightlife

As well as dance, theatre and classical, the **Southbank Centre** (p73) programmes a terrific range of rock, jazz and world-music gigs.

Arches

NEW *51-53 Southwark Street, SE1 1RU (7403 9643/www.the-arches. com). London Bridge tube/rail.* **Map** p61 D2 **36**
Among the railway arches, this huge (40,000sq ft) space has a 22hr licence for drinks and dancing – and the sound system, lighting rig and bar areas with which to exploit it. See box p72.

Corsica Studios

Units 4/5, Elephant Road, SE17 1LB (7703 4760/www.corsicastudios.com). Elephant & Castle tube/rail. No credit cards. **Map** p61 D5 **37**
This flexible performance space is increasingly being used as one of London's most adventurous live music venues and clubs, featuring acts such as Silver Apples, Acoustic Ladyland and Lydia Lunch. It's open until midnight or 1am for gigs, and until 6am for some club nights.

Jacks

NEW *7-9 Crucifix Lane, SE1 3JW (www.myspace.com/valveincorporated). London Bridge tube/rail.* **Map** p61 F3 **38**
James Manero, formerly of the West End's Bar Rumba (p137), kicked off Valve Warehouse Projekt in this two-room industrial space in spring 2009, 'an attempt to get back some of that original underground spirit for which London used to be so famous'. Expect the likes of DDD to be found here, kicking out a mix of techno, disco and dubstep each month.

Ministry of Sound

103 Gaunt Street, SE1 6DP (0870 060 0010/www.ministryofsound.com). Elephant & Castle tube/rail. **Open** 10.30pm-late Fri; 11pm-7am Sat. **Map** p61 D4 **39**
Cool it ain't (there's little more naff in all London than the VIP rooms here), but home to a killer sound system the Ministry most certainly is. Post-Turnmills, long-running trance night the Gallery has made its home here on Fridays (expect large sets from Paul Oakenfold and Sander van Doorn), while the Saturday Sessions chop and change between deep techno, fidget house and electro.

Southwark Arches

NEW *29 Great Suffolk Street, SE1 0NR (www.shakeitlondon.com). Southwark tube.* **Map** p60 C2 **40**

Another former industrial space – this time a Victorian warehouse – made into a two-space heaven for ravers. Opening night in spring 2009 shook the walls through to 7am. See box p72.

Arts & leisure

Free-standing Pit tickets are excellent value at **Shakespeare's Globe** (p63), where new writing is showcased alongside the Bard from May to September.

BFI Southbank

South Bank, SE1 8XT (information 7928 3535/bookings 7928 3232/www. bfi.org.uk/nft). Embankment tube/ Waterloo tube/rail. **Map** p60 A2 ④
A London institution, with an unrivalled programme of retrospective seasons and previews, with regular director and actor Q&As. The Thameside seating outside the rather underpowered main café is hugely popular in good weather, and museum-

caterers Benugo run a handsome new cocktail bar/restaurant on the other side of the building alongside the terrific Mediatheque. Made-for-IMAX children's fare and wow-factor documentaries are usually what's on offer at BFI London IMAX Cinema (1 Charlie Chaplin Walk, 0870 787 2525, www.bfi.org.uk/imax), the biggest screen in the country, but watch out for monster-sized versions of mainstream films too.

National Theatre

South Bank, SE1 9PX (7452 3400/box office 7452 3000/www.nationaltheatre. org.uk). Embankment or Southwark tube/Waterloo tube/rail. **Map** p60 B2 ④
This concrete monster is the flagship venue of British theatre. Three auditoriums – small, medium and large – each allow for many different kinds of performance: in-the-round, promenade, even classic proscenium arch. Nicholas Hytner's artistic directorship, with landmark successes such as Alan

Borough Market p69

Southside party time

South London has suddenly found its dancing shoes.

The last few years have been brutal in clubland – and we don't mean the post-party comedowns. Rave pioneer Turnmills shut in 2008, and in 2009 the End – steadfast, unarguable electronic institution and the West End's finest dance option – joined it, along with the Astoria, Ghetto and SIN. So where do you go now for an epic night of clubbing? All the ravers are heading south.

A combination of lower rents, fewer licensing restrictions (Southwark council currently seem much more amenable than the West End's Westminster council) and plenty of railway arches to turn into cavernous venues, has drawn in top club promoters. That the collective behind the End has splintered into three parts, all of them making for the area around London Bridge, speaks volumes.

The first splinter group, We Fear Silence, is headed by part of the former programming team Ajay Jayaram and Ryan Ashmore. They've got irregular Friday slots at the Arches (p70). Expect good things from these guys: line-ups previously have included Buzzin' Fly's Ben Watt, Gilles Peterson, Junior Boys at Eat Your Own Ears and Hyp!Hyp!Hyp! at Chew The Fat!. CTF!'s head honcho, Paul Arnold, has been a South Londoner for 15 years. 'If you put a party on in south London you know you will attract the people who are into music.' The second camp, run by former End manager Liam O'Hare, is now shaking it up at the Southwark Arches (p70).

A final group is led by the End's co-owner, Mr C, who is planning to run Superfreq monthly in Cable, a new venue that is to occupy a cluster of arches on Bermondsey Street (p69). 'It's a bit like a homecoming for me,' he says, referring to the raves he organised two decades ago in nearby Clink Street, in the early days of acid house. 'London Bridge is where I cut my teeth and rave culture was truly born. It's the new Shoreditch, one thinks.' Check out www.myspace.com/mrcsuperfreq if you want to find out if he's right.

Bennett's *The History Boys*, has shown that the state-subsidised home of British theatre can turn out quality drama at a profit. The Travelex season ensures a widening audience, by offering two-thirds of the seats for £10, as does the excellent free outdoor performing arts stage in summer – sit down for some booty-shaking bhangra or European fire-swallowing avant-gardists by the river.

Event highlights *Mother Courage* (opens Sept 2009); *Nation* (opens Nov 2009); *Danton's Death* (opens 2010).

Old Vic

Waterloo Road, SE1 8NB (0870 060 6628/www.oldvictheatre.com). Waterloo tube/rail. **Map** p60 B3 ㊸

The combination of double-Oscar winner Kevin Spacey and top producer David Liddiment at this grand, boxy 200-year-old theatre continues to be a commercial success, if not always a critical one. Programming runs from grown-up Christmas pantomimes to the Bridge Projects, transatlantic collaborations on big plays by Shakespeare and Chekhov.

Shunt

Joiner Street, SE1 (7378 7776/www.shunt.co.uk). London Bridge tube/rail. **Open** 6-11pm Wed-Fri. **Map** p61 E2 ㊹

Run by an artist collective in the depths of London Bridge station, Shunt isn't like other members' bars. For a start, everyone is welcome – non-members with photo ID can pay at the door, then stay until late in the rather lovely bar. Each week a different member decides the programme (cabaret, film, installations, free jazz or punk) in these vast musty arches. Shunt is under threat of redevelopment – go while you still can.

Siobhan Davies Dance Studios

85 St George's Road, SE1 6ER (7091 9650/www.siobhandavies. com). Elephant & Castle tube/rail. **Map** p60 C4 ㊻

Opened in 2006, this award-winning studio was designed in consultation with dancers – the building not only meets their needs, but looks amazing. Davies, who founded the company in 1988, often explores spaces outside her theatre, so check with the venue for performance details before setting out.

Southbank Centre

Belvedere Road, SE1 8XX (0871 663 2501/bookings 0871 663 2500/www. southbankcentre.co.uk). Embankment tube/Waterloo tube/rail. **Map** p60 A2 ㊻

The 3,000-capacity Royal Festival Hall reopened in 2007 after a £90m renovation to the whole brutalist concrete Southbank complex. Access has been made easier, but the real meat of the project is the acoustic refurbishment of the main hall. The RFH's free foyer gigs have been expanded to include concerts in the ballroom, but annual showcase events remain Meltdown (where guests such as David Bowie, Morrissey and Ornette Coleman curate a two-week programme of arts and music) and the Shell Classic International Season. Next door, the 900-seat Queen Elizabeth Hall houses pop and jazz gigs, while the much smaller Purcell Room (capacity 365) is used for anything from chamber concerts to poetry readings.

Event highlights London Sinfonietta play Steve Reich (31 Oct 2009); Meltdown 2010 (mid June 2010).

Young Vic

66 The Cut, SE1 8LZ (7922 2922/ www.youngvic.org). Waterloo tube/rail. **Map** p60 B3 ㊼

The Young Vic finally returned to its refurbished home in the Cut in 2007, and director David Lan's eclectic programming of rediscovered European classics has proved popular with the critics. The bar and restaurant, with an open-air balcony terrace for smokers, comes with young, discerning crowd attached; the volume of chat in the upstairs bar can be deafening.

St Martin-in-the-Fields p78

Westminster & St James's

Westminster

More formal than it is inviting, Westminster remains for many the heart of London. Home to the **Houses of Parliament**, the area has been the seat of government power for 1,000 years; Britain's very first Parliament met in **Westminster Abbey**, the site of almost every British coronation. Here too is **Trafalgar Square** – tourist photo-op by day, host of diverse festivals by night.

Sights & museums

Banqueting House

Whitehall, SW1A 2ER (0844 482 7777/www.hrp.org.uk). Westminster tube/Charing Cross tube/rail. **Open** 10am-5pm Mon-Sat. **Admission** £4.50; free-£3.50 reductions. **Map** p75 C2 ❶

This Italianate mansion was built in 1620 and is the sole surviving part of the Tudor and Stuart kings' Whitehall Palace. It features a lavish ceiling by Rubens that glorifies James I, 'the wisest fool in Christendom'. Sometimes closed for corporate dos – phone ahead.

Cabinet War Rooms & Churchill Museum

Clive Steps, King Charles Street, SW1A 2AQ (7930 6961/www.iwm.org.uk). St James's Park or Westminster tube. **Open** 9.30am-6pm daily. **Admission** £12; free-£9.50 reductions. **Map** p75 C2 ❷

Beneath Whitehall, the cramped and spartan bunker where Winston Churchill planned the Allied victory in World War II remains exactly as it was left on 16 August 1945. There's a tangible sense of wartime hardship, reinforced by wailing sirens and wartime speeches on the free audio guide.

74 **Time Out** Shortlist | London 2010

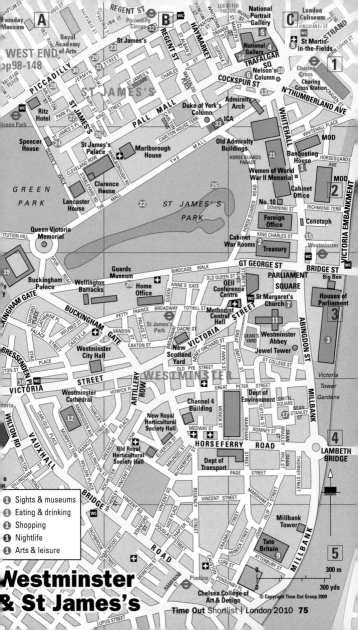

Westminster & St James's

Adjoining the War Rooms, the engaging Churchill Museum is devoted to the great man and his famous speeches.

Houses of Parliament

Parliament Square, SW1A 0AA (tours information 0870 906 3773/ www.parliament.uk). Westminster tube. **Open** phone or check website for details. **Admission** *Visitors' Gallery* free. *Tours* £12; free-£8 reductions. **Map** p75 C3 ❸

Visitors are welcome to observe the debates at the House of Lords and House of Commons – Prime Minister's Question Time at noon on Wednesday is often fiery – but tickets must be arranged in advance through your embassy or MP. The best time to visit is during the summer recess, when tours – taking in ancient Westminster Hall – are organised (book in advance). Most of the original Parliament buildings were destroyed by fire in 1834, with the current neo-Gothic extravaganza completed in 1860.

National Gallery

Trafalgar Square, WC2N 5DN (7747 2885/www.nationalgallery.org.uk). Leicester Square tube/Charing Cross tube/rail. **Open** 10am-6pm Mon-Thur, Sat, Sun; 10am-9pm Fri. *Tours* 11.30am, 2.30pm daily. **Admission** free. *Special exhibitions* prices vary. **Map** p75 C1 ❹

Founded in 1824 to display a collection of just 36 paintings, today the National Gallery is home to more than 2,000 works. There are masterpieces from virtually every European school of art, from austere 13th-century religious paintings to the visceral delights of Van Gogh. Straight ahead on entry, in the North Wing, are 17th-century Dutch, Flemish, Italian and Spanish Old Masters, including Velázquez's *Rokeby Venus*, while the East Wing contains hugely popular French Impressionist and Post-Impressionist paintings by Monet, Renoir and Seurat. You can't see everything in one visit,

but free guided tours and audio guides can point you to the highlights.

Event highlights 'The Sacred Made Real: Spanish Painting & Sculpture 1600-1700' (21 Oct 2009-24 Jan 2010); *Hoerengracht* installation (18 Nov 2009-21 Feb 2010).

National Portrait Gallery

2 St Martin's Place, WC2H 0HE (7306 0055/www.npg.org.uk). Leicester Square tube/Charing Cross tube/rail. **Open** 10am-6pm Mon-Wed, Sat, Sun; 10am-9pm Thur, Fri. **Admission** free. *Special exhibitions* prices vary. **Map** p75 C1 ❺

Portraits don't have to be stuffy. The National Portrait Gallery has everything from oil paintings of stiff-backed royals to photos of soccer stars and gloriously unflattering political caricatures. The portraits of musicians, scientists, artists, philanthropists and celebrities are arranged in chronological order from the top to the bottom of the building.

Event highlights BP Portrait Awards (18 June-20 Sept 2009).

Routemaster buses

Cockspur Street, Stops B & (opposite) S. **Map** p75 C1 ❻

The iconic red double-deckers were withdrawn from service in 2005, but beautifully refurbished Routies run Routes 9 (Stop B) and 15 (Stop S) every 15mins, 9.30am to 6.30pm. No.9 goes west to the Royal Albert Hall, no.15 east via St Paul's to Tower Hill. Unless you already have an Oyster or travelcard (p213), you must buy a ticket before boarding.

St Margaret's Church

Parliament Square, SW1P 3JX (7654 4840/www.westminster-abbey.org). St James's Park or Westminster tube. **Open** 9.30am-3.30pm Mon-Fri; 9.30am-1.30pm Sat; 2-5pm Sun (times vary due to services). **Admission** free. **Map** p75 C3 ❼

This small church was founded in the 12th century and has impressive

Fourth columnist?

There's new spice in an age-old controversy.

In the north-west corner of Trafalgar Square (p79) is the so-called Fourth Plinth – built in 1841 in anticipation of an equestrian statue that never arrived. After more than 150 years of discussion about which royal or martial hero might be a suitable occupant, in 1999 the Royal Society of Arts (RSA) decided to put a temporary contemporary sculpture there, starting a rolling commission (www.fourthplinth.co.uk) beside the National Gallery (p76).

The latest instalment of this popular programme is the most interactive: Antony Gormley's *The One and the Other* involves more than 2,400 volunteers (members of the public who registered at www.oneandother.co.uk) standing for an hour each on the plinth for 100 complete days, which began on 6 July 2009.

The sense that a martial hero would be more appropriate has, however, lingered. Most recently, support has been gathering behind a proposal to honour Battle of Britain hero – and New Zealander – Sir Keith Park, whose RAF squadrons protected London from the Nazis in 1940, earning him the nickname 'defender of London'. A maquette has been produced by Leslie Johnson (*pictured above*) and funding found for the statue, but it now won't become the permanent occupant of the plinth. Instead, it will stand there for six months, and be moved in 2010 to Waterloo Place, just behind the ICA (p83).

Intriguingly, the sculpture selected to follow Gormley – and also Sir Keith's temporary stay – is Yinka Shonibare's *Nelson's Ship in a Bottle*. This work – by a black Londoner who grew up in Lagos – is a replica of Nelson's warship HMS *Victory*, in a giant bottle, a cheeky commentary both on Britain's colonial history and its attitude to war.

St James's Park p81

pre-Reformation stained glass: the east window (1509) commemorates the betrothal of Arthur, Henry VIII's elder brother, who died young, to Catherine of Aragon. More recently a memorial to freed slave and key abolitionist Olaudah Equiano – baptised here in 1759 – was unveiled for his 250th anniversary.

St Martin-in-the-Fields

Trafalgar Square, WC2N 4JJ (7766 1100/Brass Rubbing Centre 7766 1122/www.smitf.org). Leicester Square tube/Charing Cross tube/rail. **Open** 8am-6pm daily. *Brass Rubbing Centre* 10am-7pm Mon-Wed; 10am-10pm Thur-Sat; noon-7pm Sun. *Tours* 11.30am Thur. **Admission** free. *Brass rubbing* £4.50. **Map** p75 C1 ❽
Built in 1726 by James Gibbs, the church has recently benefited from a £36m refurbishment. The bright interior has been fully restored, with Victorian furbelows removed and the addition of a controversial altar window that shows the Cross, stylised as if rippling on water. The crypt, its fine

café and the London Brass Rubbing Centre have all been modernised.
Event highlights Regular candlelit evening concerts provide lashings of Mozart and Vivaldi; lunchtime recitals (Mon, Tue, Fri) offer less predictable fare.

Tate Britain

Millbank, SW1P 4RG (7887 8888/ www.tate.org.uk). Pimlico tube. **Open** 10am-5.50pm daily; 10am-10pm 1st Fri of mth. *Tours* 11am, noon, 2pm, 3pm Mon-Fri; noon, 3pm Sat, Sun.
Admission free. *Special exhibitions* prices vary. **Map** p75 C5 ❾
Tate Modern (p65) gets all the attention, but the original Tate Gallery has a broader and more inclusive brief. Housed in a stately Portland stone building on the riverside, it's second only to the National (p76) for historical art in London. The collection of British art includes work by Hogarth, Gainsborough, Reynolds, Constable, and Turner (in the Clore Gallery). Modern Brits Stanley Spencer, Lucian Freud and Francis Bacon are well represented, and the Art Now installations

showcase up-and-comers. The handy Tate-to-Tate boat service (p65) zips to Tate Modern every 40mins.

Event highlights 'Turner & the Masters' (23 Sept 2009-24 Jan 2010); Turner Prize (6 Oct 2009-16 Jan 2010).

Trafalgar Square

Charing Cross tube/rail. **Map** p75 C1 ⑩
The centrepiece of London, Trafalgar Square was conceived in the 1820s as a homage to Britain's naval power. It has always been a natural gathering point – more so since semi-pedestrian-isation in 2003. The focus is Nelson's Column, a Corinthian pillar topped by a statue of naval hero Horatio Nelson, but the Fourth Plinth (see box p77) brings some colour and modern controversy. The square is a frequent venue for concerts and festivals.

Westminster Abbey

20 Dean's Yard, SW1P 3PA (7222 5152/tours 7654 4900/www. westminster-abbey.org). St James's Park or Westminster tube. **Open** *Nave & Royal Chapels* 9.30am-3.30pm Mon, Tue, Thur, Fri; 9.30am-6pm Wed; 9.30am-1.30pm Sat. *Abbey Museum & Chapter House* 10am-4pm daily. **Admission** £12; free-£9 reductions; £26 family. *Abbey Museum* free. *Tours* £3. **Map** p75 C3 ⑪
The cultural significance of the Abbey is hard to overstate. Edward the Confessor commissioned it on the site of a 7th-century version, but it was only consecrated on 28 December 1065, eight days before he died. William the Conqueror had himself crowned here on Christmas Day, 1066. With just two exceptions, every coronation since then has taken place in the Abbey, and many royal, military and cultural notables are interred here. The Abbey Museum, which occupies one of the oldest parts of the Abbey, celebrated its centenary in 2008. Here you'll find effigies and waxworks of British monarchs, among them Edward II and Henry VII, wearing the robes they donned in life.

Westminster Cathedral

42 Francis Street, SW1P 1QW (7798 9055/www.westminstercathedral.org.uk). Victoria tube/rail. **Open** 7am-6pm Mon-Fri; 8am-6.30pm Sat; 8am-7pm Sun. *Bell tower* 9.30am-5pm Mon-Fri; 10am-4.30pm Sat, Sun. **Admission** free; donations appreciated. *Bell tower* £5; £2.50 reductions. **Map** p75 A4 ⑫
With its domes, arches and soaring tower, the most important Catholic church in England was built between 1895 and 1903, its architecture heavily influenced by Istanbul's Hagia Sophia mosque. Inside are impressive marble columns and mosaics, and Eric Gill's sculptures of the Stations of the Cross. A lift runs to the top of the 273ft bell tower for dizzying views.

Eating & drinking

In Old Westminster Library, the grand Cinnamon Club (30-32 Great Smith Street, SW1P 3BU, 7222 2555, www.cinnamonclub.com) serves exemplary haute Indian cuisine; Cinnamon Kitchen (p165) is its new City outpost.

Albannach

66 Trafalgar Square, WC2N 5DS (7930 0066/www.albannach.co.uk). Charing Cross tube/rail. **Open** noon-1am Mon-Wed; noon-3am Thur-Sun. **Cocktail bar**. **Map** p75 C1 ⑬
Albannach (as opposed to 'sassanach') specialises in Scotch whiskies and cocktails thereof. Notwithstanding the impressive location facing on to the square, kilted staff, illuminated rein-deer and loud office groups can detract from the quality of booze on offer.

National Dining Rooms

Sainsbury Wing, National Gallery, Trafalgar Square, WC2N 5DN (7747 2525/www.thenationaldiningrooms.co. uk). Charing Cross tube/rail. **Open** 10am-5.30pm Mon, Tue, Thur-Sun; 10am-8.30pm Wed. **£££**. **British**. **Map** p75 C1 ⑭

LONDON BY AREA

Oliver Peyton's finest restaurant is still in fine shape. Cultured, cheeky afternoon teas can be taken, though the real attraction remains the main menu of British staples, immaculately cooked and presented in a nicely relaxed atmosphere. The East Wing's darkly romantic National Café bar-restaurant (7747 2525, www.thenationalcafe.com) opens until 11pm daily.

Red Lion

48 Parliament Street, SW1A 2NH (7930 5826). Westminster tube. **Open** 10am-11pm Mon-Fri; 10am-9.30pm Sat; noon-9pm Sun. **Pub**. **Map** p75 C2 ⓯
A 600-year-old boozer distinguished by a division bell (to call errant MPs in to vote) and TVs that tirelessly screen BBC Parliament. Half a dozen real ales are on offer, while beer fodder fish and chips and steaks are served upstairs.

Nightlife

Pacha London

Terminus Place, Victoria, SW1V 1JR (0845 371 4489/www.pachalondon.com). Victoria tube/rail. **Open** 10pm-5am Fri, Sat. **Admission** £15-£20. **Map** p75 A4 ⓰
The über-glamorous Ibizan superclub is located in… a bus depot. Attracting the suited, booted and minted with sassy house parties, it's a swanky place for clubbers who have money to burn.

Arts & leisure

St John's, Smith Square

Smith Square, SW1P 3HA (7222 1061/www.sjss.org.uk). Westminster tube. **Map** p75 C4 ⓱
With its distinctive four towers, this elegant church was completed in 1728. It now hosts orchestral and chamber concerts more or less every night, along with occasional recitals on its magnificent Klais organ. In the crypt, the Footstool restaurant opens for weekday lunches and also dinner on concert nights.

Victoria Palace Theatre

Victoria Street, SW1E 5EA (0870 895 5577/www.victoriapalacetheatre.co.uk). Victoria tube/rail. **Map** p75 A4 ⓳
Billy Elliot, scored by Elton John, is set during the 1984 miners' strike. A northern, working-class lad realises he loves ballet – much to the consternation of his salt-of-the-earth dad. Production subject to change.

St James's

Traditional, quiet and terribly exclusive, St James's is where **Buckingham Palace** presides over lovely **St James's Park**. Everything is dignified rather than hurried, whether you're shopping at **Fortnum's** and on **Jermyn Street**, or entertaining in **Dukes** or the **Wolseley**.

Sights & museums

Buckingham Palace & Royal Mews

The Mall, SW1A 1AA (Palace 7766 7300/Queen's Gallery 7766 7301/Royal Mews 7766 7302/www.royalcollection.org.uk). Green Park or St James's Park tube/Victoria tube/rail. **Open** *State Rooms* mid July-Sept 9.45am-6pm (last entry 3.45pm) daily. *Queen's Gallery* 10am-5.30pm daily. *Royal Mews* Mar-July, Oct 11am-4pm Mon-Thur, Sat, Sun; Aug, Sept 10am-5pm daily. **Admission** *Palace* £15.50; free-£14 reductions; £39.75 family. *Queen's Gallery* £8.50; free-£7.50 reductions; £21.50 family. *Royal Mews* £7.50; free-£6.75 reductions; £19.80 family. **Map** p75 A3 ⓳
The present home of the British royals is open to the public each year while the family Windsor are away on their summer holidays; you'll be able to see the State Apartments, which are still used to entertain dignitaries and guests of state. At other times of year, visit the Queen's Gallery to see the Queen's personal collection of treasures. Further along Buckingham Palace Road, the

Royal Mews is the home of the royal Rolls-Royces, the splendid royal carriages and the horses that pull them.
Event highlights Changing of the Guard (except in rain: 11.30am alternate days, daily Apr-July); 'The Conversation Piece: Scenes of Fashionable Life' (Queen's Gallery, 30 Oct 2009-14 Feb 2010).

Guards Museum

Wellington Barracks, Birdcage Walk, SW1E 6HQ (7414 3428/www.the guardsmuseum.com). St James's Park tube. **Open** 10am-4pm daily. **Admission** £3; free-£2 reductions. **Map** p75 B3 ⑳
This small museum tells the 350-year story of the Foot Guards, using flamboyant uniforms, medals, period paintings and intriguing memorabilia, such as the stuffed body of Jacob the Goose, the Guard's Victorian mascot.

Household Cavalry Museum

Horse Guards, Whitehall, SW1A 2AX (7930 3070/www.householdcavalry.co. uk). Embankment tube/Charing Cross tube/rail. **Open** *Mar-Sept* 10am-6pm daily. *Oct-Feb* 10am-5pm daily. **Admission** £6; free-£4 reductions; £15 family. **Map** p75 C2 ㉑
The Household Cavalry, the Queen's official escort, get to tell their stories through video diaries at this small but entertaining museum. Separated from the stables by a mere pane of glass, you'll also get a peek – and sniff – of the magnificent horses that parade just outside every day.
Event highlights Changing of the Guard (except in rain: 11am Mon-Fri; 10am Sat).

St James's Park

St James's Park or Westminster tube. **Map** p75 B2 ㉒
St James's Park, founded as a deer park, was remodelled on the orders of George IV. The central lake is home to numerous species of wildfowl, including pelicans that are fed at 3pm daily, and the bridge offers a great snap of the palace.

ICA revival

Now free to all, the art centre is finding its voice.

Ekow Eshun has been quietly transforming the **ICA** (p83) since 2005 – when he took over as artistic director from Philip Dodd, who had spent nearly a decade in the job – but things have really begun to take shape over the last year. Entrance, formerly requiring a nominal daily membership fee, is now free; there was the start of the CinematICA fundraising drive to refurbish the venue's two screens; and, to spiff up the bar-restaurant area, there was the arrival of Oliver Peyton, the man whose National Dining Rooms (p79) persuaded us museum eats could be a real pleasure.

Not only is the stylish new bar-café a place of refreshment, but it's also a happening location for guest DJs, film screenings and live music. Events here are even justifying the 'contemporary' part of the Institute's name, and without obliging visitors to pull on a hairshirt in the name of art: witness 'A Recent History of Writing and Drawing' and the iTunes Festival, both drawing, in very different ways, on modern communications technology.

We asked Eshun what he used to love about the ICA before taking over, and he talked about the bookshop: 'I go in there looking for one thing, then end up stumbling across all sorts of different stuff. Philosophy, culture, memoir, politics, art... It stretches your brain in a very pleasurable way.' His aspiration, maybe, for the place as a whole.

St James's Piccadilly

197 Piccadilly, W1J 9LL (7734 4511/ www.st-james-piccadilly.org). Piccadilly Circus tube. **Open** 8am-6.30pm daily. **Admission** free. **Map** p75 B1 ㉓

Consecrated in 1684, St James's is the only church Sir Christopher Wren built on an entirely new site. This is a busy church, providing a home for the William Blake Society and hosting markets in the churchyard: antiques on Tuesday, arts and crafts from Wednesday to Saturday.

Event highlights Free recitals (1.10pm Mon, Wed, Fri).

Eating & drinking

Dukes Hotel

35 St James's Place, SW1A 1NY (7491 4840/www.dukeshotel.co.uk). Green Park tube. **Open** noon-11pm Mon-Sat; noon-10.30pm Sun. **Cocktail bar.** **Map** p75 A2 ㉔

This centenarian hotel was renovated in 2007, transforming its discreet, highly regarded but old-fashioned bar into a swish landmark destination. Dukes' famous dry martinis are flamboyantly made at guests' tables – you pay plenty for the privilege, but won't regret it.

Inn The Park

St James's Park, SW1A 2BJ (7451 9999/www.innthepark.com). St James's Park tube. **Open** 8am-9pm Mon-Fri; 9am-9pm Sat, Sun. **££. British café- restaurant.** **Map** p75 B2 ㉕

Self-service customers fight over tables at the back, while the front terrace overlooking the lake is reserved for the fatter of wallet. The restaurant is open from (build your own) breakfast to dinner, with the accent on in-season, British ingredients.

Red Lion

23 Crown Passage, SW1Y 6PP (7930 4141). Green Park or St James's Park tube. **Open** 11am-11pm Mon-Sat. **££.** **Pub.** **Map** p75 A2 ㉖

Hidden down a dark and narrow passageway, this pub is an in-the-know location for local workers who treasure the traditional British boozer.

Sake No Hana

23 St James's Street, SW1A 1HA (7925 8988). Green Park tube. **Open** noon-3pm, 6pm-midnight Mon-Sat; noon-3pm, 6-11pm Sun. **££££.** **Japanese.** **Map** p75 A1 ㉗

Sake No Hana is discreet and coolly designed, winning our 2008 Award for Best Restaurant Design. Cedar tables with foot-wells sit amid acres of tatami (there's Western-style seating too). Some dishes are modern and playful, but many are orthodox and simple. All are works of culinary art.

Wolseley

160 Piccadilly, W1J 9EB (7499 6996/ www.thewolseley.com). Green Park tube. **Open** 7am-midnight Mon-Fri; 8am- midnight Sat; 8am-11pm Sun. **££££.** **Brasserie.** **Map** p75 A1 ㉘

In its gorgeous 1920s room, the Wolseley shimmers with glamour and excitement, the dining room is filled with a lively social energy and battalions of waiters. No wonder it's a sought-after venue at all times of day: breakfast, brunch, lunch, tea or dinner.

Shopping

Fortnum & Mason

181 Piccadilly, W1A 1ER (7734 8040/ www.fortnumandmason.co.uk). Green Park or Piccadilly Circus tube. **Open** 10am-8pm Mon-Sat; noon-6pm Sun. **Map** p75 A1 ㉙

The revamped F&M is stunning: a sweeping spiral staircase soars through the four-storey building, while light floods down from a central glass dome. The iconic eau de nil blue and gold colour scheme with flashes of rose pink abound on both the store design and the packaging of the fabulous ground-floor treats, like the chocolates, biscuits, teas and preserves.

Fortnum & Mason

Jeffery-West

16 Piccadilly Arcade, SW1Y 6NH
(7499 3360/www.jeffery-west.co.uk).
Green Park or Piccadilly Circus tube.
Open 10am-6pm Mon-Wed, Fri, Sat;
10am-7pm Thur. **Map** p75 A1 ③⓪
With its playboy vampire's apartment
feel – red walls, interesting objets d'art,
an unexpected skeleton in the window
– this shop is the perfect showcase for
rakish men's shoes, much loved by
modern-day dandies.

Jermyn Street

Green Park or Piccadilly Circus tube.
Map p75 A1 ③①
If you've got £200 to drop on a shirt,
you've come to the right place:
Hilditch & Key (no.73, 7930 5336,
www.hilditchandkey.co.uk), Emma
Willis (no.66, 7930 9980, www.emma
willis.com) and Turnbull & Asser
(nos.71-72, 7808 3000, www.turnbull
andasser.co.uk) all continue the proud
bespoke tradition of this street. You
can finish the outfit off with headwear
from Bates the Hatter (no.21A, 7734
2722, www.bates-hats.co.uk), with its
wonderful topper-shaped sign and fine
old-fashioned interior.

Nightlife

Pigalle Club

215 Piccadilly, W1J 9HN (box office
0845 345 6053/www.vpmg.net/pigalle).
Piccadilly Circus tube. **Open** 7pm-2am
Mon-Wed; 7pm-3am Thur-Sat.
Admission free-£65. **Map** p75 B1 ③②
The Pigalle is an old-fashioned, 400-
capacity, basement supper club that's
all about 1940s-style glamour. The
programming is often jazzy, with occasional big-name soul belters thrown in.

Arts & leisure

ICA (Institute of
Contemporary Arts)

The Mall, SW1Y 5AH (7930 0493/box
office 7930 3647/www.ica.org.uk).
Piccadilly Circus tube/rail. **Open** varies. *Galleries (during*
exhibitions) noon-7pm Mon-Wed, Fri-
Sun; noon-9pm Thur. **Admission** free.
Map p75 B1 ③③
Founded in 1947 by a collective of poets,
artists and critics, the ICA is a venue
for arthouse cinema, performance art,
debates, art-themed clubbing and anything in-between. See box p81.

Science Museum p88

South Kensington & Chelsea

South Kensington

This is the land of plenty as far as cultural and academic institutions are concerned: the area was once known as 'Albertopolis', in honour of the prince who oversaw the inception of its world-class museums, colleges and concert hall, using the profits of the 1851 Great Exhibition. The **Natural History Museum**, **Science Museum** and **Victoria & Albert Museum** are clustered together, but such is the wealth of exhibits in each you'd be foolish to try to 'do' more than one of them in a single day. The grandiose **Royal Albert Hall** and overblown, splendidly restored **Albert Memorial** pay homage to the man behind it all, and **Kensington Gardens** provides a refreshing green backdrop.

Sights & museums

Albert Memorial
Kensington Gardens, SW7 (7495 0916). South Kensington tube. **Tours** *Mar-Dec* 2pm, 3pm 1st Sun of mth. **Admission** *Tours* £5; £4.50 reductions. No credit cards. **Map** p86 B1 ❶
Hard to imagine what the unassuming Prince Albert would have made of this extraordinary thing, unveiled 15 years after his death. Created by Sir George Gilbert Scott, it centres on a gilded, seated Albert holding a catalogue of the Great Exhibition. The 180ft spire is inlaid with semi-precious stones.

Brompton Oratory
Thurloe Place, Brompton Road, SW7 2RP (7808 0900/www.brompton oratory.com). South Kensington tube. **Open** 6.30am-8pm daily. **Admission** free; donations appreciated. **Map** p86 C3 ❷

The second-biggest Catholic church in the country (after Westminster Cathedral, p79) was completed in 1884, but it feels older – partly because of its baroque Italianate style, partly because much of the decoration pre-dates the structure: Mazzuoli's late 17th-century apostle statues are from Siena cathedral, for example.

Kensington Palace & Gardens

Kensington Gardens, W8 4PX (0844 482 7777/booking line 0844 482 7799/ www.hrp.org.uk). Bayswater, High Street Kensington or Queensway tube. **Open** *Mar-Oct* 10am-5pm daily. *Nov-Feb* 10am-4pm daily. **Admission** £12.30; free-£10.75 reductions; £34 family. **Map** p86 A1 ❸

At the end of the 17th century, Sir Christopher Wren extended this Jacobean mansion to palatial proportions on the instructions of William III. The King's Apartments are pretty grand, while the Queen's Apartments are more intimate. The lavish ensembles of the Royal Ceremonial Dress Collection include dresses worn by Diana, Princess of Wales, the palace's most famous resident. In front of the palace, Kensington Gardens is only delineated from Hyde Park (p90) by the Serpentine and the Long Water. Diana's presence is strong: summer visitors paddle in the ring-shaped Princess Diana Memorial Fountain, by US architect Kathryn Gustafson, while children make a bee-line for the pirate ship climbing frame in the Diana, Princess of Wales Playground.

Natural History Museum

Cromwell Road, SW7 5BD (7942 5725/switchboard 7942 5000/www. nhm.ac.uk). South Kensington tube. **Open** 10am-5.50pm daily. **Admission** free. *Tours* free. *Special exhibitions* prices vary. **Map** p86 B3 ❹

The NHM opened in a magnificent, purpose-built, Romanesque palazzo in 1881. Now, the vast entrance hall is

Nude and rued?

South Ken's controversial 'naked road' initiative.

In early 2009, Exhibition Road – the heart of London's South Kensington cultural quarter, access route to the Natural History Museum, V&A (p88), Science Museum (p88), Hyde Park (p90) and the Royal Albert Hall (p89), magnet for 23 million visitors a year – embarked on some radical changes. They're inspired by the late Dutch traffic engineer Hans Monderman – according to whom all the props that are meant to make an urban space safe for cars as well as those on foot (traffic lights, railings, kerbs, road markings) are removed, thereby compelling both motorists and pedestrians to 'negotiate' with each other.

So how will Exhibition Road look? It won't be as clean as a sci-fi cartoon, but it will be a sort of utopia: trees where signs and lamps used to stand; road markings, underpasses, bins, barriers and all those crossings with zoological names (zebra, pelican) either reconfigured or removed; the dank pedestrian tunnel that links South Ken tube to the museums upgraded with airport-style travelators.

Until the work is completed here, you can check on progress in the West End, where another iconic part of our roadscape – Oxford Circus – has begun the process of transformation into a diagonal crossing on the model of Tokyo's Shibuya junction.

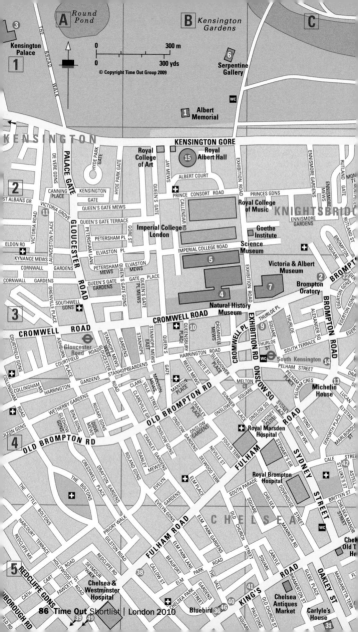

Round Pond **A**

B Kensington Gardens

C

3

1 Kensington Palace

0   300 m

0   300 yds

© Copyright Time Out Group 2009

6 Serpentine Gallery

wc

1 Albert Memorial

KENSINGTON

KENSINGTON GORE

Royal College of Art

15 Royal Albert Hall

DE VERE GDNS

HYDE PARK GATE

JAY MEWS

PRINCE CONSORT ROAD

EXHIBITION ROAD

PRINCES GDNS

ENNISMORE GARDENS

RUTLAND GATE

ENNISMORE GATE

2

ST ALBANS GR

CANNING PLACE

VICTORIA ROAD

11

GLOUCESTER   ROAD

HYDE PARK GATE

KENSINGTON

Queen's Gate Mews

QUEEN'S GATE

ALBERT COURT

CALLENDAR RD

Royal College of Music

Goethe Institute

KNIGHTSBRIDGE

ENNISMORE GARDENS

BROMPTON

PALACE GATE

LAUNCESTON PLACE

VICTORIA GROVE

Queen's Gate Terrace

GORE ST

Imperial College London

Science Museum

2 Brompton Oratory

SQUARE

Victoria & Albert Museum

ELDON RD

PETERSHAM LANE

Elvaston PL

IMPERIAL COLLEGE ROAD

EGERTON GDNS

KYNANCE MEWS

CORNWALL GARDENS

GREENVILLE PLACE

PETERSHAM MEWS

ELVASTON MEWS

QUEEN'S GATE

Gate Place

5

EXHIBITION ROAD

7

EGERTON

CORNWALL GARDENS

Queen's Gate Gdns

QUEEN'S GATE PL MEWS

4

Natural History Museum

THURLOE PL

9

ALEXANDER SQ

3

SOUTHWELL GDNS

CROMWELL ROAD

CROMWELL PL

THURLOE SQUARE

CROMWELL   ROAD

Gloucester Road

ASHBURNHAM GDNS

STANHOPE MEWS

STANHOPE MEWS

STANHOPE GARDENS

STANHOPE

QUEEN'S GATE

QUEENSBURY PLACE

CROMWELL MEWS

HARRINGTON ROAD

10

CROMWELL PL

EXHIBITION RD

THURLOE ST

SOUTH TERRACE

wc

South Kensington

14

PELHAM STREET

13

COURTFIELD GDNS

COLLINGHAM GDNS

COURTFIELD ROAD

GLOUCESTER RD

STANHOPEGARDENS

HARRINGTON GARDENS

REECE MEWS

BUTE ST

GARDEN

ONSLOW GDNS

PELHAM CRES

Michelin House

LUCAN

COLLINGHAM

HARRINGTON

CLAREVILLE GROVE

CLARE

MANSON

MELTON

STONE

SYDNEY

OLD BROMPTON ROAD

WETHERBY GARDENS

BINA GDNS

ROSARY GDNS

CLAREVILLE ST

MANSON PLACE

CRANLEY PLACE

SUMNER PLACE

ONSLOW SQUARE

SYDNEY PLACE

BURY WK

POND PL

FULTON GDNS

BOLTON GDNS

DOVE MEWS

HEREFORD SQUARE

SELWOOD TERR

ONSLOW GDNS

FOULIS TERR

SYDNEY STREET

STEWART'S GR

CALE

4 OLD BROMPTON RD

ELM PLACE

NEVILLE ST

Royal Marsden Hospital

ST LUKE'S ST

BRITTEN ST

THE BOLTONS

CRESSWELL PLACE

DRAYTON GARDENS

ROLAND GARDENS

CRANLEY MEWS

CRANLEY GDNS

EVELYN

EVELYN GDNS

ELM PARK GARDENS

SOUTH PARADE

Royal Brompton Hospital

DOVEHOUSE STREET

MANRESA RD

CHELSEA MANOR ST

THE LITTLE BOLTONS

HARCOURT TERRACE

REDCLIFFE MS

PRIORY WALK

GILSTON ROAD

BEAUFORT ST

ELM PARK ROAD

THE VALE

CHELSEA

CHELSEA SQUARE

OLD CHURCH STREET

CARLYLE SQUARE

wc

Chelsea Old T He

5 REDCLIFFE GDNS

HOLLYWOOD RD

FAWCETT ST

CATH

SEYMOUR WALK

REDCLIFFE RD

FULHAM ROAD

ELM PARK LANE

CALLOW ST

ELM

BEAUFORT

GARDENS

THE VALE

CHELSEA PARK GDNS

PAULTONS

Chelsea Antiques Market

DARTREY RD

OAKLEY ST

GLEBE PLACE

BRAMERTON ST

Carlyle's House

31

MBOROUGH RD

CART

HARBOROUGH RD

39 **49**

Chelsea & Westminster Hospital

38

41

40

KING'S ROAD

Bluebird

36 **46**

86 Time Out Shortlist | London 2010

South Kensington & Chelsea

HYDE PARK

D E F 1

Serpentine

NTINE ROAD

ROTTEN ROW

SOUTH CARRIAGE DRIVE

GREEN PARK

Apsley House

Wellington Arch

Hyde Park Corner

CONSTITUTION HILL

KNIGHTSBRIDGE

Knightsbridge

RAPHAEL ST

Knightsbridge

TREVOR SQ

Harrods

HANS RD

BROMPTON PL

BEAUFORT GDNS

BEAUCHAMP PL

PONT ST

OMPTON

WILLIAM

SLOANE STREET

LOWNDES SQUARE

HARRIET WALK

MOTCOMB ST

WEST HALKIN PLACE

LOWNDES ST

PONT ST

CHESHAM PL

CADOGAN

SLOANE STREET

CADOGAN PLACE

CADOGAN LANE

KNIGHTSBRIDGE

OLD BARRACK YARD

WILTON ROW

BELGRAVE MEWS NORTH

CRESCENT

BELGRAVE SQUARE

HALKIN STREET

HEADFORT PL

MONTROSE PL

CHAPEL STREET

BROOM PL

CHESTER STREET

WILTON CRES

WILTON ST

UPPER BELGRAVE STREET

BELGRAVE SQUARE SOUTH

ECCLESTON STREET

EATON

EATON MEWS

LOWER BELGRAVE STREET

GROSVENOR PLACE

Buckingham Palace Gardens

Royal Mews

HOBART PL

LWR GROS PL

GROSVENOR GDNS

GROSY GDNS

GROSVENOR GDNS RD

LOWER BELGRAVE ST

BELGRAVE MEWS

2

3

BELGRAVIA

KING'S ROAD

EATON PL

SOUTH EATON MEWS WEST

CHESTER SQUARE

EATON MEWS

ELLIS ST

GERALD RD

ELIZABETH ST

ECCLESTON ST

EBURY STREET

EBURY ST

PALACE STREET

BUCKINGHAM

Victoria Station

ECCLESTON

ELIZABETH BR

HUGH STREET

Victoria Coach Station

KING'S ROAD

Saatchi Gallery

LOWER SLOANE ST

SLOANE SQUARE

Sloane Square

BOURNE ST

CAROLINE TERRACE

GRAHAM TERRACE

WHITTAKER ST

HOLBEIN PL

CHESTER

HOLBEIN MEWS

PASSMORE ST

GRAHAM TERRACE

CUNDY ST

SEMLEY PL

ELIZABETH BR

4

WESTMINSTER & ST JAMES'S pp74-83

PIMLICO ROAD

BLOOMF'D TERR

BARNABAS ST

EBURY BRIDGE RD

EBURY BR

WARWICK WAY

WESTMORELAND TERRACE

5

KING'S ROAD

ELYSTAN PLACE

SPRIMONT PLACE

BRAY PLACE

BLACKLANDS TERR

DRAYCOTT PLACE

CULFORD GDNS

COULSON ST

MARKHAM SQUARE

MARKHAM ST

JUBILEE PL

WELLINGTON SQUARE

SMITH STREET

ROYAL AVE

CHELTENHAM TERRACE

WALPOLE ST

ST LEONARD'S TERRACE

FRANKLIN'S ROW

TURKS ROW

WOODFALL

SMITH TERRACE

ORMONDE

Royal Hospital Chelsea

National Army Museum

ROYAL HOSPITAL ROAD

CHELSEA BRIDGE ROAD

WEST ROAD

DILKE ST

PARADISE WK

SWAN WK

TITE STREET

CHRISTCHURCH

TEDWORTH

REDESDALE ST

RADNOR WALK

SHAWFIELD ST

FLOOD ST

SMITH STREET

KING'S ROAD

BYWATER ST

TRYON ST

ANDERSON ST

CADOGAN GDNS

Sights & museums
Eating & drinking
Shopping
Nightlife
Arts & leisure

taken up by a cast of a diplodocus skeleton, the Blue Zone has a 90ft model of a blue whale, and the Green Zone displays a cross-section through a giant sequoia tree – as well as an amazing array of stuffed birds, among which you can compare the fingernail-sized egg of a hummingbird with an elephant bird egg as big as a football. Some 22 million insect and plant specimens are housed in the Darwin Centre, due to open in September 2009, where the brand-new eight-storey 'cocoon' enables you to watch the museum's research scientists at work.

Science Museum

Exhibition Road, SW7 2DD (7942 4000/booking & information 0870 870 4868/www.sciencemuseum.org.uk). South Kensington tube. **Open** 10am-5.45pm daily. **Admission** free. *Special exhibitions* prices vary. **Map** p86 B3 **5**

Only marginally less popular with the kids than its natural historical neighbour, the Science Museum is a celebration of the wonders of technology in the service of our daily lives: from *Puffing Billy*, the world's oldest steam locomotive (built in 1815), via classic cars, to the Apollo 10 command module. In the Wellcome Wing, the Who Am I? gallery explores discoveries in genetics, brain science and psychology. Back in the main body of the museum, the third floor is dedicated to flight, including the hands-on Launchpad gallery which features levers, pulleys, explosions and all manner of experiments for children (and their grown-ups).

Event highlights 'Plasticity' (until 31 Jan 2010); 'Listening Post' (until 21 Feb 2010); 'Fast Forward: 20 ways F1 is Changing Our World' (until 5 Apr 2010).

Serpentine Gallery

Kensington Gardens, W2 3XA (7402 6075/www.serpentinegallery.org). Lancaster Gate or South Kensington tube. **Open** 10am-6pm daily. **Admission** free; donations appreciated. **Map** p86 B1 **6**

This secluded, small and airy gallery mounts rolling, two-monthly exhibitions by up-to-the-minute artists, along with the annual Serpentine Pavilion project (June-Sept), a specially commissioned temporary structure designed by an internationally renowned architect who has never built in the UK.

Victoria & Albert Museum

Cromwell Road, SW7 2RL (7942 2000/ www.vam.ac.uk). South Kensington tube. **Open** 10am-5.45pm Mon-Thur, Sat, Sun; 10am-10pm Fri. *Tours* hourly, 10.30am-3.30pm daily. **Admission** free. *Special exhibitions* prices vary. **Map** p86 C3 **7**

The V&A is a superb showcase for applied arts from around the world. Among the unmissable highlights are the seven Raphael Cartoons (painted in 1515 as tapestry designs for the Sistine Chapel), the Great Bed of Ware and the Ardabil carpet, the world's oldest and arguably most splendid floor covering. On the first floor, the new Theatre and Performance Galleries showcase the best of the performing arts, the newly opened William & Judith Bollinger Gallery of European jewellery showcases Catherine the Great's diamonds and the Gilbert Collection shows off gold snuffboxes and urns. Ten new galleries, occupying an entire wing, are to open in November 2009 to display medieval and Renaissance art.

Event highlights Canova's *Three Graces*; 'Maharajas: Splendour of India's Royal Courts' (10 Oct 2009-17 Jan 2010); '80s fashion (spring 2010); contemporary architecture (summer 2010).

Eating & drinking

Barts

NEW *Past the lobby down the corridor at the left, Chelsea Cloisters, 87 Sloane Avenue, SW3 3DW (7581 3355/www. barts-london.com). South Kensington tube.* **Open** phone reservations only. **Bar**. **Map** p86 C4 **8**

See box p91.

Casa Brindisa

NEW *7-9 Exhibition Road, SW7 2HQ
(7590 0008/www.casabrindisa.com).
South Kensington tube.* **Open** noon-11pm Mon-Sat; noon-9pm Sun. **Tapas**.
££. Map p86 C3 **9**

The original Tapas Brindisa (18-20 Southwark Street, 7357 8880) has spawned two siblings – here and in Soho (46 Broadwick Street, 7534 1690). The basement deli, bar area, 'Jamoneria' and dining room (with open kitchen) are appropriately rustic, but the general atmosphere has moved too far from the boisterous bar settings familiar from Seville. Still, the Brindisa group imports the finest Spanish produce – and it shows in every dish.

Ghost Inc

NEW *Basement, 7-11 Queensberry Place, SW7 2DL (7589 8979/www.ghostbar.co.uk). Gloucester Road or South Kensington tube.* **Open** 9.30pm-2.30am Thur-Sat. **Bar. Map** p86 B3 **10**
See box p91.

Launceston Place

1A Launceston Place, W8 5RL (7937 6912/www.danddlondon.com). Gloucester Road tube. **Open** 6-10.30pm Mon; noon-2.30pm, 6-10.30pm Tue-Fri; noon-3pm, 6.30pm-10.30pm Sat, Sun. **£££. Modern British**. **Map** p86 A2 **11**

Launceston Place is sultry, chic and elegant, all chocolate-brown and sexy low lighting, with superb cooking and glamorous presentations. Mains such as suckling pig with creamed onions or warm potato salad and Cornish mackerel bring English classics bang up-to-date. Traditionalists take note: Sunday roasts are served here too.

Tini

NEW *87-89 Walton Street, SW3 2HP (7589 8558/www.tinibar.com). South Kensington tube.* **Open** 6pm-noon Mon-Wed; 6pm-1am Thur-Sat; 6pm-12.30am Sun. **Bar. Map** p86 C3 **12**
See box p91.

Shopping

Conran Shop

Michelin House, 81 Fulham Road, SW3 6RD (7589 7401/www.conran.co.uk). South Kensington tube. **Open** 10am-6pm Mon, Tue, Fri; 10am-7pm Wed, Thur; 10am-6.30pm Sat; noon-6pm Sun. **Map** p86 C4 **13**

Sir Terence Conran's flagship store in the beautiful 1909 Michelin Building showcases furniture and design for every room in the house, as well as the garden; plenty of portable accessories, gadgets, books, stationery and toiletries make great gifts.

Library

268 Brompton Road, SW3 2AS (7589 6569). South Kensington tube. **Open** 10am-6.30pm Mon, Tue, Thur-Sat; 10am-7pm Wed; 12.30-5.30pm Sun. **Map** p86 C3 **14**

Designer labels and literature may seem an unlikely combination, but this fantastic emporium will convince you otherwise. For men, stock from seasoned greats like McQueen and Westwood hangs alongside that of newer fashion stars. There's also gift-friendly womenswear (such as cashmere and Balenciaga bags).

Arts & leisure

Royal Albert Hall

Kensington Gore, South Kensington, SW7 2AP (information 7589 3203/box office 7589 8212/www.royalalberthall. com). South Kensington tube/9, 10, 52, 452 bus. **Map** p86 B2 **15**

Built as a memorial to Queen Victoria's husband, this vast rotunda is best approached for the annual BBC Proms, despite acoustics that do orchestras few favours. Look out for recitals on the great Willis pipe organ and grand ballet extravaganzas at Christmas. **Event highlights** Jools Holland (27-28 Nov 2009); Royal Philharmonic Orchestra presents Grand Opera Gala (28 June 2010); the Proms (mid July-mid Sept 2010).

LONDON BY AREA

Knightsbridge

Knightsbridge is about be-seen-in restaurants and designer shops, but that doesn't mean it's particularly stylish. There are terrific people-watching opportunities, though.

Sights & museums

Apsley House

149 Piccadilly, W1J 7NT (7499 5676/ www.english-heritage.org.uk). Hyde Park Corner tube. **Open** *Nov-Mar* 10am-4pm Wed-Sun. *Apr-Oct* 10am-5pm Wed-Sun. **Admission** £5.50; £4.40 reductions. **Map** p87 E1 ⑯
Called No.1 London because it was the first London building encountered on the road to the City from the village of Kensington, Apsley House was the Duke of Wellington's residence for 35 years. His descendants still live here, but several rooms open to the public and give a superb feel for the man and his era.

Hyde Park

7298 2000/www.royalparks.gov.uk. Lancaster Gate or Queensway tube. **Map** p87 D1 ⑰
At 1.5 miles long and a mile wide, Hyde Park (7298 2000, www.royalparks.gov. uk) is one of the largest Royal Parks. It was a hotspot for mass demonstrations in the 19th century and remains so today – a march against war in Iraq in 2003 was the largest in British history. The legalisation of public assembly in the park led to the establishment of Speakers' Corner in 1872 (close to Marble Arch tube), where political and religious ranters – sane and otherwise – still have the floor. Marx, Lenin, Orwell and the Pankhursts have all spoken here. Rowing boats can be hired on the Serpentine.

Wellington Arch

Hyde Park Corner, W1J 7JZ (7930 2726/www.english-heritage.org.uk). Hyde Park Corner tube. **Open** *Apr-Oct* 10am-5pm Wed-Sun. *Nov-Mar* 10am-4pm Wed-Sun. **Admission** £3.30; free-£2.60 reductions. **Map** p87 F1 ⑱
Built in the 1820s and initially topped by an out-of-proportion equestrian statue of Wellington, since 1912 the 38-ton bronze *Peace Descending on the Quadriga of War* has finished the Arch with a flourish. Three floors of displays cover its history and that of the Blue Plaques scheme; the third gives great winter views from its balcony.

Eating & drinking

Amaya

19 Motcomb Street, Halkin Arcade, SW1X 8JT (7823 1166/www.realindian food.com). Knightsbridge tube. **Open** 12.30-2.15pm, 6.30-11.15pm Mon-Sat; 12.45-2.30pm, 6.30-10.15pm Sun. **£££**.
Indian. **Map** p87 E2 ⑲
Glamorous, stylish and seductive, Amaya is sleekly appointed with sparkly chandeliers, splashes of modern art and a groovy bar. The restaurant's calling card is its sophisticated Indian creations, chosen from a menu that cleverly links dressed-up street food with regal specialities.

Handi

7 Cheval Place, SW3 1HY (7823 7373). Knightsbridge tube. **Open** noon-3pm, 5.30-11pm Mon-Thur, Sun; noon-3pm, 5.30-11.30pm Fri, Sat. **£**. **East African Indian**. **Map** p87 D2 ⑳
Get a seat close to the cooks: the glass-fronted kitchen allows diners to watch all manner of culinary theatrics. The cooking isn't very sophisticated, but is seriously satisfying – try Punjabi classic chole masaledar (curried chickpeas) or Kenyan favourite jeera (cumin) chicken. Speedy lunch specials too.

Library

Lanesborough, 1 Lanesborough Place, Hyde Park Corner, SW1X 7TA (7259 5599/www.lanesborough.com). Hyde Park Corner tube. **Open** 11am-1am Mon-Sat; noon-10.30pm Sun. **Bar**. **Map** p87 F1 ㉑

Aspirational drinking

Three new bars in the heartland of paparazzi boozing.

It may have been a while since Prince Harry was last seen with girlfriend Chelsey at Boujis, but that doesn't mean the area's bijou party spots are going to start letting any old joe or joanna past the velvet rope. Newcomer **Barts** (p88) just might, but you mustn't say we said so. This so-called speakeasy should, for the sake of all involved, have genuinely tried to keep schtum about itself. The only thing it puts 'shh' into is shambolic: the food belongs on a kids' menu circa 1975, but never mind, because it's like, ironic, and the regulars consist of Chelsea renegades at their most subversive – namely, feeling smug about having got in.

Perhaps try **Ghost Inc** (p89), down in the basement of the Gainsborough Hotel. It's done up with 'graffiti' that was specially commissioned from 'The Don'. If that isn't 'precinct' enough, the LA biker-chic extends to the bar's own Harley. The wallpaper – black, festooned with skulls – would be happy wrapped around Russell Brand, which it wasn't. Perhaps though he could afford one of the eight low tables (£500 minimum spend) surrounded by plush child-sized Louis XV armchairs. The most popular cocktail on offer? The Porn Star: vodka alcopop with peche, passion fruit and apple.

Marginally more grown-up than either is **Tini** (p89), transporting its clientele into a pastiche of a Fellini film, where charcoal leather banquettes await beneath framed portraits of Pirelli girls. Aperitivi include the Mar-Tini, served in a sherry glass. The men's loo, plastered with stills from *La Dolce Vità*, has a notice on the back of the door: 'God gave man a brain and a penis and only enough blood to run once [sic] at a time'. Oh Tini, you are awful!

Surprisingly, those books are real. Whereas bars at other nearby hotels – the Berkeley, say, or the Mandarin Oriental – draw a younger, more boisterous crowd, the Library remains gentle and mellow long into the night, in part thanks to a tinkling pianist and perpetually low lighting.

Racine

239 Brompton Road, SW3 2EP (7584 4477). Knightsbridge or South Kensington tube/14, 74 bus. **Open** noon-3pm, 6-10.30pm Mon-Sat; 6-10pm Sun. **£££. French. Map** p86 C3 ㉒
Heavy curtains inside the door allow diners to make a grand entrance into the warm, vibrant 1930s retro atmosphere here. The food, though not cutting edge, has bags of character: perhaps a veal chop with roasted globe artichoke or juicy rabbit fricassee.

Zuma

5 Raphael Street, SW7 1DL (7584 1010/www.zumarestaurant.com). Knightsbridge tube. **Open** noon-11pm Mon-Fri; 12.30-11pm Sat; noon-10pm Sun. **££££. Japanese fusion. Map** p87 D2 ㉓
One of London's smartest top restaurants, there's more to this 'contemporary izakaya' (Japanese tapas bar, effectively) than a striking wood-and-stone interior. The surprise is that the mix of Japanese and fusion food on the long menu fully justifies the high prices. Zuma's younger sibling Roka/Shochu Lounge (p118) is as good.

Shopping

Harrods

87-135 Brompton Road, SW1X 7XL (7730 1234/www.harrods.com). Knightsbridge tube. **Open** 10am-8pm Mon-Sat; noon-6pm Sun. **Map** p87 D2 ㉔
In the store that boasts of selling everything, it's hard not to leave with at least one thing you'll like. New additions to the legendary food halls and restaurants include the Andronicas world of

Boisdale

coffee on the fourth floor, and the 5J ham and tapas bar from Sanchez Romero Carvajal, Spain's oldest Jabugo ham-producing company. It's on the fashion floors that Harrods really comes into its own, though: perhaps something from Halston, the iconic revived 1970s design house, or from the Oscar de la Renta boutique.

Harvey Nichols

109-125 Knightsbridge, SW1X 7RJ (7235 5000/www.harveynichols.com). Knightsbridge tube. **Open** 10am-8pm Mon-Sat; noon-6pm Sun. **Map** p87 D2 ㉕
The swanky department store feels like it's coasting a little, but you'll still find a worthy clutch of unique brands. In beauty, there's Rodial and New York fave Bliss; for shoes, there are exclusives from the likes of Alejandro Ingelmo and Camilla Skovgaard; in womenswear, check out Derek Lam and Les Chiffoniers. There's a fine food hall on the fifth floor, as well as a bar with private vodka-tasting room.

Belgravia

Belgravia is characterised by a host of embassies and the fact that everyone living here is very rich. Enjoy strolling through tiny mews, then settle into some plush dining, drinking or shopping.

Eating & drinking

Motcomb Street has a branch of the fine bakery-café **Ottolenghi** (no.13, 7823 2707, www.ottolenghi.co.uk; for the Islington branch, see p172).

Boisdale
13-15 Eccleston Street, SW1W 9LX (7730 6922/www.boisdale.co.uk). Victoria tube/rail. **Open**/food served noon-1am Mon-Fri; 7pm-1am Sat. **Admission** £12 (£4.50 before 10pm) after 10pm Mon-Sat. **Whisky bar.** Map p87 F3 ㉖
From the labyrinthine bar and restaurant spaces and heated cigar terrace to overstated tartan accents, there's something preposterous about this entire operation. Which we write with utmost affection: there's nowhere quite like this posh, Scottish-themed enterprise, and that includes its sister in the City. Single malts are the tipple of choice.

Nag's Head
53 Kinnerton Street, SW1X 8ED (7235 1135). Hyde Park Corner or Knightsbridge tube. **Open** 11am-11pm Mon-Sat; noon-10.30pm Sun. **Pub.** Map p87 E2 ㉗
It's unusual to see a landlord's name plastered on the front of a pub, but then there aren't many like Kevin Moran left in the trade. The Nag's Head reflects Moran's exuberant eccentricity, both by design (mobiles are banned) and, most strikingly, by accident (the rooms themselves could scarcely be wonkier).

Olivomare
10 Lower Belgrave Street, SW1W 0LJ (7730 9022). Victoria tube/rail.

Open noon-2.30pm, 7-11pm Mon-Sat. **£££. Fish.** Map p87 F3 ㉘
The stark minimalist monochrome fish-patterned decor here is as single-minded as the fish-only menu, but then you are about to eat impeccably fresh, intelligently cooked seafood. Even the waiters are, in a good way, fresh.

Shopping

Daylesford Organic
44B Pimlico Road, SW1W 8LP (7881 8060/www.daylesfordorganic. com). Sloane Square tube. **Open** 8am-8pm Mon-Sat; 10am-4pm Sun. Map p87 E4 ㉙
Part of a new wave of chic purveyors of health food, this impressive offshoot of Lady Carole Bamford's Cotswold-based farm shop is set over three floors, and includes a café. Goods include ready-made dishes, and such storecupboard staples as pulses and pasta.

Elizabeth Street
Sloane Square tube. Map p87 F4 ㉚
The location by Victoria Coach Station doesn't inspire confidence, but this is a fine shopping street. You'll find Erickson Beamon's show-stopping jewellery (no.38, 7259 0202, www.ericksonbeamon.com), fine perfumes at Les Senteurs (no.71, 7730 2322, www.lessenteurs.com) and hats by Philip Treacy (no.69, 7730 3992, www.philiptreacy.co.uk), the king of couture headgear. Tomtom (no.63, 7730 1790, www.tomtom.co.uk) sells finest Cuban cigars, while gratification for the stomach is found at French bakery Poilâne (no.46, 7808 4910) and the Chocolate Society (no.36, 7259 9222).

Chelsea

It's been more than four decades since *Time* magazine declared that London – by which was meant the **King's Road** – was 'swinging'. These days you're more likely to find suburban swingers wondering where it went than the next Jean Shrimpton, but places like **Shop at Bluebird** have improved the retail opportunities and the arrival of the **Saatchi Gallery** has put it back on the tourist map. Chelsea proper begins with Sloane Square, spoiled by traffic but redeemed by the edgy **Royal Court Theatre**.

Sights & museums

Carlyle's House

24 Cheyne Row, SW3 5HL (7352 7087/www.nationaltrust.org.uk). Sloane Square tube/11, 19, 22, 49, 211, 239, 319 bus. **Open** *Apr-Oct* 2-5pm Wed-Fri; 11am-5pm Sat, Sun. **Admission** £4.75; £2.40 reductions; £11.90 family. **Map** p86 C5 ③①

Thomas Carlyle and his wife Jane, both towering intellects, moved to this Queen Anne house in 1834. In 1896, 15 years after Carlyle's death, the house was preserved as a museum, and it's an intriguing snapshot of Victorian life.

Chelsea Physic Garden

66 Royal Hospital Road (entrance on Swan Walk), SW3 4HS (7352 5646/ www.chelseaphysicgarden.co.uk). Sloane Square tube/11, 19, 239 bus. **Open** Apr-Oct noon-5pm Wed-Fri; noon-6pm Sun. **Admission** £7; free-£4 reductions. **Map** p87 D5 ③②

The 165,000sq ft grounds of this gorgeous botanic garden are filled with healing herbs and vegetables, rare trees and dye plants. The garden was founded in 1673 by Sir Hans Sloane with the purpose of cultivating and studying plants for medical purposes.

National Army Museum

Royal Hospital Road, SW3 4HT (7730 0717/www.national-army-museum. ac.uk). Sloane Square tube/11, 137, 239 bus. **Open** 10am-5.30pm daily. **Admission** free. **Map** p87 D5 ③③

More entertaining than its rather dull exterior suggests, this museum of the history of the British Army kicks off

with 'Redcoats', a gallery that starts at Agincourt in 1415 and ends with the American War of Independence. You'll also find some fingertips, frostbitten on Everest, and Dame Kelly Holmes' Olympic gold medals.

Royal Hospital Chelsea

Royal Hospital Road, SW3 4SR (7881 5200/www.chelsea-pensioners.org.uk). Sloane Square tube/11, 19, 22, 137, 211, 239 bus. **Open** *Oct-Apr* 10am-noon, 2-4pm Mon-Sat. *May-Sept* 10am-noon, 2-4pm Mon-Sat; 2-4pm Sun. **Admission** free. **Map** p87 E5 ③④

About 350 scarlet-coated Chelsea Pensioners (retired soldiers) live here, men and – since early 2009 – women. Their quarters, the Royal Hospital, was founded in 1682 by Charles II and the building was designed by Sir Christopher Wren. The museum has more about their life.

Saatchi Gallery

NEW *Duke of York's HQ, off King's Road, SW3 4SQ (7823 2363/www. saatchi-gallery.co.uk). Sloane Square tube.* **Open** 10am-6pm daily. **Admission** free. **Map** p87 E4 ③⑤

Charles Saatchi's new gallery, which opened after numerous delays in October 2008, has three floors, providing more than 50,000sq ft of space for temporary exhibitions. It will surprise some that the opening show from this erstwhile champion of Brit Art was of new Chinese art, but some of his more famous British acquisitions – among the marvellous sump-oil installation *20:50* – remain on permanent display. **Event highlights** 'Newspeak: British Art Now' (27 Oct 2009-17 Jan 2010).

Eating & drinking

Bluebird

350 King's Road, SW3 5UU (7559 1000/www.danddlondon.com). Sloane Square tube then 11, 19, 22, 49, 319 bus. **Open** 12.30-2.30pm, 6-10.30pm Mon-Fri; noon-3.30pm, 6-10.30pm Sat;

Napket p96

noon-3.30pm, 6-9.30pm Sun. *Bar* noon-midnight Mon-Thur; noon-1am Fri, Sat; noon-11.30pm Sun. **£££. Modern European**. Map p86 B5 ③⑥

Part of a cunning conversion of an amazing art deco garage, comprising this restaurant, a café, an expensive épicerie and a shop (p97), Bluebird remains a popular meeting place for Chelsea residents. The menu is eclectic and please-all, with French accents. Prices reflect the swanky location.

Botanist

7 Sloane Square, SW1W 8EE (7730 0077/www.thebotanistonsloanesquare. com). Sloane Square tube. **Open** 8am-10.30pm Mon-Sat; noon-10.30pm Sun. **££. British bar-restaurant**. Map p87 E4 ③⑦

This rather beautiful dining room and bar serves food most of the day and there are majestic roasts on Sundays. The wonderful breakfasts comprise all the usual cooked and continental options; dinner might be poached gull's egg with chorizo, alsace bacon and fresh peas, followed by an assiette of Scottish Blackface lamb.

Haché

329-331 Fulham Road, SW10 9QL (7823 3515/www.hachebugars.com).

South Kensington tube. **Open** noon-10.30pm Mon-Fri; noon-11.15 Sat, Sun. **£. Burgers**. Map p86 B5 ③⑧

Haché is the French term for 'chopped', but the only Gallic twist on the great American burger here is attention to detail. Rather than the now-ubiquitous underpinning with skewers, Haché's crisply toasted ciabattas are left ajar so that you can admire the ingredients – and they're worth admiring.

Harwood Arms

NEW *27 Walham Grove, SW6 1QP (7386 1847). Fulham Broadway tube.* **Open** noon-11pm Mon-Thur, Sun; noon-midnight Fri, Sat. *Restaurant* noon-3pm, 6.30-9.30pm Tue-Thur; noon-3pm, 6.30-10pm Fri, Sat; noon-5pm, 6-9pm Sun. **££. Gastropub**. Map p86 A5 ③⑨

The decor has been inspired by the style bible 'for people whose heart is in the country' – hessian napkins tied with raffia – but, more importantly, the claim of using 'seasonal, local and natural produce' is fully realised. Despite the quality of the food, the owners haven't forgotten this is a pub, even if the locals seem more interested in wine than the fine real ales on draught. We could do with a raffia bow or two less, but this is a terrific new place.

LONDON BY AREA

Napket

342 King's Road, SW3 5UR (7352 9832/www.napket.com). Sloane Square tube then 11, 19, 22 bus. **Open** 8am-8pm daily. **£. Brasserie.** Map p86 B5 ④⓪

Looks are everything at this stylish café that goes under the tag-line 'snob food'. The interior is all chic black gloss and space-age perspex, accessorised with iPods on the tables. Food features terrific bread generously filled with high-quality ingredients: try the meal-in-itself club sandwich layered with roast chicken, ham, bacon and emmental. Salads come in pots of two sizes.

Sushinho

NEW *312-314 King's Road, SW3 5UH (7349 7496/www.sushinho.com). South Kensington tube.* **Open** noon-3pm, 6-10.30pm Mon-Sat; 6-10pm Sun. *Bar* 6pm-midnight daily. **££. International.** Map p86 C5 ④①

A very Chelsea take on fantasy Orientalism – dark wood, screens of bamboo poles, artfully arranged sushi – until you read the cocktail list, which mixes up Brazilian batidas ('shaken' cocktails of cachaça and fruit juice) and sakes. Amazingly, this marriage of convenience between Japanese food and Brazilian bar culture is remarkably good. Just don't expect it to be either quite Brazilian – or quite Japanese.

Tom's Kitchen

27 Cale Street, SW3 3QP (7349 0202/www.tomskitchen.co.uk). South Kensington or Sloane Square tube. **Open** 7-10am, noon-3pm, 6pm-midnight Mon-Fri; 10am-3pm, 6pm-midnight Sat, Sun. **££. Brasserie.** Map p86 C4 ④②

This is home from home for Chelsea's super-rich, but don't let that put you off. The warm, welcoming room, framed in gleaming white tiles and homespun prints, feels as if it was set up just to make everybody happy. The menu is superb, covering much of what you'd want to eat at any time of day,

from the down-home (macaroni cheese) through brasserie classics (moules and steak and chips) to a fine Sunday lunch.

Shopping

Antiquarius

131-141 King's Road, SW3 5PH (7823 3900/www.antiquarius.co.uk). Sloane Square tube, then 11, 19, 22, 319, 211 bus. **Open** 10am-6pm Mon-Sat. Map p87 D5 ④③

This long-standing King's Road landmark has lost some dealers during partial redevelopment, but there's still plenty of variety: specialisms range from sporting collectibles to vintage trunks, from Islamic art to military antiques, from glassware to film art.

Duke of York Square

King's Road, SW3 4LY. Map p87 D4 ④④

West London's first new public square for over a century is a former barracks (now home to the Saatchi, p94) transformed into a pedestrian area with

Sloane Square

fountains and stone benches. Among the high-end high-street clothes shops and terrace cafés, Liz Earle's flagship beauty store (no.53, 7730 9191, www. lizearle.com) and the ultra-modern Michel Guillon Vision Clinic (no.35, 7730 2142, www.michelguillon.com) stand out. There's also a very popular Saturday food market.

John Sandoe
10 Blacklands Terrace, SW3 2SR (7589 9473/www.johnsandoe.com). Sloane Square tube. **Open** 9.30am-5.30pm Mon, Tue, Thur-Sat; 9.30am-7.30pm Wed; noon-6pm Sun. **Map** p87 D4 ⓘ

Tucked away on a Chelsea side street, this 50-year-old independent looks just as a bookshop should. The stock is literally packed to the rafters, and of the 25,000 books here, 24,000 are a single copy – so there's serious breadth.

Shop at Bluebird
350 King's Road, SW3 5UU (7351 3873/www.theshopatbluebird.com). Sloane Square tube. **Open** 10am-7pm Mon-Sat; noon-6pm Sun. **Map** p86 B5 ⓘ

The Shop at Bluebird is part lifestyle boutique – DJs play at weekends – and part design gallery. The 10,000sq ft space is a shifting showcase of clothing (for men, women and children – think Ossie Clark, Chris Benz and store-exclusive Andy & Deb), accessories, furniture, books and gadgets. An on-site spa has opened and, from 2009, menswear covered Marc Jacobs, Kitsune and PS by Paul Smith.

Sloane Square
Sloane Square tube. **Map** p87 E4 ⓘ

The shaded benches and fountain in the middle of the square provide a lovely counterpoint to the looming façades of Tiffany & Co and the enormous 1930s Peter Jones department store, as well as the grinding traffic. Come summer, the brasserie terraces teem with stereotypical blonde Sloane Rangers

sipping rosé; expect an artier crop of whatever replaces the Agyness Deyn platinum bob to have taken up residence outside the Royal Court Theatre. Nearby, Ortigia's sleek flagship (no.55, 7730 2826, www.ortigia-srl.com) sells divinely packaged smellies.

Arts & leisure

Cadogan Hall
5 Sloane Terrace, Chelsea, SW1X 9DQ (7730 4500/www.cadoganhall.com). Sloane Square tube. **Map** p87 E3 ⓘ

Built a century ago as a Christian Science church, this austere building was transformed into a light and airy auditorium. It's hard to imagine how the renovations could have been bettered: the 905-capacity hall is comfortable and the acoustics excellent.
Event highlights Nordland Music Festival (16-17 Oct 2009); Ladysmith Black Mambazo (23-24 Oct 2009).

Chelsea Football Club
Stamford Bridge, Fulham Road, SW6 1HS (0871 984 1955/www.chelseafc.com). Fulham Broadway tube. **Map** p86 A5 ⓘ

The capital's most recent Premiership winners have lost way to Manchester United over the last couple of seasons, but you're still unlikely to be able to get tickets to see Chelsea's megastars in Premiership action. Instead, check out the new museum or seek tickets for cup ties against lower league opposition.

Royal Court Theatre
Sloane Square, SW1W 8AS (7565 5000/www.royalcourttheatre.com). Sloane Square tube. **Map** p87 E4 ⓘ

A hard-hitting theatre in a well-heeled location, the emphasis here has always been on new voices in British theatre – from John Osborne's *Look Back in Anger* in the inaugural year, 1956, to numerous discoveries over the past decade: Sarah Kane, Joe Penhall and Conor McPherson among them. All tickets cost £10 on Mondays.

LONDON BY AREA

Covent Garden Piazza p140

The West End

Marylebone

The relentless trade on Oxford Street accounts for ten per cent of all spending in the capital, but few Londoners esteem the historic thoroughfare. Clogged pavements make it unpleasant for shopping, although it is home to impressive **Selfridges**, doughty **John Lewis** and chain flagships such as **Uniqlo**. Improvements are on the way, beginning with new diagonal Shibuya-style crossings at Oxford Circus, but escape the crowds into quiet squares and pretty boutiques along Marylebone High Street to the north. Among the sights, the **Wallace** is too often overlooked, and **Regent's Park** is one of London's finest green spaces.

Sights & museums

Madame Tussauds
Marylebone Road, NW1 5LR (0870 400 3000/www.madame-tussauds.co.uk).
Baker Street tube. **Open** 9.30am-6pm daily. **Admission** £25; £21 reductions. **Map** p99 A1 ❶

Founded in Paris in 1770, Madame Tussaud brought her show to London in 1802. There are 300 figures in the collection now, among them a suspiciously clear-skinned Amy Winehouse. Kylie, who's always being recast, sits in a large sequinned crescent moon. Be here before 10am to avoid the queues, or come after 5.30pm and take advantage of the reduced admission charge.

Regent's Park
Camden Town, Baker Street or Regent's Park tube. **Map** p99 B1 ❷

Regent's Park (open 5am-dusk daily) is one of London's most popular open spaces. Attractions run from the animal noises and odours of London Zoo (p171) to enchanting Open Air Theatre performances of *A Midsummer Night's Dream* that are an integral part of the London summer. Rowing boat hire, some spectacular rose gardens, ice-cream stands and the fine Garden Café

Marylebone & Mayfair

(7935 5729, www.thegardencafe.co.uk) complete the picture.

Wallace Collection

Hertford House, Manchester Square, W1U 3BN (7935 0687/www.wallace collection.org). Bond Street tube. **Open** 10am-5pm daily. **Admission** free. Map p99 A2 ❸

This handsome house, built in 1776, contains an exceptional collection of 18th-century French painting and objets d'art, as well as a fine array of armour and weapons. Open to the public since 1900, room after room contains Louis XIV and XV furnishings and Sèvres porcelain, while the galleries are hung with paintings by Titian, Velázquez, Fragonard and Gainsborough.

Event highlights 'Damien Hirst: The Blue Paintings' (14 Oct 2009-24 Jan 2010).

Eating & drinking

Artesian

Langham, 1C Portland Place, W1B 1JA (7636 1000/www.artesian-bar.co.uk). Oxford Circus tube. **Open** 10am-2am Mon-Sat; 10am-midnight Sun. **£££**. **Bar**. Map p99 C2 ❹

Order any three of the extraordinary cocktails here, add service, and you won't get much change from a £50 note. But at least you'll be drinking them in style: David Collins has done a fine job on the decor, the back bar dramatically lit by huge hanging lamps.

L'Autre Pied

5-7 Blandford Street, W1U 3DB (7486 9696/www.lautrepied.co.uk). Baker Street tube. **Open** noon-2.45pm, 6-10.30pm Mon-Sat; noon-3pm, 6.30-9.30pm Sun. **£££**. **French**. Map p99 A2 ❺

Sister restaurant to the fabled Pied à Terre, the cooking here is accomplished and precise, with imaginative, well-considered flavour combinations. The food looks stunning too. It won our Best New Restaurant award in 2008 and was a runner-up for Best Design.

Regent's Park p98

Fairuz

3 Blandford Street, W1U 3DA (7486 8108/8182/www.fairuz.uk.com). Baker Street or Bond Street tube. **Open** noon-11.30pm Mon-Sat; noon-11pm Sun. **££**. **Middle Eastern**. Map p99 B2 ❻

Fairuz is a rough-hewn one-off. A youngish crowd are attracted by the relatively low prices at this singularly rustic and well-regarded Lebanese. Check out the makloobeh, which is a terrific stew made of aubergine, rice, lamb and almonds.

La Fromagerie

2-6 Moxon Street, W1U 4EW (7935 0341/www.lafromagerie.co.uk). Baker Street or Bond Street tube. **Open** 10.30am-7.30pm Mon; 8am-7.30pm Tue-Fri; 9am-7pm Sat; 10am-6pm Sun. **£**. **Café/deli**. Map p99 A2 ❼

Famed with foodies for its dedicated cheese room, Patricia Michelson's high-end deli also dishes out freshly cooked café food. Its communal tables are often packed with devotees.

Naughty, with ice

The new lingerie shop that's more than a store.

'More tonic?' No, you're not in a bar, you're in the Library area of Marylebone High Street's brand, er, spanking new concept lingerie store **Apartment C** (p105) – and you're about to drink a speakeasy-style teacup of gin and tonic straight from the shop's original 1930s cocktail cabinet.

The front door of Apartment C opens into the Lounge, where all manner of alluring naughtiness is displayed under chandeliers and against black walls, with a Louis XV wardrobe opening to display health and beauty products, including Parisian perfumes. But it's the Library section of the shop that's really fun: pick up a trash exploitation paperback while reclining on Laura Berens silk cushions with that teacup of mother's ruin.

Kenya Cretegny, Apartment C's owner, is a pretty exotic creature herself: following a track scholarship at university, she worked as a model, then a TV presenter in New York, and

spent some time running the hip Blue Door restaurant at Miami's chic Starck-Schrager hotel the Delano. She finished off her education in London, where she studied design at Central Saint Martins. With that kind of background, it's no surprise that Apartment C is quite out-there – witness the Jericho Hands light fittings made from stuffed pigeons, those Arne Jacobsen hip modernist Egg chairs and the vintage chaise longue.

While the black and gold art deco stylings are certainly chic, a shop is nothing without its stock, and here you'll find new and exclusive lingerie from US labels The Lake and Stars and VPL, Dutch Marlies Dekkers, German Wundervoll and French Elise Aucoutourier, offering everything from lacy loungewear to handcrafted bras. As you'd expect, service is thoroughly professional too – staff are fully trained to offer specialist fitting and contour advice.

Galvin Bistrot de Luxe

66 Baker Street, W1U 7DJ (7935 4007/www.galvinuk.com). Baker Street tube. **Open** noon-2.30pm, 6-11pm Mon-Sat; noon-5pm, 6-9.30pm Sun. **££**. **French**. **Map** p99 A2 ❽
On a rather impersonal stretch of Baker Street, the comforting 1930s decor and friendly, efficient staff here are most welcoming. Fresh ingredients and contrasting textures dominate the menu. Long may it flourish.

Giusto

NEW *43 Blandford Street, W1U 7HF (7486 7340). Bond Street or Baker Street tube.* **Open** noon-3pm, 6.30-10.30pm Mon-Sat. **£**. **Pizza**. **Map** p99 A2 ❾
On the small ground-floor shop-front is a bar-cum-takeaway for Italian favourites such as lasagne. But descend to the terracotta-tiled basement restaurant and you'll find a large, friendly pizzeria with an imposing white wood-fired oven.

Golden Eagle

59 Marylebone Lane, W1U 2NY (7935 3228). Bond Street tube. **Open** 11am-11pm Mon-Sat; noon-7pm Sun. **££**. No credit cards. **Pub**. **Map** p99 B2 ❿
Every year, we like this pub a bit more. A paint job has brightened it up, but the Golden Eagle remains what it's always been: an unpretentious little boozer (just a clutch of bar stools lined up by the window), not hugely charismatic, but pleasingly untouched by corporate hands.

Golden Hind

73 Marylebone Lane, W1U 2PN (7486 3644). Bond Street tube. **Open** noon-3pm Mon-Fri; 6-10pm Mon-Sat. **£**. **Fish & chips**. **Map** p99 B2 ⓫
The pastel-hued art deco fryer at this marvellous chip shop is only used to store menus these days (the cooking's done in a kitchen at the back), but the Golden Hind still oozes local character, entirely in keeping with its Marylebone

Lane location. Big portions hit the spot, and the Greek owners and staff really make a fuss over customers – even more so if they have children.

imbiss

NEW *14 Seymour Place, W1H 7NF (7723 2574/www.imbiss.co.uk). Marble Arch tube.* **Open** noon-2pm, 6pm-11pm Tue-Fri; noon-11pm Sat; noon-10.30pm Sun. **££**. **Austrian bar**. **Map** p99 A3 ⓬
A small bar-cum-deli-cum-coffee shop that's recognisably Austrian but has opted for an avant-garde Alpine approach; think future *Sound of Music* with mountain-scape pictures, modern art, and actually quite cosy. 'Imbiss' is the German word for snack or light meal, but loosen your lederhosen as some serious Austrian fare is on offer.

Providores & Tapa Room

109 Marylebone High Street, W1U 4RX (7935 6175/www.theprovidores. co.uk). Baker Street or Bond Street tube. **Open** noon-2.45pm, 6-10.30pm

Providores & Tapa Room

Mon-Sat; noon-2.45pm, 6-10pm Sun. *Tapa Room* 9-10.30am, noon-10.30pm Mon-Fri; 10am-3pm, 4-10.30pm Sat; 4-10pm Sun. **£££. Global tapas**. Map p99 B2 ⑬

Chef Peter Gordon dazzles here with such epicurean obscurities as barrel-aged Banyuls vinegar, and produce from his native New Zealand like kumara (a uniquely flavoured sweet potato). The flavours of his complex dishes work in blissful harmony.

Trishna London

NEW *15-17 Blandford Street, W1U 3DG (7935 5624/www.trishnalondon. com)*. **Open** noon-3pm, 6-11pm Mon; 6-11pm Tue-Sat; noon-3.30pm, 6.30-10.30pm Sun. **£££. Indian**. Map p99 A2 ⑭

Anyone who's eaten at the legendary Trishna restaurant in Mumbai might be disappointed by the absence of kitsch plastic flowers and tawdry posters: the decor here is wannabe-chic. Nonetheless, the cooking damn near perfectly captures the essence of the mouthwatering seafood that is characteristic of the western Indian state of Maharashtra.

Shopping

Held in the cobbled yard of St Marylebone Parish Church on Saturdays, **Cabbages & Frocks** market (7794 1636, www.cabbages andfrocks.co.uk) sells retro and vintage clothing, snacks, and work from independent designers. On Sunday mornings, you can drop in on the **Marylebone Farmers' Market**, in Cramer Street carpark, at the corner of Moxton Street.

Apartment C

NEW *70 Marylebone High Street, W1U 5JL (7935 1854/www.apartment-c.com)*. Baker Street tube. **Open** 10am-6pm Mon-Sat; noon-5pm Sun. **Map** p99 B1 ⑮

See box p102.

Cadenhead's Whisky Shop & Tasting Room

26 Chiltern Street, W1U 7QF (7935 6999). Baker Street tube. **Open** 10.30am-6.30pm Mon-Sat. **Map** p99 A2 ⑯

Cadenhead's is a survivor of a rare breed: the independent whisky bottler. Cadenhead's selects barrels from distilleries all over Scotland and bottles them without filtration or any other intervention. One of a kind.

John Lewis

278-306 Oxford Street, W1A 1EX (7629 7711/www.johnlewis.co.uk). Bond Street or Oxford Circus tube. **Open** 9.30am-8pm Mon-Wed, Fri; 9.30am-9pm Thur; 9.30am-7pm Sat; noon-6pm Sun. Map p99 B3 ⑰

Recently renovated – new transparent-sided escalators and a partly glazed roof allow in plenty of natural light – and renowned for solid reliability and the courtesy of its staff, John Lewis also deserves a medal for its breadth of stock. The spacious ground-floor cosmetics hall, for example, has glam Crème de la Mer and Eve Lom, but also natural brands like Neal's Yard and Burt's Bees.

KJ's Laundry

74 Marylebone Lane, W1U 2PW (7486 7855/www.kjslaundry.com). Bond Street tube. **Open** 10am-7pm Mon-Wed, Fri, Sat; 10am-8pm Thur; 11am-5pm Sun. **Map** p99 B3 ⑱

This unintimidating, understated boutique is a good bet for highly wearable clothes with an edge. Jane Ellis and Kate Allden work hard to source little-seen lines, such as handmade slip dresses from Lee Mathews or Hiromi Tsuyoshi's buttonless cardies.

Margaret Howell

34 Wigmore Street, W1U 2RS (7009 9009/www.margarethowell.co.uk). Bond Street tube. **Open** 10am-6pm Mon-Wed, Fri, Sat; 10am-7pm Thur. **Map** p99 B2 ⑲

Howell's wonderfully wearable clothes are made in Britain with an old-fashioned attitude to quality. These principles combine with her elegant designs to make for the best 'simple' clothes for sale in London. These are clothes that get better with time – as will the new bags she's designed with Japanese label Porter.

Marylebone High Street

Bond Street or Baker Street tube.
Map p99 B2 ⑳
With tube stations at the top and bottom of the street, this is one of the most accessible strips of boutiques in London. Browse the likes of L'Artisan Parfumeur (no.36, 7486 3435), elegant lifestyle store Brissi (no.22, 7935 6733), inspirational Daunt Books (nos.83-84, 7224 2295, www.dauntbooks.co.uk), the Scandinavian design classics at Skandium (no.86, 7935 2077) and Kabiri's avant-garde jewellery (no.37, 7224 1808, www.kabiri.co.uk). One of the newest arrivals is concept lingerie store Apartment C (see box p102). Need a snack? Try 1950s timewarp café Paul Rothe & Son (no.35, 7935 6783).

Mint

70 Wigmore Street, W1U 2SF (7224 4406/www.mintshop.co.uk). Bond Street tube. **Open** 10.30am-6.30pm Mon-Wed, Fri, Sat; 10.30am-7.30pm Thur. **Map** p99 B3 ㉑
Surprising and inspirational, Mint is a compact two-level space full of globally sourced pieces from established designers and recent graduates alike. As well as contemporary statement furniture, there are plenty of smaller, more affordable items here, such as Doris Banks' paper-thin ceramics glazed in gorgeous greens and oranges.

Selfridges

400 Oxford Street, W1A 1AB (0800 123 400/www.selfridges.com). Bond Street tube. **Open** 9.30am-8pm Mon-Wed, Fri, Sat; 9.30am-9pm Thur; noon-6pm Sun. **Map** p99 A3 ㉒

Margaret Howell p105

It's no surprise Selfridges won our Shopping Award for Best Department Store in 2008: its concession boutiques, store-wide themed events and collections from the hottest new brands make it the first port-of-call for stylish one-stop shopping, while useful floor plans make navigating the store easypeasy. On the ground floor, the Wonder Room – 19,000sq ft of luxury brands – goes from strength to strength, and the fashion selections are superb.

Topshop

214 Oxford Street, W1W 8LG (7636 7700/www.topshop.com). Oxford Circus tube. **Open** 9am-9pm Mon-Sat; 11.30am-6pm Sun. **Map** p99 C3 ㉓
Topshop's massive, throbbing flagship is a teenage Hades at weekends, but there's nowhere on the high street that's more on-trend. You'll find a boutique of high-fashion designer capsule ranges, vintage clothes, even a Hersheson hairstylist among cheap and well-cut jeans, the Kate Moss range and all manner of other temptations. A whole new floor opens in 2009.

Radio 3, are excellent value, as are the Sunday morning coffee concerts, and pianist Brad Mehldau's involvement in the programming ensures some fine jazz and jazz-classical collaborations.

Mayfair

Mayfair means money. And these days that doesn't necessarily translate into stuffy exclusivity. Even the tailors of **Savile Row**, low be it spoken, have loosened their ties a little, and the **Royal Institution** has been given a fantastic, user-friendly makeover. Even so, there's enough old-world decorum here to satisfy the most fastidious visitor, from elegant shopping arcades to five-star hotels. **Piccadilly Circus** remains its infuriating self.

Sights & museums

Handel House Museum

25 Brook Street (entrance Lancashire Court), W1K 4HB (7399 1953/www. handelhouse.org). Bond Street tube. **Open** 10am-6pm Tue, Wed, Fri, Sat; 10am-8pm Thur; noon-6pm Sun. **Admission** £5; free-£4.50 reductions. **Map** p99 B3 ㉖
George Frideric Handel settled in this Mayfair house aged 37, remaining here until his death in 1759. The house has been beautifully restored with original and recreated furnishings, paintings and a welter of the composer's scores (in the same room as photos of Jimi Hendrix, who lived next door). There are recitals every Thursday.

Haunch of Venison

NEW *6 Burlington Gardens, W1S 3ET (7495 5050/www.haunchofvenison. com). Piccadilly Circus tube.* **Open** 10am-6pm Mon-Wed, Fri; 10am-7pm Thur; 10am-5pm Sat. **Admission** free. **Map** p99 C4 ㉗
Zippy contemporary art gallery Haunch has moved into the grand, neo-

Tracey Neuls

29 Marylebone Lane, W1U 2NQ (7935 0039/www.tn29.com). Bond Street tube. **Open** 11am-6.30pm Mon-Fri; noon-5pm Sat. **Map** p99 B2 ㉔
Tracey Neuls challenges footwear conventions, right down to the way her shoes are displayed – here they dangle from the ceiling, suspended on ribbons. Her TN_29 label has gathered a cult following all the way from Seattle to Sydney, but the Cordwainers-trained Canadian designer is based in this small shop/studio.

Arts & leisure

Wigmore Hall

36 Wigmore Street, W1U 2BP (7935 2141/www.wigmore-hall.org.uk). Bond Street tube. **Map** p99 B2 ㉕
Built in 1901 as the display hall for Bechstein Pianos, but now boasting perfect acoustics, art nouveau decor and an excellent basement restaurant, the Wiggy is one of the world's top chamber-music venues. The Monday-lunch recitals, broadcast live on BBC

LONDON BY AREA

classical building behind the Royal Academy, home until 1997 of the ethnographical collections of the British Museum. The gallery's opening show, 'Mythologies', self-consciously echoed those tribal masks and canoes.

Royal Academy of Arts

Burlington House, Piccadilly, W1J 0BD (7300 8000/www.royalacademy.org.uk). Green Park or Piccadilly Circus tube. **Open** 10am-6pm Mon-Thur, Sat, Sun; 10am-10pm Fri. **Admission** free. *Special exhibitions* prices vary. **Map** p99 C4 ❷❽

Britain's first art school was founded in 1768 and moved to the extravagantly Palladian Burlington House a century later. It is now best known for the galleries. Expect to pay for blockbusters in the Sackler Wing or main galleries, while shows in the John Madejski Fine Rooms are drawn from the RA's holdings – ranging from Constable to Hockney – and are free. **Event highlights** 'JW Waterhouse: Modern Pre-Raphaelite' (until 13 Sept 2009); Summer Exhibition (June-Aug 2010).

Royal Institution & Faraday Museum

NEW *21 Albemarle Street, W1S 4BS (7409 2992/www.rigb.org). Green Park tube.* **Open** 9am-5pm Mon-Fri. **Admission** free. **Map** p99 C4 ❷❾

The Royal Institution has been at the forefront of London's scientific achievements for more than 200 years. Following a complete rebuild, accessibility is now the key word: a revamp of the Michael Faraday Laboratory – a complete replica of electromagnetic pioneer Faraday's former workspace; a new events programme, with lighthearted Family Fun Days; and a brand new Time & Space restaurant-café.

Shepherd Market

Green Park tube. **Map** p99 B5 ❸❶ Named after a food market set up by architect Edward Shepherd in the early 18th century, from 1686 this was home

to the raucous May Fair (eventually shut down due to 'drunkenness, fornication, gaming and lewdness'). It's now a pleasant, upscale area with a couple of good pubs and some of London's most agreeable pavement dining.

Eating & drinking

Chisou

4 Princes Street, W1B 2LE (7629 3931/www.chisou.co.uk). Oxford Circus tube. **Open** noon-2.30pm, 6-10.15pm Mon-Sat. **££**. **Japanese**. **Map** p99 C3 ❸❶

In spite of the black-clad staff, plain wooden tables, smart blond chairs and black slate floor, Chisou has a friendly izakaya tavern-style atmosphere that lures regulars back time and again. It puts a bright contemporary spin on Japanese classics.

Connaught Bar

NEW *16 Carlos Place, W1K 2AL (7499 7070/www.theconnaught.com). Bond Street or Green Park tube.* **Open** 4pm-1am Mon-Sat. **££££**. **Cocktail bar**. **Map** p99 B4 ❸❷

The Connaught is one of London's most properly old-fashioned luxury hotels – but this is one hell of a sexy bar, with a sleek, black-and-chrome, cruise-liner style interior. The range of spirits covers just about every desirable and fashionable drink you can name. Across the corridor, the equally impressive sibling Coburg Bar (7499 7070) specialises in more traditional mixed drinks.

Corrigan's Mayfair

NEW *28 Upper Grosvenor Street, W1K 7EH (7499 9943/www.corrigans mayfair.com). Marble Arch tube.* **Open** noon-3pm, 6-11pm Mon-Fri; 6-11pm Sat; 6-10pm Sun. **££££**. **British**. **Map** p99 A4 ❸❸

Richard Corrigan's surefooted blend of haute cuisine and trad Irish cooking is up and running at this new venture. The restaurant is both sophisticated

Haunch of Venison p107

and down-to-earth in its decor, and dishes are presented with immaculate attention to detail. Also worth seeking out is Bentley's (11-15 Swallow Street, 7734 4756), Corrigan's grand seafood operation off Piccadilly.

Galvin at Windows

28th floor, London Hilton, 22 Park Lane, W1K 1BE (7208 4021/www. galvinatwindows.com). Hyde Park Corner tube. **Open** 10am-1am Mon-Wed; 10am-3am Thur- Sat; 10am-10.30pm Sun. **Bar**. Map p99 B5 ❸❹
With the possible exception of Vertigo 42 (p166), there's no more remarkable site for a bar in London: 28 floors up, at the top of the Park Lane Hilton, with an extraordinary panoramic view of the capital, and a sleek interior that mixes art deco glamour with a hint of '70s petrodollar kitsch.

Gaucho Piccadilly

25 Swallow Street, W1B 4DJ (7734 4040/www.gauchorestaurants.co.uk). Piccadilly Circus tube. **Open** noon-midnight Mon-Sat; noon-10.30pm Sun. **£££**. **Steakhouse**. Map p99 C4 ❸❺
Steakhouse chic is what the Gaucho chain's flagship restaurant is all about – from its well-stocked Cavas wine

shop to a pitch-dark cocktail bar and penchant for cowskin wallpaper and pouffes. The steaks? Good, with the bife de lomo (fillet) often outstanding.

Guinea

30 Bruton Place, W1J 6NL (7409 1728/www.theguinea.co.uk). Bond Street or Oxford Circus tube. **Open** 11.30am-11pm Mon-Fri; 6-11pm Sat. **Pub**. Map p99 C4 ❸❻
Tucked away in an attractive West End mews, the Guinea is a proper boozer. The largely besuited punters sup from a limited but well-kept range of ales. The steak and kidney pies, served on weekday lunchtimes, have won awards, and for more refined palates there's a proper restaurant, the Guinea Grill, next door.

Hibiscus

29 Maddox Street, W1S 2PA (7629 2999/www.hibiscusrestaurant.co.uk). Oxford Circus tube. **Open** noon-2.30pm, 6.30-10pm Mon-Fri. **£££**. **Modern European**. Map p99 C3 ❸❼
Small and intimate, Hibiscus is one of the capital's most exciting places to eat. Chef-patron Claude Bosi is a kitchen magician, playing with texture and flavour in ways that challenge and

excite, without making diners feel they're in some weird experiment.

Maze

10-13 Grosvenor Square, W1K 6JP (7107 0000/www.gordonramsay.com). Bond Street tube. **Open** noon-midnight daily. **£££**. **Modern European**. Map p99 B3 ➌➑
Although part of Gordon Ramsay's stable, Maze owes its success to star chef Jason Atherton. He has earned accolades for a line-up of sophisticated tapas, miniature main courses and awe-inspiring desserts. This is a modern, spacious set-up, with a glamorous cocktail bar by the entrance.

Momo

25 Heddon Street, W1B 4BH (7434 4040/www.momoresto.com). Piccadilly Circus tube. **Open** noon-2.30pm, 6.30-11pm Mon-Sat; 6.30-10.30pm Sun.
£££. **North African**. Map p99 C4 ➌➒
A big reputation, cool Marrakech-style decor, great Maghrebi soundtrack and some of the best North African food in London keep punters pouring in to Momo for an experience to savour.

Nobu Berkeley Street

15 Berkeley Street, W1J 8DY (7290 9222/www.noburestaurants.com). Green Park tube. **Open** noon-2.15pm Mon-Fri; 6-11pm Mon-Wed; 6pm-midnight Thur-Sat; 6-9pm Sun. *Bar* noon-1am Mon-Wed; 1pm-2am Thur, Fri; 6pm-2am Sat; 6-9pm Sun. **££££**.
Japanese fusion. Map p99 C4 ➍➓
Three years after opening, the upstairs restaurant and sushi bar here continue to buzz with celeb-studded glamour, and the cooking remains sublime. The cocktail bar's plenty swish too.

Only Running Footman

5 Charles Street, W1J 5DF (7499 2988/www.therunningfootman.biz). Green Park tube. **Open** 7.30am-midnight daily. **Pub**. Map p99 B4 ➍➊
Recently reopened after a huge refurb, this place still looks as if it's been here

Scott's p110

forever. On the ground floor, jolly chaps prop up the mahogany bar, enjoying three decent ales on draught and an extensive menu: anything from a bacon buttie takeaway to Welsh rarebit with watercress. A full English breakfast is served for only £7.50.

La Petite Maison

54 Brooks Mews, W1K 4EG (7495 4774/www.lpmlondon.co.uk). Bond Street tube. **Open** noon-3pm, 6-11pm Mon-Sat; 12.30-4pm Sun. **£££**.
French. Map p99 B3 ➍➋
Part of the buzz around this place is that its namesake in Nice is so good; part is that it's co-owned by Arjun Waney, the owner of Roka (p118) and Zuma (p92). It's usually full of couples, financiers and socialites, all audibly excited by the quality of food that is served to be shared, tapas-style.

Scott's

20 Mount Street, W1K 2HE (7495 7309/www.caprice-holdings.co.uk). Bond Street or Green Park tube. **Open** noon-midnight Mon-Sat; noon-10pm Sun. **££££**. **Fish**. Map p99 B4 ➍➌

Of the celebrity hangouts in the capital, Scott's is the one that most justifies the hype: from the greeting by doorman Sean to the look-at-me contemporary British art on the walls and the glossy Rich List crowd. The food – perhaps tiny boar sausages with chilled rock oysters – gets better and better.

Tamarind

20-22 Queen Street, W1J 5PR (7629 3561/www.tamarindrestaurant.com). Green Park tube. **Open** noon-2.45pm, 6-11.30pm Mon-Fri; 6-11.30pm Sat; noon-2.45pm, 6-10.30pm Sun. **£££**. **Indian**. Map p99 B5 ④

Chef Alfred Prasad has maintained Tamarind in the top rank of Indian restaurants. The big basement space has grandiose, burnished gold pillars and walls, but Prasad relies on innovative spicing, expert presentation and a lightness of touch to make his mark.

Tibits

NEW *12-14 Heddon Street, W1B 4DA (7758 4110/www.tibits.ch). Oxford Circus tube.* **Open** 9am-10.30pm Mon-Wed; 9am-midnight Thur-Sat; 10am - 10.30pm Sun. **££**. **Vegetarian**. Map p99 C4 ④

It's all California-cool in this groovy vegetarian export from Switzerland. The buffet-cum-pay-per-100g concept left us sceptical at first, but the global offerings have proven to be notches above the usual all-you-can-eat gaff.

Wild Honey

12 St George Street, W1S 2FB (7758 9160/www.wildhoneyrestaurant.co.uk). Bond Street or Oxford Circus tube. **Open** noon-2.30pm, 6-10.30pm Mon-Sat; noon-3pm, 6-10.30pm Sun. **£££**. **Modern European**. Map p99 C3 ④

This sister of Arbutus (p128) has both charm and professionalism. The oak-panelled walls could be stifling, but modern artworks banish thoughts of the old world, and a happy buzz predominates. The menu ranges across the best of the UK and Europe.

Shopping

Browns

23-27 South Molton Street, W1K 5RD (7514 0000/www.brownsfashion.com). Bond Street tube. **Open** 10am-6.30pm Mon-Wed, Fri, Sat; 10am-7pm Thur. Map p99 B3 ④

Joan Burstein's venerable store has reigned supreme for nearly 40 years. Among the 100-odd designers jostling for attention in its five interconnecting shops are Chloé, Dries Van Noten and Balenciaga. New labels include cult legging label Les Chiffoniers and ethical denim by Shakrah Chakra, as well as exclusives from Balmain, Ossie Clark and Vince. Browns Focus (nos.38-39, 7514 0063) is younger and more casual, while Labels for Less (no.50, 7514 0052) is loaded with last season's leftovers.

Burlington Arcade

Piccadilly, W1 (7630 1411/www. burlington-arcade.co.uk). Green Park tube. **Open** 9.30am-5.30pm Mon-Fri; 10am-6pm Sat. Map p99 C4 ④

The Royal Arcades in the vicinity of Piccadilly are a throwback to shopping past – Burlington is the largest, and commissioned by Lord Cavendish in 1819, oldest of them. Highlights include collections of classic watches, Luponde Teas, iconic British brands Globe-Trotter and Mackintosh… and the top-hatted beadles who keep order.

Dover Street Market

17-18 Dover Street, W1S 4LT (7518 0680/www.doverstreetmarket.com). Green Park tube. **Open** 11am-6pm Mon-Wed; 11am-7pm Thur-Sat. Map p99 C4 ④

Comme des Garçons designer Rei Kawakubo's ground-breaking six-storey space combines the energy and edginess of London's indoor markets – concrete floors, Portaloo dressing rooms – with rarefied labels. Recent additions include Oscar de la Renta and exclusive range by Stefano Pilati's Yves Saint Laurent 24.

LONDON BY AREA

Elemis Day Spa

2-3 Lancashire Court, Mayfair, W1S 1EX (7499 4995/www.elemis.com). Bond Street tube. **Open** 9am-9pm Mon-Sat; 10am-6pm Sun. **Map** p99 B3 🐾

This leading British spa brand's exotic, unisex retreat is tucked away down a cobbled lane off Bond Street. The elegantly ethnic treatment rooms are a lovely setting in which to relax and enjoy a spot of pampering, from wraps to results-driven facials.

Georgina Goodman

44 Old Bond Street, W1F 4GD (7493 7673/www.georginagoodman.com). Green Park tube. **Open** 10am-6pm Mon-Wed, Fri, Sat; 10am-7pm Thur. **Map** p99 C4 🐾

Goodman started her business crafting sculptural, made-to-measure footwear from a single piece of untreated vegetan leather, and a couture service is still available at her airy, gallery-like shop. The ready-to-wear range (from £165 for her popular slippers) brings Goodman's individualistic approach to a wider customer base.

Grays Antique Market & Grays in the Mews

58 Davies Street, W1K 5LP & 1-7 Davies Mews, W1K 5AB (7629 7034/www.graysantiques.com). Bond Street tube. **Open** 10am-6pm Mon-Fri. **Map** p99 B3 🐾

More than 200 dealers run stalls in this smart covered market – housed in a Victorian lavatory showroom – selling everything from antiques, art and jewellery to vintage fashion and, with the permanent book fair that is the Biblion section (7629 1374, www.biblionmayfair.co.uk), some 20,000 used and antiquarian tomes.

Luella

25 Brook Street, W1K 4HB (7518 1830/www.luella.com). Bond Street tube. **Open** 10am-6pm Mon-Wed, Fri, Sat; 10am-7pm Thur. **Credit** AmEx, MC, V. **Map** p99 B3 🐾

Luella originally made her name with strappy, charm-laden bags, but her fun, sexy prom dresses have also been gaining momentum, with young London hipsters such as Alexa Chung and Lily Allen regularly snapped in them.

Miller Harris

21 Bruton Street, W1J 6QD (7629 7750/www.millerharris.com). Bond Street or Green Park tube. **Open** 10am-6pm Mon-Sat. **Map** p99 B4 🐾

Grasse-trained British perfumer Lyn Harris's distinctive, long-lasting scents, in their lovely decorative packaging, are made with quality natural extracts and oils.

Mount Street

Bond Street or Green Park tube. **Map** p99 B4 🐾

Mount Street, with its dignified Victorian terracotta façades and by-appointment art galleries, master butcher Allens (no.117) and cigar shop Sautter (no.106), has taken on a new, cutting-edge persona. At no.12, near the Connaught's new cocktail bars (p108), Balenciaga has set its super-chic clothes in a glowing sci-fi interior. Here too you will find Britain's first Marc Jacobs (nos.24-25) boutique (to be joined, as we go to press, by a cheaper, stand-alone Marc by Marc Jacobs at no.44), revered shoe-designer Christian Louboutin (no.17), Parisian perfumer Annick Goutal (no.109) and a five-floor Lanvin (no.128). Further shopping delights (such as Rick Owens) can be found on South Audley Street.

Paul Smith Sale Shop

23 Avery Row, W1X 9HB (7493 1287/www.paulsmith.co.uk). Bond Street tube. **Open** 10.30am-6.30pm Mon-Wed, Fri, Sat; 10.30am-7pm Thur; 1-5.30pm Sun. **Map** p99 B3 🐾

Samples and previous season's stock can be found here at a 30%-50% discount. The stock includes clothes for men, women and children, as well as a range of accessories.

Dover Street Market p111

Postcard Teas

9 Dering Street, W1S 1AG (7629 3654/ www.postcardteas.com). Bond Street or Oxford Circus tube. **Open** 10.30am-6.30pm Tue-Sat. **Map** p99 B3 ❺⑦
The range in this exquisite little shop is not huge, but it is selected with care: for instance, all its Darjeeling teas are currently sourced from the Goomtee estate, regarded as the best in the region. There's a central table for those who want to try a pot.

Savile Row

Oxford Circus tube. **Map** p99 C4 ❺⑧
Even Savile Row is moving with the times, with mid-brow US import Abercrombie & Fitch (0844 412 5750, www.abercrombie.co.uk) ensconced here with hip b store (7734 6846, www.bstorelondon.com), where cutting-edge designers meet established iconoclasts such as Eley Kishimoto and Bï La Lï. Still, reassuringly expensive bespoke tailoring remains the principal activity: suit-shopping becomes an almost otherworldly experience at generations-old emporiums such as Gieves & Hawkes (no.1, 7434

2001, www.gievesandhawkes.com) or Churchill's tailor Henry Poole (no.15, 7734 5985, www.henrypoole.com).

Timothy Everest

35 Bruton Place, W1J 6NS (7629 6236/www.timothyeverest.co.uk). Bond Street tube. **Open** 10am-6pm Mon-Fri; 11am-5pm alternate Sat. **Map** p99 C4 ❺⑨
One-time apprentice to the legendary Tommy Nutter, Everest is a star of the current generation of London tailors. He is well known for his relaxed 21st-century definition of style.

Uniqlo

311 Oxford Street, W1C 2HP (7290 7701/www.uniqlo.co.uk). Bond Street or Oxford Circus tube. **Open** 10am-8pm Mon-Wed; 10am-9pm Thur-Sat; noon-6pm Sun. **Map** p99 B3 ❻⓪
There are two outposts of Uniqlo, Japan's biggest clothes retailer, on Oxford Street alone – but this one is 25,000sq ft and three storeys of flagship. Not as cheap as Primark but more stylish, Uniqlo sells simple staples for men and women.

Mount Street p112

Fitzrovia

West of Tottenham Court Road and north of Oxford Street, Fitzrovia retains enough subtle traces of bohemianism to appeal to the media types that now frequent it, with its reputation as a gathering point for radicals, writers and boozers – mostly in reverse order. Some of the capital's hippest restaurants and hotels cluster near strollable Charlotte Street, but (apart from the **Newman Arms**) we don't list any traditional boozers – **Bradley's** or the **Long Bar** are more satisfying than the Fitzroy Tavern or Wheatsheaf unless you're walking your way through a Dylan Thomas biography.

Sights & museums

All Saints

7 Margaret Street, W1W 8JG (7636 1788/www.allsaintsmargaretstreet.org. uk). Oxford Circus tube. **Open** 7am-7pm daily. **Admission** free. **Map** p116 B4 ❶
Respite from the tumult of Oxford Street, this 1850s church was designed by William Butterfield, one of the great Gothic Revivalists. Behind the poly-chromatic brick façade, the shadowy, lavish interior is one of the capital's ecclesiastical triumphs.

BBC Broadcasting House

Portland Place, Upper Regent Street, W1A 1AA (0870 603 0304/www. bbc.co.uk/tours). Oxford Circus tube. **Admission** *Tours* £6.50; £4.50-£5.50 reductions; £15 family. **Map** p116 A4 ❷
Since 2008, there have been weekly tours round the BBC's headquarters, Britain's first purpose-built broadcast centre, completed in 1932. There are nine tours of various radio studios here each Sunday; booking ahead is essential. Tours are also available at BBC Television Centre (Wood Lane, Shepherd's Bush, W12 7RJ, 0370 603 0304), taking in a visit to the news desk, TV studios and Weather Centre.

Pollock's Toy Museum

1 Scala Street (entrance Whitfield Street), W1T 2HL (7636 3452/www. pollockstoymuseum.com). Goodge Street tube. **Open** 10am-5pm Mon-Sat. **Admission** £5; free-£4 reductions. **Map** p116 C4 ❸

Housed in a wonderfully creaky Georgian townhouse, Pollock's is named after Benjamin Pollock, the last of the Victorian toy theatre printers. By turns beguiling and creepy, the museum is a nostalgia-fest of old board games, tin trains, porcelain dolls and Robertson's gollies.

Royal Institute of British Architects

66 Portland Place, W1B 1AD (7580 5533/www.architecture.com). Great Portland Street tube. **Map** p116 A3 **❹**
Temporary exhibitions are held in RIBA's Grade II-listed HQ, which houses a bookshop, café and library, and hosts an excellent lecture series.

Eating & drinking

Benito's Hat

NEW *56 Goode Street, W1T 4NB (7637 3732/www.benitos-hat.com). Goodge Street tube.* **Open** 11.30am-10pm Mon-Wed, Sun; 11.30am-11pm Thur-Sat. **£.** **Burritos.** **Map** p116 B4 **❺**
London's TexMex eateries are suddenly ten a peso, and while there's only one Benito's Hat, the branded interior looks ripe for replication. The production line compiles some of the best burritos in town, with the fiery salsa brava made freshly several times daily. For drinks, the margaritas are suitably merciless.

Bradley's Spanish Bar

42-44 Hanway Street, W1T 1UT (7636 0359). Tottenham Court Road tube. **Open** noon-11pm Mon-Sat; 3-10.30pm Sun. **££.** **Pub.** **Map** p116 C5 **❻**
Is it the jukebox? Is it the tatty velvet furniture and wobbly stools? Is it just habit? Whatever the reason, people love Bradley's. A hotchpotch of local workers, shoppers and amorous foreign exchange students fills the cramped two-floor space.

Hakkasan

8 Hanway Place, W1T 1HD (7907 1888). Tottenham Court Road tube.
Open noon-12.30am Mon-Wed; noon-1.30am Thur-Sat; noon-midnight Sun. **££££.** **Chinese.** **Map** p116 C4 **❼**
When Alan Yau opened this glamtastic take on the Shanghai teahouse in 2001, he redefined Chinese dining in the UK. Its moody, nightclub feel, lounge music and high-ticket dining still pull one of the liveliest, monied crowds in town. To enjoy the Hakkasan experience for less, visit for the brilliant lunchtime dim sum.

Lantana

NEW *13 Charlotte Place, W1T 1SN (7637 3347). Goodge Street tube.* **£.** **Café.** **Map** p116 B4 **❽**
The super salads (smoky aubergine or a crunchy sugar snap and red cabbage combo, for example), cakes and sunny breakfasts have drawn a band of regulars to this Antipodean-style eatery ever since it opened. The espresso machine is the coffee connoisseur's choice – La Marzocco – and the beans come from the excellent Monmouth.

Long Bar

Sanderson, 50 Berners Street, W1T 3NG (7300 1400/www.sanderson london.com). Oxford Circus or Tottenham Court Road tube. **Open** 11.30am-2am Mon-Wed; 11.30am-3am Fri, Sat; noon-10.30pm Sun. **££££.** **Bar.** **Map** p116 B4 **❾**
The Long Bar's early noughties glory days may be a faded memory, but there's still easy glamour for the taking. The bar in question is a long, thin onyx affair, though nabbing one of the eyeball-backed stools is an unlikely prospect. A better bet is the lovely courtyard, where table service, candlelight and watery features make a much nicer setting for cocktails.

Match Bar

37-38 Margaret Street, W1G 0JF (7499 3443/www.matchbar.com). Oxford Circus tube. **Open** 11am-midnight Mon-Sat; 4pm-midnight Sun. **Cocktail bar.** **Map** p116 B4 **❿**

LONDON BY AREA

Fitzrovia & Bloomsbury

① Sights & museums
① Eating & drinking
① Shopping
① Nightlife
① Arts & leisure

Numbered locations refer to the Fitzrovia and Bloomsbury sections on pp114-128

London's Match cocktail bars celebrate the craft of the bartender with a selection of authentic concoctions, such as juleps and fizzes, made from high-end liquor. DJs spin from 7.30pm Thur-Sat.

Newman Arms

23 Rathbone Street, W1T 1NG (7636 1127/www.newmanarms.co.uk). Goodge Street or Tottenham Court Road tube. **Open** noon-midnight Mon-Fri. Food served noon-3pm, 6-9pm Mon-Fri. **Pub**. **Map** p116 C4 ⑪

The cabin-like Newman Arms has had the decorators in, but is still in touch with its history: a poster for Michael Powell's *Peeping Tom*, filmed here in 1960, faces a black and white portrait of former regular George Orwell. In the Famous Pie Room upstairs (you may have to book), pies with a variety of fillings cost just under a tenner.

Ooze

62 Goodge Street, W1T 4NE (7436 9444/www.ooze.biz). Goodge Street tube. **Open** noon-11pm Mon-Sat. **££**. **Risotto café**. **Map** p116 B4 ⑫

Risotto is the selling point, though there are plenty of alternatives. Most of the risottos come in two sizes: small isn't very small and costs around £7; large is £8.50-£13.95. Service is smiley, and there's a nicely priced wine list.

Roka & Shochu Lounge

37 Charlotte Street, W1T 1RR (7580 6464/www.rokarestaurant.com). Goodge Street or Tottenham Court Road tube. **Open** noon-3pm, 5.30-11.30pm Mon-Fri; 12.30-3pm, 5.30-11.30pm Sat; 5-10.30pm Sun. **££££**. **Japanese restaurant-bar**. **Map** p116 C4 ⑬

Roka is where to come for restaurant theatre at its best. Smack-bang in the middle of the dining room is the sushi bar and robata grill, putting the chefs centre stage. There's a great saké list, and the brilliant and buzzy basement cocktail bar Shochu Lounge (7580 9666, www.shochulounge.com) – part classy 21st-century cosmopolitan, part feudal Japan – opens until midnight.

Salt Yard

54 Goodge Street, W1T 4NA (7637 0657/www.saltyard.co.uk). Goodge Street tube. **Open** noon-11pm Mon-Fri; 5-11pm Sat. **££**. **Spanish-Italian tapas**. **Map** p116 B4 ⑭

After four years of popularity, Salt Yard spawned a second branch (Dehesa, p133) in 2008. This is tapas, but not as we knew it, bringing together Spanish and Italian ideas and ingredients with brilliant results. Confit of Gloucester Old Spot with cannellini beans is a sensation, and one of the only perennials on the alluring, frequently changing menu. Book ahead, and try to get a table upstairs.

Scandinavian Kitchen

61 Great Titchfield Street, W1W 7PP (7580 7161/www.scandikitchen.co.uk). Oxford Street tube. **Open** 8am-7pm Mon-Fri; 10am-6pm Sat; 10am-4pm Sun. **£**. **Café**. **Map** p116 B4 ⑮

A lively multicultural crowd of local office workers is kept entertained here by flirty male staff breaking into song (no Abba in our experience) and a self-deprecating sheet of instructions for eating open sandwiches: chicken and green-pepper salad, perhaps, Norwegian smoked salmon, or three types of herring. Soup and hot dogs are also on offer, as well as Gevalia filter coffee. A fun spot for a healthy lunch.

Shopping

Our favourite place for laptop repairs is **Einstein Computer Services** (07957 557065, www.einsteinpcs.co.uk), which operates on a call-out basis only and costs around £20 per hour.

Contemporary Applied Arts

2 Percy Street, W1T 1DD (7436 2344/ www.caa.org.uk). Goodge Street or

Scandinavian Kitchen

Tottenham Court Road tube. **Open** 10am-6pm Mon-Sat. **Map** p116 C4 ⑯
This airy gallery, run by the charitable arts organisation, represents more than 300 makers. Work embraces both the functional (jewellery, textiles, tableware) and unique decorative pieces.

HMV
150 Oxford Street, W1D 1DJ (0845 602 7800/www.hmv.co.uk). Oxford Street or Tottenham Court Road tube. **Open** 9am-8.30pm Mon-Wed, Fri, Sat; 9am-9pm Thur; 11.30am-5.30pm Sun. **Map** p116 B5 ⑰
With the departure of Zavvi in early 2009, HMV is the last of the mammoth Oxford Street music stores. Plenty of space is now given over to DVDs and games, but world, jazz and classical have a whole floor downstairs – and the ground floor has loads of pop, rock and dance music, including some vinyl.

Sniff
1 Great Titchfield Street, W1W 8AU (7299 3560/www.sniff.co.uk). Oxford Circus tube. **Open** 10am-7pm Mon-Fri; 10am-6.30pm Sat; noon-6pm Sun. **Map** p116 B4 ⑱
Sniff aims to be an alternative to the average high-street shoe shop, cover-ing every eventuality from sports to parties. There's a well-balanced mix of brands, established – Paco Gil, Birkenstock, Ed Hardy – and up-and-coming – strawberry motif wedges from British designer Miss L Fire.

Nightlife

Lowdown at the Albany
240 Great Portland Street, W1W 5QU (7387 5706/www.lowdownatthealbany. com). Great Portland Street tube. **Map** p116 A3 ⑲
This rough-around-the-edges base-ment venue hosts very cool comedy nights. Our personal recommendation is the monthly Clark's at Lowdown: a reliable roster of smart, young, left-field comedians is MCed by the thor-oughly genial Dan Clark. Excellent for Edinburgh previews as well.

100 Club
100 Oxford Street, W1D 1LL (7636 0933/www.the100club.co.uk). Oxford Circus or Tottenham Court Road tube. **Map** p116 C5 ⑳
Perhaps the most adaptable venue in London, this wide, 350-capacity base-ment room has provided a home for trad jazz, pub blues, northern soul and

punk. These days, it offers jazz, indie acts and ageing rockers such as Nine Below Zero and the Blockheads.

Social

5 Little Portland Street, W1W 7JD (7636 4992/www.thesocial.com). Oxford Circus tube. **Map** p116 B4 ㉑
A discreet, opaque front hides this daytime diner and DJ bar of supreme quality, a place that still feels more like a displaced bit of Soho than a resident of chic Marylebone a decade after Heavenly Records opened it up.

Bloomsbury

In bookish circles, Bloomsbury is a name to conjure with: it is the HQ of London University and home to the superb **British Museum**. The name was famously attached to a group of early 20th-century artists and intellectuals (Virginia Woolf and John Maynard Keynes among them), and more recently to the (Soho-based) publishing company that gave us Harry Potter. It is an area that demands an idle browse: perhaps the bookshops of Great Russell Street, Marchmont Street or Woburn Walk, maybe along lovely **Lamb's Conduit Street**.

Sights & museums

British Museum

Great Russell Street, WC1B 3DG (7323 8000/information 7323 8783/www. britishmuseum.org). Russell Square or Tottenham Court Road tube. **Open** 10am-5.30pm Mon-Wed, Sat, Sun; 10am-8.30pm Thur, Fri. *Great Court* 9am-6pm Mon-Wed, Sun; 9am-11pm Thur-Sat. **Admission** free; donations appreciated. *Special exhibitions* prices vary. **Map** p117 D4 ㉒
Officially the country's most popular tourist attraction, the British Museum is a neoclassical marvel that was built in 1847 – and finished off with the magnificent glass-roofed Great Court in 2000. This £100m landmark surrounds the domed Reading Room, where Marx, Lenin, Dickens, Darwin, Hardy and Yeats once worked. Star

British Museum

exhibits include ancient Egyptian arte-facts – the Rosetta Stone on the ground floor, mummies upstairs – and Greek antiquities including marble friezes from the Parthenon. The King's Library is a calming home to a 5,000-piece collection devoted to the extraordinary formative period of the museum during the Enlightenment. You won't be able to see everything in one day, so buy a guide and pick some showstoppers, or plan several visits. Highlights tours (£8, £5 reductions) focus on specific aspects of the huge collection; the free Eye Opener tours offer introductions to particular world cultures.

Cartoon Museum

35 Little Russell Street, WC1A 2HH (7580 8155/www.cartoonmuseum. org). Tottenham Court Road tube. **Open** 10.30am-5.30pm Tue-Sat; noon-5.30pm Sun. **Admission** £4; free-£3 reductions. **Map** p117 D4 ❷

On the ground floor of this former dairy, a brief chronology of British cartoon art is displayed, from Hogarth via Britain's cartooning 'golden age' (1770-1830) to examples of wartime cartoons, ending up with modern satirists such as Ralph Steadman and the *Guardian*'s Steve Bell, alongside fine temporary exhibitions. Upstairs is a celebration of UK comics and graphic novels.

Charles Dickens Museum

48 Doughty Street, WC1N 2LX (7405 2127/www.dickensmuseum.com). Chancery Lane or Russell Square tube. **Open** 10am-5pm Mon-Sat; 11am-5pm Sun. **Admission** £5; £3-£4 reductions; £14 family. **Map** p117 E3 ❷

London is scattered with plaques marking addresses where the peripatetic Charles Dickens lived, but this is the only one of them still standing. He lived here from 1837 to 1840, during which time he wrote *Nicholas Nickleby* and *Oliver Twist*. Ring the doorbell to gain access to four floors of Dickensiana, collected over the years from various other of his residences.

Foundling Museum

40 Brunswick Square, WC1N 1AZ (7841 3600/www.foundlingmuseum. org.uk). Russell Square tube. **Open** 10am-5pm Tue-Sat; 11am-5pm Sun. **Admission** £5; free-£4 reductions. **Map** p117 D3 ❷

Returning to England from America in 1720, Captain Thomas Coram was appalled by the number of abandoned children on the streets and persuaded artist William Hogarth and composer GF Handel to become governors of a new hospital for them. Hogarth decreed the hospital should also be Britain's first public art gallery, and work by such as Gainsborough and Reynolds is still shown upstairs. The most heart-rending display is a tiny case of mementos that were all mothers were allowed to leave the children they abandoned here.

Petrie Museum of Egyptian Archaeology

University College London, Malet Place, WC1E 6BT (7679 2884/www.petrie. ucl.ac.uk). Euston Square, Goodge Street or Warren Street tube. **Open** 1-5pm Tue-Fri; 10am-1pm Sat. **Admission** free; donations appreciated. **Map** p116 C3 ❷

The museum, set up in 1892, is named after Flinders Petrie, tireless excavator of ancient Egypt. Where the British Museum's Egyptology collection is strong on the big stuff, the Petrie is dim case after dim case of minutiae. Among the oddities are a 4,000-year-old skeleton of a man ritually buried in an earthenware pot. Wind-up torches help you peer into the gloomy corners.

St George's Bloomsbury

Bloomsbury Way, WC1A 2HR (7405 3044/www.stgeorgesbloomsbury.org.uk). Holborn or Tottenham Court Road tube. **Open** 11am-4pm Mon-Fri; 11.30am-5pm Sat; 10.30am-5pm Sun. **Admission** free. **Map** p117 D4 ❷

Consecrated in 1730, St George's is a grand and typically disturbing work by Nicholas Hawksmoor, with an off-set, stepped spire that was inspired by Pliny's account of the Mausoleum at Halicarnassus. Highlights include the mahogany reredos, and 10ft-high sculptures of lions and unicorns clawing at the base of the steeple. There are guided tours and regular concerts.

Eating & drinking

Hummus Bros

37-63 Southampton Row, WC1B 4DA (7404 7079/www.hbros.co.uk). Holborn tube. **Open** noon-9pm Mon-Fri. **£**. **Café**. **Map** p117 D4 ❷❾
The simple and hugely successful formula at this café/takeaway is to serve houmous as a base for a selection of toppings, which you scoop up with excellent pitta bread. The food is nutritious and good value. There's a second Hummus Bros in Soho (88 Wardour Street, 7734 1311).

Lamb

94 Lamb's Conduit Street, WC1N 3LZ (7405 0713/www.youngs.co.uk). Holborn or Russell Square tube. **Open** 11am-midnight Mon-Sat; noon-10.30pm Sun. **Pub**. **Map** p117 E3 ❷❾
Founded in 1729, this Young's pub is the sort of place that makes you misty-eyed for a vanishing era. The Lamb found fame as a theatrical haunt when the A-list included Sir Henry Irving and sundry stars of music hall; they're commemorated in vintage photos, surrounded by well-worn seats, polished wood and vintage knick-knacks.

Meals

1st floor, Heal's, 196 Tottenham Court Road, W1T 7LQ (7580 2522/www.heals.co.uk). Goodge Street or Warren Street tube. **Open** 10am-6pm Mon-Wed, Fri; 10am-7.30pm Thur; 9.30am-6.30pm Sat; noon-6pm Sun. **£**. **Café**. **Map** p116 C3 ❸⓪
Crossing an alpine lodge with a toddler's bedroom, with cut-out cupboards that suggest a fairytale landscape, the

decor here is the ironic side of twee. The food doesn't quite taste as well as it reads, but it's enjoyable, cultured and surprisingly generous.

Museum Tavern

49 Great Russell Street, WC1B 3BA (7242 8987). Holborn or Tottenham Court Road tube. **Open** 11am-11.30pm Mon-Thur; 11am-midnight Fri, Sat; noon-10.30pm Sun. **££**. **Pub**. **Map** p117 D4 ❸❶
When a boozer boasts logoed T-shirts and its own history book, you might be wary; but this venerable corner pub opposite the British Museum pulls in locals as well as tourists. Past customers have included JB Priestley, Sir Arthur Conan Doyle and Karl Marx, who unwound here after hours spent in the old British Library. Today, the excellent guest ales are well worth anyone's *Kapital*, though the food is basic proletarian pub fare.

Norfolk Arms

28 Leigh Street, WC1H 9EP (7388 3937/www.norfolkarms.co.uk). Euston tube/rail. **Open** 11am-11pm Mon-Sat; 11am-10.30pm Sun. **£££**. **Gastropub**. **Map** p117 D2 ❸❷
A glossy gastropub reinvention means that while the tiled exterior, ornate ceiling and etched-glass windows remain, a businesslike charcuterie slicer now takes pride of place behind the stately mahogany bar, with lomo, chorizo and salchichon hanging overhead. Dining, not drinking, is the focus, but the Norfolk Arms is far from formal; half the menu is starters and mains, half an eclectic tapas list.

Wagamama

4A Streatham Street, WC1A 1JB (7323 9223/www.wagamama.com). Holborn or Tottenham Court Road tube. **Open** noon-11pm Mon-Sat; noon-10pm Sun. **££**. **Oriental canteen**. **Map** p117 D4 ❸❸
Since starting life in the basement here in 1992, this chain of shared-table

Mighty Moctezuma

Mexico's Ruling Lord conquers the British Museum.

You may only know of him as a brand of luxury chocolates, or maybe you've suffered his famous 'revenge', a severe attack of the runs in Acapulco perhaps, but now's your chance to right those wrongs to the memory of one of central America's most awe-inspiring and misunderstood rulers, properly called Moctezuma II. The **British Museum** (p120) will be opening its fourth and final exploration of the lives of great leaders on 24 September 2009, running until 24 January 2010.

'Moctezuma: Aztec Ruler' is the culmination of a series of hugely popular shows here that began in 2007 by looking at the First Emperor of China, Qin Shihuangdi, and his terracotta warriors. They were followed up by exhibitions on the Roman Emperor Hadrian, and 17th-century Persian Shah 'Abbas.

The Moctezuma exhibition is being timed to coincide with the bicentenary of Mexican independence, as well as the centenary of the revolution, both falling in 2010. Yet the last ruler of the Aztecs, the most prodigious of Mexico's indigenous empire-builders, has an ambivalent reputation in his own country, largely because the circumstances surrounding his demise and abject defeat in the face of Cortés and his few hundred Conquistadors in 1520 remain a riddle. After welcoming the invaders as guests in his palace, possibly because he thought them to be gods, was he stoned to death by his own people? Or was he murdered by the duplicitous Spanish, perhaps forced to drink molten gold by Cortés himself?

The British Museum promises to examine all the available evidence in mapping out the extraordinary details of Moctezuma's life. On display will be a scale model of the Great Temple where he presided over human sacrifices to his god Quetzalcoatl, as well as architectural fragments that remain from his great island city of Tenochtitlán. Highlights will be the Teocalli of Sacred Warfare, a stone throne inscribed with textual imagery, on loan from Mexico City's National Anthropology Museum, and an amazing turquoise and gold mask.

If your thirst for things Mexican hasn't yet been sated, from 22 October 2009 to 28 February 2010 there will also be a free exhibition of post-revolutionary Mexican drawings by the likes of Diego Rivera, José Clemente Orozco and David Alfaro Siqueiros.

Norfolk Arms p122

players, radios, laptops as well as hi-fis and TVs and all the accessories, concentrating on the major brands. Prices are competitive.

Ben Pentreath Ltd

NEW *17 Rugby Street, WC1N 3QT (7430 2526/www.benpentreath.com). Russell Square tube.* **Open** 11am-6pm Tue-Sat. **Map** p117 E3 ③⑤

This tiny homeware store, just off Lamb's Conduit Street (below), stocks a magical variety of items – crockery, vintage books, masonry fragments, soft furnishings – all in accord with with architect Ben's aesthetic. 'Good things for your home', indeed.

Gosh!

39 Great Russell Street, WC1B 3NZ (7636 1011/www.goshlondon.com). Tottenham Court Road tube. **Open** 10am-6pm Mon-Wed, Sat, Sun; 10am-7pm Thur, Fri. **Map** p117 D4 ③⑥

Half of the basement room at this comics specialist is given over to comics while the other holds a fine stash of manga. It's graphic novels that take centre stage, though, from early classics like *Krazy Kat* and *Little Nemo* to Alan Moore's *Lost Girls*.

Lamb's Conduit Street

Holborn or Russell Square tube. **Map** p117 E3 ③⑦

Tucked away among residential back streets, Lamb's Conduit Street is perfect for browsing, whether you fancy a custom-made suit from Pokit (no.53, 7430 9782, www.pokit.co.uk), cult menswear and cute women's knitwear from Folk (no.49, 7404 6458, www.folk clothing.com), a photographic book from Matchless Prints & Steidlville London (no.36, 7405 8899, www. steidlville.com) or classic vinyl reissues at Synphonic (no.47, 7242 9876). Refuel at the Lamb (p122), then head just off the main drag to Rugby Street to check out Ben Pentreath (above) or the deco accessories at French's Dairy (no.13, 7404 7070, www.frenchsdairy.com).

LONDON BY AREA

restaurants has become a global phenomenon – there are now branches as far as Cyprus and Boston. The British Wagamamas all serve the same menu: rice plate meals and Japanese noodles, cooked teppanyaki-style on a flat griddle or simmered in huge bowls of spicy soup, all served in double-quick time. Satisfying food, well priced.

Shopping

Ask

248 Tottenham Court Road, W1T 7QZ (7637 0353/www.askdirect.co.uk). Tottenham Court Road tube. **Open** 10am-7pm Mon-Wed, Fri, Sat; 10am-8pm Thur; noon-6pm Sun. **Map** p116 C4 ③④

Some shops on Tottenham Court Road – London's main street for consumer electronics – feel gloomy and claustrophobic, and give you the real hard sell. Ask has four capacious, well-organised floors that give you space to browse stock that spans digital cameras, MP3

London Review Bookshop

14 Bury Place, WC1A 2JL (7269 9030/www.lrbshop.co.uk). Holborn or Tottenham Court Road tube. **Open** 10am-6.30pm Mon-Sat; noon-6pm Sun. **Map** p117 D4 ㊳

An inspiring bookshop, from the stimulating presentation to the quality of the selection. Politics, current affairs and history are well represented on the ground floor, while downstairs, audio books lead on to exciting poetry and philosophy sections. Lovely café too.

Skoob

Unit 66, Brunswick Centre, WC1N 1AE (7278 8760/www.skoob.com). Russell Square tube. **Open** 10.30am-8pm Mon-Sat; 10.30am-6pm Sun. **Map** p117 D3 ㊴

A back-to-basics concrete basement that showcases 50,000 titles covering virtually every subject, from philosophy and biography to politics and the occult. You probably won't find what you were looking for – but rarely come away without buying something else.

Nightlife

Bloomsbury Bowling Lanes

Basement, Tavistock Hotel, Bedford Way, WC1H 9EU (7183 1979/www. bloomsburybowling.com). Russell Square tube. **Open** noon-2am Mon-Thur; noon-3am Fri, Sat; 1pm-midnight Sun. **Map** p117 D3 ㊵

Already a hip destination for local students and those wanting a late drink away from Soho, BBL started putting on live bands and DJs on Mondays, Fridays and Saturdays, sometimes with a 1950s theme. If you get bored of the bands or the bowling, hole up in one of the karaoke booths.

King's Cross

North-east of Bloomsbury, the once-insalubrious area of King's Cross is undergoing massive redevelopment

London Review Bookshop

around the amazing new **St Pancras International** and now well-established 'new' **British Library**. The gaping badlands to the north are being transformed (to the tune of £500m) into a mixed-use nucleus called King's Cross Central, with **Kings Place** arts complex perhaps the sign of things to come.

Sights & museums

St Pancras International (Pancras Road, 7843 4250, www. stpancras.com; see also p212) welcomes the high-speed Eurostar train from Paris with William Barlow's gorgeous Victorian glass-and-iron train shed. For all the public art, high-end boutiques and eateries (notably St Pancras Grand, p127), it's the beauty of the original structure that's the real hit. The magnificent neo-Gothic hotel building that fronts the station is due to reopen in 2010.

British Library

96 Euston Road, NW1 2DB (7412 7332/www.bl.uk). Euston Square tube/ Euston or King's Cross tube/rail. **Open** 9.30am-6pm Mon, Wed-Fri; 9.30am-8pm Tue; 9.30am-5pm Sat; 11am-5pm Sun. **Admission** free; donations appreciated. **Map** p117 D1 ㊹

'One of the ugliest buildings in the world,' opined a Parliamentary committee on the opening of the new British Library in 1997. But don't judge a book by its cover: the interior is a model of cool, spacious functionality. This is one of the greatest libraries in the world, holding over 150 million items. In the John Ritblat Gallery, the library's main treasures are displayed: the Magna Carta, original manuscripts from Chaucer and Beatles lyrics. The focal point of the building is the King's Library, a six-storey glass-walled tower housing George III's collection.

London Canal Museum

12-13 New Wharf Road, N1 9RT (7713 0836/www.canalmuseum.org.uk). King's Cross tube/rail. **Open** 10am-4.30pm Tue-Sun. **Admission** £3; free-£2 reductions. **Map** p117 E1 ㊷

The museum is housed in a former 19th-century ice warehouse, used by Carlo Gatti for his ice-cream, and includes an interesting exhibit on the history of the ice trade. The part of the collection looking at the history of the waterways and those who worked on them is rather sparse by comparison.

Wellcome Collection

183 Euston Road, NW1 2BE (7611 2222/www.wellcomecollection.org). Euston Square tube/Euston tube/rail. **Open** 10am-6pm Tue, Wed, Fri, Sat; 10am-10pm Thur; 11am-6pm Sun. **Admission** free. **Map** p116 C2 ㊸

Founder Sir Henry Wellcome, a pioneering 19th-century pharmacist and entrepreneur, amassed a vast, grisly and idiosyncratic collection of implements and curios – ivory carvings of pregnant women, used guillotine blades, Napoleon's toothbrush – mostly relating to the medical trade. It's now displayed in this swanky little museum, along with works of modern art. The temporary exhibitions are usually wonderfully interesting.

Eating & drinking

The **Peyton & Byrne** café on the ground floor of the Wellcome (above) is a handy stop, and tea at **Rough Luxe** (see box p205) is fun.

Camino

3 Varnishers Yard, Regents Quarter, N1 9AF (7841 7331/www.camino.uk. com). King's Cross tube/rail. **Open** 8am-3pm, 6.30-11pm Mon-Fri; 7-11pm Sat. *Bar* noon-midnight Mon-Wed; noon-1am Thur-Sat. **£££**. **Spanish bar-restaurant**. **Map** p117 D1 ㊹

A big, Spanish-themed bar-restaurant in the heart of the King's Cross construction zone, Camino is a shining beacon of things to come. In the bar you can order good tapas, but it's worth sitting down for a proper meal in the restaurant, where the cooking adheres wonderfully to the central principle of traditional Spanish food: the finest ingredients, simply cooked.

King Charles I

55-57 Northdown Street, N1 9BL (7837 7758). King's Cross tube/rail. **Open** noon-11pm Mon-Fri; 5-11pm Sat, Sun. **Pub**. **Map** p117 E1 ㊺

The King Charles is frequented by loyal (mainly male) regulars who are pleased as punch to partake of great beers in such a conspiratorial setting. The global range baffles the first-time visitor, as might the quirky decor: an old bar billiards table, an advert for Leu Family Tattoo Parlour, ethnic figures and carnival masks.

Konstam

2 Acton Street, WC1X 9NA (7833 5040/www.konstam.co.uk). King's Cross tube/rail. **Open** 12.30-3pm,

6.30-10.30pm Mon-Fri; 6.30-10.30pm Sat. **£££. Eco-restaurant**. Map p117 E2 **46**

The USP at this small, eco-conscious restaurant is that 'over 85% of the produce... is grown or reared within the area covered by the London Underground network'. Which is not to say that owner/chef Oliver Rowe's menu is limited or unimaginative: how about sea bass with almond sauce and purple sprouting broccoli, for example?

St Pancras Grand

NEW *Upper Concourse, St Pancras International, Euston Road, NW1 2QP (7870 9900/www.searcys.co.uk/ stpancrasgrand). King's Cross tube/rail.* **Open** 7.30am-10.30pm daily. **£££. British brasserie**. Map p117 D1 **47**

Their 'longest in Europe' trackside Champagne Bar got all the attention when St Pancras station reopened, but Searcys' even newer restaurant is better, a romantic beauty clearly inspired by the Oyster Bar in New York's Grand Central Station. Rediscovering British dishes is the culinary trend du jour, but the superbly accomplished menu here reaches back further than most: braised beef ribs with 17th-century spices a case in point.

Snazz Sichuan

New China Club, 37 Chalton Street, NW1 1JD (7388 0808). Euston tube/ rail. **Open** noon-midnight daily. **££. Sichuanese**. Map p116 C2 **48**

The bizarre decor (flimsy magenta curtains, Cultural Revolution poster), the enthusiasm of the staff, the skill of the chef and the wonderful aromas are all testament to authenticity. This is mala (hot and numbing) fare, so don't expect familiar Cantonese dishes – instead try the likes of spicy pigs' ears.

Nightlife

Big Chill House

257-259 Pentonville Road, N1 9NL (7427 2540/www.bigchill.net). King's Cross tube/rail. **Open** noon-midnight Mon-Wed, Sun; noon-1am Thur; noon-3am Fri, Sat. **Map** p117 E1 **49**

The Big Chill empire rolls on: the festival that became a record label and a bar most recently opened this three-floor house. There's a great terrace, but the real reasons to attend are the chill vibe and terrific DJs. It costs £5 to enter after 10pm on Friday and Saturday.

Scala

275 Pentonville Road, N1 9NL (7833 2022/www.scala-london.co.uk). King's Cross tube/rail. **Map** p117 E1 **50**

One of London's best-loved gig venues, this multi-floored monolith is the frequent destination for one-off superparties now that many of London's superclubs have bitten the dust. Built as a cinema shortly after World War I, it is surprisingly capacious and hosts a laudably broad range of indie, electronica, avant hip hop and folk. Funky, electro and tech house bash Smartie Partie has relocated here from Turnmills with a monthly residency.

Arts & leisure

Kings Place

NEW *90 York Way, N1 9AG (0844 264 0321/www.kingsplace.co.uk). King's Cross tube/rail.* **Map** p117 E1 **51**

Part of a complex of galleries and office space (housing the *Guardian* and *Observer* newspapers), the main 400-seat auditorium opened in late 2008 with a wide-ranging series of concerts. Although Kings Place will be the permanent home of both the London Sinfonietta and the Orchestra of the Age of Enlightenment, there's also jazz, folk, leftfield rock and spoken word – sometimes in the second, smaller room.

Place

17 Duke's Road, WC1H 9PY (7121 1000/www.theplace.org.uk). Euston tube/rail. **Map** p116 C2 **52**

For genuinely emerging dance, look to the Place. The Robin Howard Dance

Theatre has 300 seats raked to a stage 15m by 12m wide – an electrifying space in which to showcase the best new choreographers and dancers.
Event highlights Resolution! Dance Festival (Jan-Feb 2010).

Soho

Forever unconventional, packed with restaurants, clubs and bars, Soho remains London at its most game. Shoppers and visitors mingle with the musos, gays, boozers and perverts who have colonised the area since the late 1800s. Poseurs, spivs, chancers, loud girls and wide boys still spend their money here. If you want to drink or eat, you could hardly find a better part of London to do so. Have a wander among the skinny streets that radiate off **Old Compton Street**, Soho's main artery – and see if you can't still find yourself a bit of mischief.

Sights & museums

Leicester Square

Leicester Square tube. **Map** p130 C3 ❶
Leicester Square is reasonably pleasant by day, but by night a sinkhole of semi-undressed inebriates out on a big night 'up west'. How different it once was. Satirical painter William Hogarth had a studio here (1733-64), as did 18th-century artist Sir Joshua Reynolds; both are commemorated in the small central gardens, although it's the statue of Charlie Chaplin that gets all the attention. Apart from the excellent tkts booth (p140) and unlikely neighbours the Prince Charles cinema (p140) and Notre Dame de France (no.5, 7437 9363, www.notredamechurch.co.uk), with its Jean Cocteau murals, there's little reason to spend time here.

Photographers' Gallery

NEW *16-18 Ramillies Street, W1A 1AU (0845 262 1618/www.photonet.org.uk). Oxford Circus tube.* **Open** 11am-6pm

Tue-Wed, Sat, Sun; 11am-8pm Thur, Fri. **Map** p130 A1 ❷
In late 2008, this excellent photographic gallery moved, with its café and shop, to this transitionary space. New six-storey premises will open on the same site, with a target date of 2011.

Ripley's Believe It or Not!

NEW *1 Piccadilly Circus, W1J 0DA (3238 0022/www.ripleyslondon.com). Piccadilly Circus tube.* **Open** 10am-midnight daily. **Admission** £19.95; free-£17.95 reductions; £65 family. **Map** p130 B3 ❸
Over five floors of the Trocadero, this 'odditorium' follows a formula more or less unchanged since Robert Ripley opened his first display at the Chicago World Fair in 1933: an assortment of 800 curiosities is displayed, ranging from a two-headed calf to the world's smallest road-safe car.

Soho Square

Tottenham Court Road tube.
Map p130 C1 ❹
This tree-lined quadrangle was once King's Square – a weather-beaten statue of Charles II stands at the centre, very at home beside the mock Tudor gardeners' hut. On sunny days, the grass is covered with smoochy couples, the benches with snacking workers.

Eating & drinking

Since the 1950s, Gerrard and Lisle Streets have been the centre of **Chinatown**, marked by oriental gates, stone lions and pagoda-topped telephone boxes. Stalwart old-style diners like Mr Kong (21 Lisle Street, 7437 7341) and Wong Kei (41-43 Wardour Street, 0871 332 8296) are still here, but we prefer the likes of newbie Ba Shan (below).

Arbutus

63-64 Frith Street, W1D 3JW (7734 4545/www.arbutusrestaurant.co.uk). Tottenham Court Road tube. **Open**

noon-2.30pm, 5-11pm Mon-Sat; 12.30-3.30pm, 5.30-9.30pm Sun. **£££**. **Modern European**. Map p130 C2 ❺

The menu here is strong on hearty British fare, accented with continental flavours, and seasonality matters. Arbutus is very popular. Book ahead, and expect the place to be full to bursting at dinner. The lunchtime set menus are a bargain.

Baozi Inn

25 Newport Court, WC2H 7JS (7287 6877). Leicester Square tube. **Open** 11am-10pm daily. **£**. No credit cards. **Beijing noodles**. Map p131 D3 ❻

The decor, inspired by Beijing hutongs circa 1952, signals kitsch rather than culture, and backless wooden pews are far from conducive to a lingering lunch, yet these Beijing- and Chengdu-style street snacks (including handmade dan dan noodles) are 100% authentic. The baozi themselves – steamed buns filled with pork, radish or egg – are great.

Barrafina

54 Frith Street, W1D 4SL (7813 8016/ www.barrafina.co.uk). Leicester Square or Tottenham Court Road tube. **Open** noon-3pm, 5-11pm Mon-Sat; 12.30-3.30pm, 5.30-10.30pm Sun. **£££**. **Tapas**. Map p130 C2 ❼

The air is redolent of frying garlic and grilling meat: an enticing aroma made more appealing by the dishes waiters carry past as you queue for a seat. And you probably will queue, as Barrafina is tiny, popular and takes no bookings. It's just an open kitchen, stainless-steel bar and tall stools, but what more do you need when the tapas are this good?

Ba Shan

NEW *24 Romilly Street, W1D 5AH (7287 3266). Piccadilly Circus tube.* **Open** noon-11pm Mon-Thur, Sun; noon-11.30pm Fri, Sat. **££**. **Chinese**. Map p130 C2 ❽

The third opening by the team behind Bar Shu (closed for a refurb as we go to press) and Baozi Inn – two of the top spots for spicy Sichuanese food – Ba Shan's black-painted frontage gives no clues to the exquisite food and cheery service within. The xiao chi menu (Mandarin for 'small eats') offers a host of tiny treats, all inspired by the snack vendors of Chengdu.

Beatroot

NEW *92 Berwick Street, W1F 0QD (7437 8591). Oxford Circus, Piccadilly Circus or Tottenham Court Road tube.* **Open** 9.15am-9pm Mon-Sat. **£**. **Vegetarian**. Map p130 B2 ❾

Soho Square

Soho & Covent Garden

© Copyright Time Out Group 2009

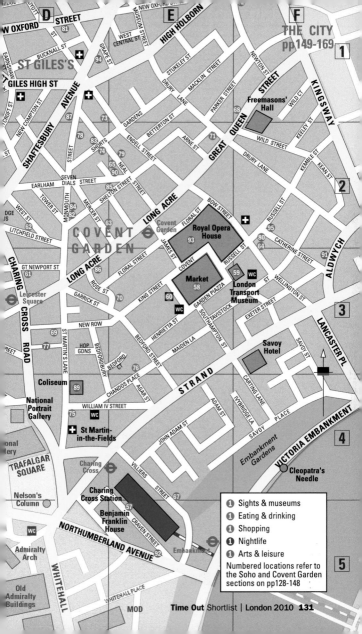

Rise of the bakery-caff

With Princi, Alan Yau is not in Canton anymore.

Best known for his wildly successful Asian eateries – quality fast-food at Wagamama (p122), Busaba Eathai (p132) and Cha Cha Moon (p133); haute Chinese at Hakkasan (p115) and Yauatcha (p135) – Alan Yau's previous attempt at an Italian restaurant was short-lived. But despite the rare failure of that 2003 enterprise, Anda, with new venture **Princi** (p135) he can feel on pretty safe ground: bakery-cafés – from Ottolenghi (p172) to the popular Peyton & Byrne minichain (www.peytonandbyrne.com) – have slyly become the discerning Londoner's favoured snack-stop.

Located in Soho, Princi is a joint venture with Rocco Princi, 'the Armani of bread'. They clearly have great empathy with each other, and Armani, on the design front. The place has that wonderfully sophisticated informality that has made Busaba such a treasure, and the glass cabinets displaying cakes, pizza, salads and hot meals make it irresistible.

Best of all, the prices are very kind. Those custard-filled cannoncini are 80p for three, and if our chicken cacciatora was typical, it was enough to feed two – especially if you factor in the bread supplied in a smart black-and-white paper bag holding some bamboo cutlery. Get a side dish like the zucchine fritte and you'll have a feast.

Beatroot has been providing reliable, healthy eats for over a decade. Cheerful staff dole out generous portions of hot dishes and salads from behind the counter. Grab your choice as a take-away, or eat at one of a handful of acid-green and sunny-orange tables.

Bob Bob Ricard

NEW *1 Upper St James Street, W1F 9DF (3145 1000/www.bobbobricard.com). Piccadilly Circus tube.* **Open** 7am-3am daily. **£££**. **Brasserie**. **Map** p130 B3 ⑩

This 'eccentric' new bar-brasserie is a spectacle, from the louche interior (lots of marble and leather, gold chainmail and retro lamp fittings) to the ridiculous, glam pink uniforms of the waiters. 'Classic British favourites', done with variable skill, dominate the menu.

Bocca di Lupo

NEW *12 Archer Street, W1D 7BB (7734 2223/www.boccadilupo.com). Piccadilly Circus tube.* **Open** 12.30-3pm, 5.30-11pm Mon-Sat. **£££**. **Italian**. **Map** p130 B3 ⑪

Take an outstanding gastronomic tour of most of Italy's 20 regions with the starter-sized portions of its 'degustation' menu – or larger portions for those who prefer a more traditional Italian meal – served up in an atmosphere of understated luxury at surprisingly reasonable prices.

Busaba Eathai

106-110 Wardour Street, W1F 0TR (7255 8686). Oxford Circus or Tottenham Court Road tube. **Open** noon-11pm Mon-Thur; noon-11.30pm Fri, Sat; noon-10pm Sun. **£**. **Thai**. Map p130 B2 ⑫

This is probably the handiest of the three branches of the excellent Thai fast food canteen – which means there's often a queue. It combines shared tables and bench seats with a touch of oriental mystique (dark wood, incense, low lighting), and food that is as good as many top-price restaurants.

Cha Cha Moon

15-21 Ganton Street, W1F 9BN (7297 9800). Oxford Circus tube. **Open** noon-11pm Mon-Thur; noon-11.30pm Fri, Sat; noon-10pm Sun. **£. Hong Kong noodles**. Map p130 A2 ⑬

Still attracting queues, Alan Yau's mini-chain offers accessible prices, communal tables and a no-booking policy to on-the-go Soho-ites after a quick pit-stop. Noodles are the order of the day, inspired by Hong Kong mein dong (noodle stalls) but with influences from across China, Malaysia and Singapore.

Chippy

NEW *38 Poland Street, W1F 7LY (7434 1933). Oxford Circus tube.* **Open** noon-9pm Mon-Sat; noon-6pm Sun. **£. Fish & chips**. Map p130 A1 ⑭

This licensed café looks as if it's been here for decades. The dark lino, primrose Formica, wood panels and bentwood chairs all reference decades past, but the retro look and menu are very conscious, and superbly accomplished.

Dehesa

25 Ganton Street, W1F 9BP (7494 4170). Oxford Circus tube. **Open** noon-11pm Mon-Sat; noon-5pm Sun. **££. Spanish-Italian tapas** Map p130 A2 ⑮

A bijou place serving top-rank Spanish-Italian tapas and a runner-up for our best new restaurant award in 2008. Expect bicultural bites such as jamón iberico, hand-sliced from a leg on display, and intensely flavoured wild boar salami. Reservations aren't taken, so expect to wait a while.

Dog & Duck

18 Bateman Street, W1D 3AJ (7494 0697). Tottenham Court Road tube. **Open** 10am-11.30pm Mon-Sat; noon-10.30pm Sun. **Pub**. Map p130 C2 ⑯

This cosy, corner pub has changed little since Orwell hung out here in the 1940s. Today's regulars take their tipples seriously; there are even ale tasting sessions on Monday evenings.

Princi

Fernandez & Wells

73 Beak Street, W1F 9SR (7287 8124/ www.fernandezandwells.com). Oxford Circus or Piccadilly Circus tube. **Open** 7.30am-7pm Mon-Fri; 9am-7pm Sat, Sun. **£. Café**. Map p130 B2 ⑰

If only there were more coffee bars like this in central London. Its sandwiches aren't cheap, but they are special – mostly made with ingredients imported from Spain for the takeaway/deli round the corner on Lexington Street. At lunchtime, seats are at a premium but worth the wait.

Floridita

100 Wardour Street, W1F 0TN (7314 4000/www.floriditalondon.com). Tottenham Court Road tube. **Open** 5.30pm-2am Mon-Wed; 5.30pm-3am Thur-Sat. **Cuban cocktail bar**. Map p130 B2 ⑱

Named after the famous Havana haunt, this tastefully glitzy basement does a Spanish cocktail menu – most of what's on it, priced at £8, involves Havana Club Anejo Blanco being expertly shaken with fresh mint, fresh

Algerian Coffee Stores p136

MANDEHLING SUMATRA

lime, sugars and a variety of dashes. Live music comes courtesy of Salsa Unica every evening. From Thursday to Saturday, admission costs £15 after 7.30pm, and is by guestlist or at the doorman's discretion.

French House

49 Dean Street, W1D 5BG (7437 2799/ restaurant 7437 2477/www.french housesoho.com). Leicester Square or Piccadilly Circus tube. **Open** noon-11pm Mon-Sat; noon-10.30pm Sun. **Pub. Map** p130 C2 ⑲

Titanic drinkers of the post-war era, the Bacons and the Behans, frequented this small but significant establishment, with the venue's French heritage having enticed De Gaulle to run a Resistance operation from upstairs. Beer is still served in half pints and bottles of Breton cider are still plonked on the famed back alcove table.

Imli

167-169 Wardour Street, W1F 8WR (7287 4243/www.imli.co.uk). Tottenham Court Road tube. **Open** noon-11pm daily. **£. Indian tapas. Map** p130 B2 ⑳

Indian tapas is the hook here, but Imli is no passing fad. Cut-price relative of the classy Tamarind (p111), this vibrant restaurant has culinary zip aplenty. Three dishes amount to a substantial two-course meal.

LAB

12 Old Compton Street, W1D 4TQ (7437 7820/www.lab-townhouse.com). Leicester Square or Tottenham Court Road tube. **Open** 4pm-midnight Mon-Sat; 4-10.30pm Sun. **Cocktail bar. Map** p130 C2 ㉑

LAB's two-floor space is invariably packed with Sohoites eager to be fuelled by London's freshest mixologists. Straight out of LAB school (LAB is the London Academy of Bartending), graduates are aided by colleagues of considerable global experience.

Little Lamb

72 Shaftesbury Avenue, W1D 6NA (7287 8078). Leicester Square or Piccadilly Circus tube. **Open** noon-

11.30pm Mon-Sat; noon-10.30pm Sun.
££. Oriental hot-pot. Map p130 C3 ㉒
Little Lamb suffers from a common
Chinatown malaise – the urge to dumb
down flavours that are beyond the mild
Cantonese norm. So despite the
Genghis Khan schtick, don't expect
Mongolian specialities. Instead, enjoy
the fondue-style fun of dipping veg,
meat and fish into the bubbling broth.

Maison Bertaux

*28 Greek Street, W1D 5DQ (7437
6007). Leicester Square, Piccadilly
Circus or Tottenham Court Road tube.*
Open 8.30am-11pm Mon-Sat; 8am-7pm
Sun. **£**. No credit cards. **Café**. Map
p130 C2 ㉓
Oozing arty, bohemian charm, this café
dates back to 1871 when Soho was
London's little piece of the Continent.
Battered old bentwood tables and
chairs add to the feeling of being in a
pâtisserie in rural France. The provisions (cream cakes, greasy pastries,
pots of tea) really aren't the point.

Nordic Bakery

*14 Golden Square, W1F 9JF (3230
1077/www.nordicbakery.com). Oxford
Circus or Piccadilly Circus tube.* **Open**
8am-8pm Mon-Fri; noon-7pm Sat. **£**.
Café. Map p130 B3 ㉔
A haven of über-stylish Scandinavian
cool warmed up with baskets, tea tow-
els, denim aprons and a nature-inspired
wall rug. Their fresh-out-of-the-oven
cinnamon buns – thick, fluffy and oozing spicy sweetness – are the real deal.

Player

*8 Broadwick Street, W1F 8HN (7292
9945/www.thplyr.com). Oxford Circus
or Tottenham Court Road tube.* **Open**
5.30pm-midnight Mon-Wed; 5.30pm-
1am Thur, Fri; 7pm-1am Sat. **Cocktail
bar**. Map p130 B2 ㉕
As the cocktail menu points out,
'don't fix what ain't broke': it remains
unchanged since 2005, and the basement space in which it is served is still
sexy. Similarly impressive cocktails

are mixed in nearby jazz-tinged
speakeasy Milk & Honey (61 Poland
Street, 7292 9949, www.mlkhny.com),
open to non-members only with an
advance booking.

Princi

NEW *135 Wardour Street, W1F 0UF
(7478 8888). Tottenham Court Road
or Oxford Circus tube.* **Open** 10am-
midnight Mon-Sat; 10am-11pm Sun.
££. Bakery-café. Map p130 B1 ㉖
See box p132.

Spiga

*84-86 Wardour Street, W1V 3LF
(7734 3444/www.vpmg.net). Leicester
Square, Piccadilly Circus or Tottenham
Court Road tube.* **Open** noon-11pm
Mon, Tue; noon-midnight Wed-Sat.
££. Pizza. Map p130 B2 ㉗
Spiga makes a refreshing change
from common or garden pizza chains,
distinguished by interesting dishes
created from super-fresh ingredients.
Decorated with mirrored walls and
Italian movie posters, it's packed most
nights. The vibe is buzzy, even noisy,
but the staff keep on top of things.

Two Floors

*3 Kingly Street, W1B 5PD (7439 1007/
www.barworks.co.uk). Oxford Circus
or Piccadilly Circus tube.* **Open** noon-
11.30pm Mon-Thur; noon-midnight Fri,
Sat. **Bar**. Map p130 A3 ㉘
Sparse, laid-back and bohemian, Two
Floors is understated and quite wonderful. Beers here are mainly bottled,
ales too. There are £4 lunchtime ciabattas too, though even the laziest daytime
rendezvous might spark into a raging
evening session along the new bar hub
of Kingly Street.

Yauatcha

*15 Broadwick Street, W1F 0DL (7494
8888). Oxford Circus, Piccadilly Circus
or Tottenham Court Road tube.* **Open**
11am-11.30pm Mon-Sat; 11am-10.30pm
Sun. **£££. Dim sum/teahouse**.
Map p130 B2 ㉙

This ground-breaking dim sum destination is a sultry lounge-like basement den, with glowing fish tanks and starry ceiling lights, where young professionals, Chinese families and suited businessmen enjoy a succession of freshly prepared, highly impressive, perennial favourites.

Shopping

Albam

23 Beak Street, W1F 9RS (3157 7000/ www.albamclothing.com). Oxford Circus tube. **Open** noon-7pm Mon-Sat; noon-5pm Sun. **Map** p130 A3 ③⓪

With its refined yet rather manly aesthetic, this menswear label dresses well-heeled gents, fashion editors and regular guys who like no-nonsense style. The focus is on classic, high-quality design with a subtle retro edge (Steve McQueen is an inspiration).

Algerian Coffee Stores

52 Old Compton Street, W1V 6PB (7437 2480/www.algcoffee.co.uk). **Open** 9am-7pm Mon-Wed; 9am-9pm Thur, Fri; 9am-8pm Sat. **Map** p130 C2 ③①

For 120 years, this unassuming little shop has been trading over the same wooden counter. The range of coffees is broad, with house blends alongside single-origin beans, and some serious teas and brewing hardware are also available.

Berwick Street

Piccadilly Circus or Tottenham Court Road tube. **Map** p130 B2 ③②

The buzzy street market (9am-6pm Mon-Sat), in an area better known for its lurid, neon-lit trades, is one of London's oldest. Dating back to 1778, it's still great for seasonal produce and cheap fabric. The indie record shops that used to be clustered here have taken a pasting over the last few years, but Revival Records (no.30, 7437 4271, www.revivalrecords.uk.com) is full of vinyl beans, and Chris Kerr (no.52, 7437 3727, www.eddiekerr.co.uk), son

of legendary 1960s tailor Eddie, is still here crafting brilliant bespoke suits.

Carnaby Street

Oxford Street tube. **Map** p130 A2 ③③

As famous as the King's Road back when the Sixties Swung, Carnaby Street was until a few years ago more likely to sell you a postcard of the Queen snogging a punk rocker than a fishtail parka. But the noughties have been kind and Carnaby is cool again. Among classy chains (Lush, Muji), Kingly Court (7333 8118, www.carnaby.co.uk) is the real highlight, a three-tiered complex containing a funky mix of chains and independents, including the traditionally styled boutique fashion, homeware and gifts at Mnini (7494 9086, www.mnini.co.uk).

Foyles

113-119 Charing Cross Road, WC2H 0EB (7437 5660/www.foyles.co.uk). Tottenham Court Road tube. **Open** 9.30am-9pm Mon-Sat; noon-6pm Sun. **Map** p130 C2 ③④

Probably London's single most impressive independent bookshop, Foyles built its reputation on the sheer volume and breadth of its stock (there are 56 specialist subjects in this flagship store). Its five storeys accommodate other shops too: Ray's Jazz, London's least beardy jazz shop, has recently moved up to the 3rd floor, giving more room to the first-floor café, which hosts low-key gigs and readings.

Liberty

Regent Street, W1B 5AH (7734 1234/ www.liberty.co.uk). Oxford Circus tube. **Open** 10am-9pm Mon-Sat; noon-6pm Sun. **Map** p130 A2 ③⑤

Charmingly idiosyncratic, Liberty is housed in a 1920s mock Tudor structure. Shopping here is about more than just spending money; artful window displays, exciting new collections and luxe labels make it an experience to savour for its own sake. A Tom Dixon-designed champagne room and a tea

Liberty

room by Roksanda Illincic are rumoured to be in the offing. And despite being fashion forward, Liberty still respects its dressmaking heritage with an extensive haberdashery department. Liberty's stand-alone store (197 Sloane Street, 7573 9695) sells a selection of their own-brand products.

Playlounge
19 Beak Street, W1F 9RP (7287 7073/ www.playlounge.co.uk). Oxford Circus or Piccadilly Circus tube. **Open** 10.30am-7pm Mon-Sat; noon-5pm Sun. **Map** p130 A3 ㊱
Compact but full of fun, this groovy little shop has action figures, gadgets, books and comics, e-boy posters, T-shirts and clothes that appeal to kids and adults alike. Those nostalgic for illustrated children's literature shouldn't miss the Dr Seuss PopUps and Where the Wild Things Are books.

Sir Tom Baker
NEW *4 D'Arblay Street, W1F 8DJ (7437 3366/www.tombakerlondon. com). Tottenham Court Road tube.* **Open** 11am-7pm Mon-Fri; 10am-6pm Sat. **Map** p130 B2 ㊲

Bringing a bit of glam attitude to the business of bespoke, Sir Tom Baker had been making suits for the rock gentry (Mick Jagger, Robert Plant) from his Berwick Street workshop since the mid-1990s. This boutique allows you to connect you with great shoes and Stephen Jones hats as well.

Nightlife

Bar Rumba
36 Shaftesbury Avenue, W1D 7EP (7287 6933/www.barrumba.co.uk). Piccadilly Circus tube. **Map** p130 C3 ㊳
Smack in the middle of the West End, Bar Rumba's small basement club was already known for its deep urban flavours and surprisingly un-West End crowd, but a relaunch saw it take on a more underground, techno and electro twist. Movement is the fortnightly junglist and drum 'n' bass session, while salsa fans love Barrio Latino.

Comedy Camp
Barcode, 3-4 Archer Street, W1D 7AP (7483 2960/www.comedycamp.co.uk). Leicester Square or Piccadilly Circus tube. **Map** p130 B3 ㊵

This intimate, straight-friendly gay Tuesday night regular is one of the best nights out in town. The audiences are always up for a great evening, and resident host and promoter Simon Happily only books fabulous acts.

Comedy Store

1A Oxendon Street, SW1Y 4EE (Ticketmaster 0870 060 2340/www.the comedystore.co.uk). Leicester Square or Piccadilly Circus tube. **Map** p130 C3 **40**
Dubbed 'Comedy's Unofficial National Theatre', the Comedy Store was founded in 1979. Through the 1980s, it became the home of alternative comedy: the Comedy Store Players improv group, now including Paul Merton and Josie Lawrence, continues to shine on Wednesdays and Sundays.

Leicester Square Theatre

NEW *6 Leicester Place, WC2H 7BX (7534 1740/box office 0844 847 2475/ www.leicestersquaretheatre.com). Leicester Square tube.* **Map** p130 C3 **41**
The main auditorium seems to be majoring in solo shows from feisty women – Joan Rivers, Sandra Bernhard – on a largely comedy-driven schedule, but we also love the goings-on in the little basement performance space, with its champagne bar.

Lo-Profile

NEW *84-86 Wardour Street, W1F 0TG (7734 1053/www.profilesoho. com). Leicester Square or Piccadilly Circus tube.* **Open** 9pm-3am Thur; 10pm-4am Fri, Sat. **Map** p130 B2 **42**
If gay dating sites are the enemy of gay clubs, what on earth is Gaydar doing opening one in the heart of Soho? The late-night counterpart of sleek, futuristic, three-floor flagship venue Profile (56 Frith Street, 7734 8300), this basement club holds around 450 people with two bars, a cruising area and a dancefloor for commercial house and live PAs. Sexy black surfaces contribute to a slightly retro, down-and-dirty vibe.

Lo-Profile

Madame JoJo's

8-10 Brewer Street, W1F 0SE (7734 3040/www.madamejojos.com). Leicester Square or Piccadilly Circus tube. **Map** p130 B3 **43**
JoJo's is a beacon for those seeking to escape post-work chain pubs. The basement space is very red and a bit shabby and hosts variety (the all-new London Burlesque Social Club; Kitsch Cabaret), Keb Darge's long-running Deep Funk and, on a Tuesday, the indie racket of White Heat.

Pizza Express Jazz Club

10 Dean Street, W1D 3RW (7439 8722/www.pizzaexpress.co.uk). Tottenham Court Road tube. **Map** p130 C1 **44**
The upstairs restaurant (7437 9595) is jazz-free, but the 120-capacity basement venue is one of Europe's best modern mainstream jazz venues.

Punk

14 Soho Street, W1D 3DN (7734 4004/ www.fabbars.com). Tottenham Court Road tube. **Map** p130 C1 **45**

When regulars include Kate Moss, Lily Allen and Mark Ronson, it seems there's little this basement space can do wrong. It accommodates 270 at a squeeze, and the Mapplethorpe-style flower prints and Rock Galpin furniture suit the mix of high-heeled girls and indie mash-ups from the Queens of Noize at their fab Smash 'n' Grab parties on Thursdays.

Ronnie Scott's

47 Frith Street, W1D 4HT (7439 0747/ www.ronniescotts.co.uk). Leicester Square or Tottenham Court Road tube. **Open** *6pm-3am Mon-Sat; 6pm-midnight Sun.* **Admission** *£25-£100.* **Map** p130 C2 ❹❻

Opened by the British saxophonist Ronnie Scott in 1959, this legendary institution was completely refurbished in 2006. Capacity has been expanded to 250, and the food is better – but the improvements have come at a cost. The bookings have declined in quality, with decent jazz heavyweights (Roy Haynes, Bill Charlap, Mark Murphy) now outnumbered by some distinctly average pop and funk artists.

Shadow Lounge

5 Brewer Street, W1F 0RF (7287 7988/www.theshadowlounge.com). Piccadilly Circus tube. **Open** *10pm-3am Mon-Sat.* **Map** p130 B3 ❹❼

For professional cocktail waiters, celebrity sightings, suits, cutes and fancy boots, this gay cocktail lounge is your venue. At weekends, expect to queue and pay a hefty cover charge, but it's worth it once you're inside.

Arts & leisure

Curzon Soho

99 Shaftesbury Avenue, W1D 5DY (information 7292 1686/bookings 0870 756 4620/www.curzoncinemas.com). Leicester Square tube. **Map** p130 C2 ❹❽

All the cinemas in the Curzon group programme a superb range of shorts, rarities, double bills and mini-festivals,

but the Curzon Soho is the best – not least because it also has a great ground-floor café and decent basement bar.

London Hippodrome

NEW *Leicester Square, 10-14 Cranbourn Street, WC2H 7JH (7907 7097/www.thelondonhippodrome.com). Leicester Square tube.* **Map** p131 D3 ❹❾

The spirit of the London Hippodrome in its heyday lives on, in aptly scuzzy form, in burlesque variety show *La Clique*. Thanks to thoughtful presentation (spivvy ushers in bowlers) and to the lead of Mario, Queen of the Circus (think Freddie Mercury with a lot of extra balls), it comes together as a whole lot of hilarious pleasure. Production subject to change.

London Palladium

NEW *Argyll Street, W1F 7TF (0844 579 1940/www.sisteractthe musical.com). Oxford Circus tube.* **Map** p130 A2 ❺⓿

New musical comedy based on the hit 1992 Whoopi Goldberg movie *Sister Act*, in which a nightclub singer takes refuge from gangsters in a convent. Production subject to change.

Odeon West End

Leicester Square, WC2H 7LQ (0871 224 4007/www.odeon.co.uk). Leicester Square tube. **Map** p130 C3 ❺❶

This art deco masterpiece is London's archetypal red-carpet star-studded site for premieres. Catch one of the occasional silent movie screenings with live organ music if you can; otherwise, it will be a comfy viewing of a pricey current blockbuster.

Palace Theatre

NEW *Shaftesbury Avenue, W1D 5AY (0844 755 0016/www.priscilla themusical.com). Leicester Square or Tottenham Court Road tube.* **Map** p130 C2 ❺❷

Priscilla, Queen of the Desert is brash, trashy and uniquely transporting, thanks to a soundtrack of super-femme

LONDON BY AREA

anthems ('I Will Survive', 'Finally') and costume design that is on a madly brilliant mission to give the whole of Australia the campest of makeovers. Production subject to change.

Prince Charles

7 Leicester Place, Leicester Square, WC2H 7BY (0870 811 2559/www. princecharlescinema.com). Leicester Square tube. **Map** p130 C3 ❻
The downstairs screen here offers the best value in town for releases that have ended their first run elsewhere. Upstairs, a new screen shows current releases at higher prices – but at under a tenner, still competitive for the West End. The weekend singalong sreenings are very popular.

Prince Edward Theatre

28 Old Compton Street, W1D 4HS (0870 040 0046/www.jerseyboys london.com). Leicester Square or Piccadilly Circus tube. **Map** p130 C2 ❺
This is the London home for *Jersey Boys*, the story of Frankie Valli and the Four Seasons. The pace is lively, the sets gritty and the doo-wop standards ('Big Girls Don't Cry', 'Can't Take My Eyes Off You') superbly performed. Production subject to change.

Soho Theatre

21 Dean Street, W1D 3NE (7478 0100/box office 0870 429 6883/www. sohotheatre.com). Tottenham Court Road tube. **Map** p130 C2 ❺
Its cool blue neon lights, front-of-house café and occasional late-night shows attract a younger, hipper crowd than most theatres. The Soho brings on aspiring writers through regular work-shops, and has regular solo comedy shows and drag performances.

tkts

Clocktower Building, Leicester Square, WC2H 7NA (www.officiallondon theatre.co.uk). Leicester Square tube. **Open** 10am-7pm Mon-Sat; noon-3pm Sun. **Map** p130 C3 ❺
This non-profit organisation is known for selling cut-price tickets for West End shows on a first-come, first-served basis on the day of performance, but also sells full-price tickets. Avoid getting ripped off by the touts and come here instead.

Covent Garden

Covent Garden is understandably popular with visitors. A traffic-free oasis in the heart of the city, replete with shops, cafés and bars – as well as the fun **London Transport Museum** – it centres on a restored 19th-century covered market. On the west side of the square, **St Paul's Covent Garden** still upstages the escapologists and jugglers that entertain crowds in front of its portico. If you're looking for great performances rather than street performances, the **Royal Opera House** is here too.

Sights & museums

Benjamin Franklin House

36 Craven Street, WC2N 5NF (7925 1405/www.benjaminfranklinhouse.org). Charing Cross tube/rail. **Open** pre-booked tours only. **Admission** £7; free-£5 reductions. **Map** p131 E5 ❺
The house where Franklin lived from 1757 to 1775 can be explored on well-run, pre-booked multimedia 'experi-ences'. Lasting an intense 45mins, they are led by an actress in character as Franklin's landlady. More straightfor-ward, 20min tours (£3.50) are given by house interns on Mondays.

Covent Garden Piazza

Covent Garden tube. **Map** p131 E3 ❺
Visitors flock here for a combination of shopping, outdoor restaurant and café seating, performances by street artists and classical music renditions in the lower courtyard. The majority of the street entertainment takes place under the portico of St Paul's (opposite). Most

tourists favour the old covered market (7836 9136, www.coventgardenlondon.uk.com), which combines a collection of small and sometimes quirky shops, many of them rather twee, with a range of upmarket gift chain stores. The Apple Market, in the North Hall, has a either arts and crafts (Tue-Sun) or antiques (Mon) stalls set up.

London Transport Museum

The Piazza, WC2E 7BB (7379 6344/ www.ltmuseum.co.uk). Covent Garden tube. **Open** 10am-6pm Mon-Thur, Sat; 11am-9pm Fri. **Admission** £8; free-£6.50 reductions. **Map** p131 F3 ⑤⑨

Reopened in 2007 after the most thorough refurbishment since its move to Covent Garden in 1980, London's Transport Museum traces the city's transport history from the horse age to the present day. As well as remodelling the interior of the magnificent old flower market building, the museum has emerged with a much more confident focus on social history and design, illustrated by a superb array of preserved buses, trams and trains. Appropriately, it's now also much easier to get around.

St Paul's Covent Garden

Bedford Street, WC2E 9ED (7836 5221/www.actorschurch.org). Covent Garden or Leicester Square tube. **Open** 9am-4.30pm Mon-Fri; 9am-12.30pm Sun. **Admission** free; donations appreciated. **Map** p131 E3 ⑥⓪

Known as the Actors' Church for its long association with Covent Garden's theatres, this magnificently spare building was designed by Inigo Jones for the Earl of Bedford in 1631. Thespians commemorated on its walls range from those lost in obscurity to those destined for immortality. Surely there's no more romantic tribute in London than Vivien Leigh's plaque, simply inscribed with words from Shakespeare's *Antony & Cleopatra*: 'Now boast thee, death, in thy possession lies a lass unparalleI'd.'

Play it again, fan

Are 20-year-old movies the future for the West End?

Another year, another hit film adaptation is announced for the West End. This time it's the Oscar-winning *Ghost* that gets the musical treatment.

You might not remember the the 1990 original – Patrick Swayze's Sam is killed by a mugger, only to return from the dead (assisted by Whoopi Goldberg's psychic Oda Mae) to preserve Demi Moore's Molly from imminent danger – but you will surely know the endlessly parodied scene where Sam takes Molly in his arms to the strains of 'Unchained Melody' and together they turn a pot that isn't going to win them a scholarship to ceramics college. Bruce Joel Rubin, who got an Oscar for his original screenplay, is behind the adaptation, aided and abetted on music by the founder of the Eurythmics, Dave Stewart, and Glen Ballard.

We'll have already had a chance to see whether Whoopi Goldberg is West End gold dust: her 1992 film comedy *Sister Act* previewed as a musical at the London Palladium (p139) in spring 2009. But it may be the Swayze factor that got the producers cracking their knuckles in excitement. The reappearance of *Ghost* follows an adaptation of Swayze's 1987 film *Dirty Dancing* that took an eye-popping £11m in advance ticket sales before its official opening in 2006.

Eating & drinking

There's a busy **Masala Zone** (48 Floral Street, 7379 0101, www. masalazone.com; see also p172) near the Opera House and market.

Abeno Too

17-18 Great Newport Street, WC2H 7JE (7379 1160/www.abeno.co.uk). Leicester Square tube. **Open** noon-11pm Mon-Sat; noon-10.30pm Sun. **££. Japanese. Map** p131 D3 ③
Okonomiyaki (hearty pancakes with nuggets of vegetables, seafood, pork and other titbits added to a disc of noodles) are cooked to order on hot-plates set into Abeno's tables and counter.

L'Atelier de Joël Robuchon

13-15 West Street, WC2H 9NE (7010 8600/www.joel-robuchon.com). Leicester Square tube. **Open** noon-2.30pm, 5.30-11.30pm Mon-Sat; noon-2.30pm, 5.30-10.30pm Sun. **£££. Modern European. Map** p131 D2 ②
The locations in Joël Robuchon's restaurant empire sound like 007 stopovers – Macau, Hong Kong, Monaco – but Robuchon is no Bond baddie, he's a French super-chef. The Japanese-inspired ground-floor L'Atelier is dimly lit, but the open kitchen is an impressively theatrical focal point. A choice of small tasting dishes is the best way to explore the work of this fine chef.

Bullet

3rd floor, Snow & Rock, 4 Mercer Street, WC2H 9QA (7836 4922). Covent Garden tube. **Open** 10am-6pm Mon-Wed, Fri, Sat; 10am-7pm Thur; 10am-4.30pm Sun. **£. Café. Map** p131 D2 ③
This gem of a café is holed up on the third floor of a lift-free extreme-sports shop, but the trek is worth the effort for the organic fair-trade coffee alone. The food menu is limited (two choices of main course, baguettes and bagels for toasting, a few fine cakes), but it's a great getaway if you've been battling the Covent Garden masses.

Coach & Horses

2 Wellington Street, Covent Garden, WC2E 7BD (7240 0553). Covent Garden tube. **Open** 11am-11pm Mon-Sat; noon-10.30pm Sun. **Pub. Map** p131 F2 ④
A genuine expat Irish boozer that packs a bundle of tradition and charm into a modest space. There's well-pulled Guinness, of course, but also a couple of real ale chasers and more than 70 single malt whiskies. Soak it up with a hot roast beef, salt beef or Limerick ham sandwich.

Food for Thought

31 Neal Street, WC2H 9PR (7836 0239). Covent Garden tube. **Open** noon-8.30pm Mon-Sat; noon-5pm Sun. **£. No credit cards. Vegetarian café. Map** p131 E2 ⑤
The menu of this very much-loved veggie café changes daily, though you can expect three or four main courses, and a selection of salads and desserts. The laid-back premises are down a steep stairway that, during lunch, usually fills with a patient queue. The ground floor offers the same food to take away.

Giaconda Dining Room

NEW *9 Denmark Street, WC2H 8LS (7240 3334/www.giacondadining.com). Tottenham Court Road tube.* **Open** noon-2.15pm, 6-9.45pm Mon-Fri. **££. Modern European. Map** p131 D1 ⑥
The simple black-and-white dining room belies the esteem in which chef Paul Merrony is held in his native Australia. This is a generous, egalitarian spot where the unpretentious food is the star. We loved the hot pillow of ham hock hash with fried egg and lightly dressed mixed leaves.

Gordon's

47 Villiers Street, WC2N 6NE (7930 1408/www.gordonswinebar.com).

London Transport Museum p141

Embankment tube/Charing Cross tube/rail. **Open** 11am-11pm Mon-Sat; noon-10pm Sun. **Wine bar**. **Map** p131 E4 ⑰
Gordon's has been serving drinks since 1890, and it looks like it – the place is a specialist in sweaty, yellowing, candle-lit alcoves. Long may it remain so. The wine list doesn't bear expert scrutiny and the food is buffet-style, but atmosphere is everything, and this is a great place for secret assignations and furtive plans.

Great Queen Street

32 Great Queen Street, WC2B 5AA (7242 0622). Covent Garden or Holborn tube. **Open** 6-10.30pm Mon; noon-2.30pm, 6-10.30pm Tue-Sat; noon-3pm Sun. **££**. **British**. **Map** p131 F1 ⑱
The pub-style room here thrumms with bonhomie. Ranging from snacks to shared mains, the menu is designed to tempt and satisfy rather than educate or impress. Booking is essential, and the robust food is worth it. At the Sunday lunch session, diners sit and are served together. The Dive bar downstairs serves snacks as well as drinks.

J Sheekey Oyster Bar

NEW *28-32 St Martin's Court, WC2N 4AL (7240 2565/www.j-sheekey.co.uk). Leicester Square tube.* **Open** noon-3pm, 5.30pm-midnight Mon-Sat; noon-3.30pm, 6-11pm Sun. **£££**. **Fish**. **Map** p131 D3 ⑲
Sheekey's Oyster Bar opened early in 2009, yet another enticement to visit this fine restaurant. Unlike many of London's period pieces (which this certainly is, it was chartered in the mid 19th century), Sheekey's buzzes with fashionable folk. Even if you opt for the main restaurant, your party of four may be crammed on to a table for two, but the accomplished menu will take your mind off it, stretching from modern European to comforting favourites (fish pie, salmon fish cakes).

Lamb & Flag

33 Rose Street, WC2E 9EB (7497 9504). Covent Garden tube. **Open** 11am-11pm Mon-Sat; noon-10.30pm Sun. **Pub**. **Map** p131 E3 ⑳
A pub for over 300 years and a fixture on Rose Street for longer, the unabashedly traditional Lamb & Flag

is always a squeeze, but no one minds. The afternoon-only bar upstairs is 'ye olde' to a fault, and sweetly localised by pictures of passed-on regulars ('Barnsey', Corporal Bill West).

Lowlander

36 Drury Lane, WC2B 5RR (7379 7446/www.lowlander.com). Covent Garden or Holborn tube. **Open** 10am-11pm Mon-Sat; noon-10.30pm Sun. **Beer bar**. Map p131 E2 71

Brightly logoed and Benelux-themed, the smart Lowlander fills its expansive, long-tabled space easily, thanks to an impressive range of draught (15 options) and bottled beer (100 varieties). The efficient table service adds extra appeal to knackered workers, shoppers and the terminally lazy. Belgian stoemp stew is perfectly made here; mussels come in four sauces.

Princess Louise

208-209 High Holborn, WC1V 7BW (7405 8816). Holborn tube. **Open** 11am-11pm Mon-Fri; noon-11pm Sat; noon-10.30pm Sun. **Pub**. Map p131 F1 72

Following refurbishment, the Grade II-listed Princess Louise has scrubbed up something wonderful. Decorated tiles, stained-glass windows, finely cut mirrors and ornate plasterwork have all been given a polish, and Victorian wood partitions have been put back to create a pleasantly confusing warren of snugs and alcoves.

Rock & Sole Plaice

47 Endell Street, WC2H 9AJ (7836 3785/www.rockandsoleplaice.com). Covent Garden tube. **Open** 11.30am-11pm Mon-Sat; noon-10pm Sun. **££**. **Fish & chips**. Map p131 D1 73

A chippie since 1874, this establishment has walls covered in theatre posters and a busy vibe. The ground-floor tables are often all taken (check whether there's space in the basement dining room), and the outside seats are never empty in summer.

Scoop

40 Shorts Gardens, WC2H 9AB (7240 7086/www.scoopgelato.com). Covent Garden tube. **Open** 11.30am-11.30pm daily. **£**. **Ice-cream**. Map p131 D2 74

Long queues are a testament to the quality of the ice-creams, even dairy-free health versions, at this Italian artisan's shop. Flavours include a very superior Piedmont hazelnut type.

Terroirs

NEW *5 William IV Street, WC2N 4DW (7036 0660/www.terroirswinebar.com). Charing Cross tube/rail.* **Open** noon-11pm Mon-Sat. **£££**. **Wine bar**. Map p131 D4 75

Gimmick or the future of wine-making we're not sure, but many of the new generation of organic and biodynamic, sulphur-, sugar- or acid-free wines on offer here are well-made. Sensational food such as duck scratchings or fat chorizo to dip into yolky Basque piperade is served up to go with.

Coco de Mer

Wahaca

66 Chandos Place, WC2N 4HG
(7240 1883/www.wahaca.co.uk).
Covent Garden or Leicester Square
tube. **Open** noon-11pm Mon-Sat;
noon-10.30pm Sun. **£**. **Mexican
canteen**. Map p131 E3 **76**
Queues snake into this colourful canteen daily, and Wahaca has a look as
cheery as its staff, created from lamps
made out of tomatillo cans dotted with
bottle tops, wooden crates packed with
fruit, and tubs of chilli plants. Choose
one of the large plato fuertes (enchi-
ladas, burritos or grilled dishes) if you
don't feel like sharing.

Shopping

Cecil Court

Leicester Square tube. **Map** p131 D3 **77**
Bookended by Charing Cross Road and
St Martin's Lane, picturesque Cecil
Court (www.cecilcourt.co.uk) is known
for its antiquarian book, map and print
dealers. Notable residents include children's specialist Marchpane (no.16,
7836 8661) and 40-year veteran David
Drummond at Pleasures of Past Times
(no.11, 7836 1142), who specialises in
theatre and magic. A more recent
arrival is Red Snapper (no.22, 7240
2075) for small-press fiction and
counter-culture classics.

Coco de Mer

23 Monmouth Street, WC2H 9DD
(7836 8882/www.coco-de-mer.co.uk).
Covent Garden tube. **Open** 11am-7pm
Mon-Wed, Fri, Sat; 11am-8pm Thur;
noon-6pm Sun. **Map** p131 D2 **78**
London's most glamorous erotic emporium sells a variety of tasteful books,
toys and lingerie, from glass dildos
that double as objets d'art to a Marie
Antoinette costume of crotchless
culottes and corset.

Freddy

NEW *30-32 Neal Street, WC2H 9PS*
(7836 5291/www.freddy.it). Covent
Garden tube. **Open** 10am-7pm Mon-

Wed, Sat; 10am-8pm Thur; noon-6pm
Sun. **Map** p131 E2 **79**
Official outfitter to the Italian Olympic
team and La Scala Ballet, Freddy has
also been Italy's essential label for
aerobics fans since the 1980s. Its first
UK branch offers three floors of own-
label sportswear.

Hope & Greenwood

*1 Russell Street, WC2B 5JD (7240
3314/www.hopeandgreenwood.co.uk).*
Covent Garden tube. **Open** 11am-
7.30pm Mon-Wed; 11am-8pm Thur,
Fri; 10.30am-7.30pm Sat; 11.30am-
5.30pm Sun. **Map** p131 F2 **80**
This adorable 1950s-style, letterbox-
red cornershop is the perfect place to
find the sherbets, chews and chocolates
that were once the focus of a proper
British childhood. Even the staff look
the part: beautifully turned out in a
pinny, ready to pop your sweets in a
striped paper bag with a smile.

James Smith & Sons

53 New Oxford Street, WC1A 1BL
(7836 4731/www.james-smith.co.uk).
Holborn or Tottenham Court Road
tube. **Open** 9.30am-5.15pm Mon-Fri;
10am-5.15pm Sat. **Map** p131 D1 **81**
For more than 175 years, this charming shop, Victorian fittings still intact,
has managed to hold its own in the
niche market of umbrellas and walking
sticks. Forget throwaway brollies that
break at the first sign of bad weather
and invest instead in a hickory-crooked
City umbrella.

Koh Samui

65-67 Monmouth Street, WC2H 9DG
(7240 4280/www.kohsamui.co.uk).
Covent Garden tube. **Open** 10.30am-
6.30pm Mon-Wed, Fri, Sat; 10.30am-
7pm Thur; noon-5.30pm Sun. **Map**
p131 D2 **82**
Vintage pieces sourced from around
the world share rail space with a
finely tuned selection of heavyweight
designers at Koh Samui, resulting in a
delightfully eclectic mix of stock,

LONDON BY AREA

including a global array of independent jewellery designers; prices start at around £50 for a pair of earrings.

Neal's Yard Dairy
17 Shorts Gardens, WC2H 9UP (7240 5700/www.nealsyarddairy.co.uk). Covent Garden tube. **Open** 11am-7pm Mon-Thur; 10am-7pm Fri, Sat. **Map** p131 D2 ⑬
Neal's Yard buys from small farms and creameries and matures the cheeses in its own cellars until they're ready to sell. Names such as Stinking Bishop and Lincolnshire Poacher are as evocative as the aromas in the shop.

Poste Mistress
61-63 Monmouth Street, WC2H 9EP (7379 4040/www.officeholdings.co.uk). Covent Garden tube. **Open** 10am-7pm Mon-Wed, Fri, Sat; 10am-8pm Thur; 11.30am-6pm Sun. **Map** p131 D2 ⑭
The 1970s boudoir decor at this shop make a suitably glam backdrop for a line-up of high-fashion footwear, plus its own designer-look label. Lulu Guinness bags and other accessories are also sold.

Rokit
42 Shelton Street, WC2 9HZ (7836 6547/www.rokit.co.uk). Covent Garden tube. **Open** 10am-7pm Mon-Sat; 11am-6pm Sun. **Map** p131 E2 ⑮
With four locations, Rokit has come a long way since its humble Camden beginnings. This flagship has the most comprehensive selection of second-hand items. You'll find tutus and military wear, cowboy boots and sunglasses, and even classic vintage homeware. Check out the live DJ sets and window performances too.

Stanfords
12-14 Long Acre, WC2E 9LP (7836 1321/www.stanfords.co.uk). Covent Garden or Leicester Square tube. **Open** 9am-7.30pm Mon, Wed, Fri; 9.30am-7.30pm Tue; 9am-8pm Thur; 10am-7pm Sat; noon-6pm Sun. **Map** p131 D3 ⑯

Three floors of travel guides, travel literature, maps, language guides, atlases and magazines. The basement houses the full range of British Ordnance Survey maps, and you can plan your next trip over Fairtrade coffee in the new Natural Café.

Unconditional
NEW *16 Monmouth Street, WC2H 9DD (7836 6931/www.unconditional.uk.com). Covent Garden tube.* **Open** 11am-7pm Mon-Wed, Fri, Sat; 11am-8pm Thur; 12.30-6.30pm Sun. **Map** p131 D1 ⑰
Adding a bit of hard-edged urban cool to the lovely but somewhat chichi Monmouth Street, Unconditional specialises in menswear and womenswear with a twist, peddling its eponymous London label alongside a small selection of other brands, including Sharon Wauchob, Rick Owens and Zucca.

Nightlife

12 Bar Club
22-23 Denmark Place, WC2H 8NL (office 7240 2120/box office 7240 2622/www.12barclub.com). Tottenham Court Road tube. **Open** 11am-3am Mon-Sat; 6pm-midnight Sun. No credit cards. **Map** p131 D1 ⑱
This cherished hole-in-the-wall – if smoking were still allowed, this is the kind of place that would be full of it – books a grab-bag of stuff. The size (capacity of 100, a stage that barely accommodates a trio) dictates a predominance of singer-songwriters.

Arts & leisure

Coliseum
St Martin's Lane, WC2N 4ES (box office 0871 911 0200/www.eno.org). Leicester Square tube/Charing Cross tube/rail. **Map** p131 D4 ⑲
The Coliseum's 2,350-seat auditorium, built as a grand music hall in 1904 by the renowned architect Frank Matcham, was restored to its former

Lauren's laurels

Meet the Royal Ballet's new principal dancer.

When the adored Darcey Bussell retired there was mild uproar as the Royal Ballet was left with no British ballerina among its female principals. But in the 2008/9 season, grumbles were muted a little by the promotion of 24-year-old Lauren Cuthbertson, a homegrown talent who is proving that there is life after Darcey.

Cuthbertson shrugs off any expectations that being Bussell's successor might bring. 'I don't feel any pressure right now. Inside the company I could still be "*corps de ballet* Lauren" – nothing's changed, nothing's different.' Originally from Devon, Cuthbertson trained at the Royal Ballet's famous White Lodge school but, despite the regimented education, she's always been a bit of a free spirit – and that's served her well as a dancer. 'I think I managed to stay an individual,' she says. 'I just don't think that there should be a mould – that doesn't create an artist. I was always inquisitive.'

While Cuthbertson has the ability to dance with a classical elegance and poise beyond her years, recent outings have seen her perform with spark, wit and a fizzing personality that are much closer to the woman herself – 'as opposed to just trying to emulate a statue', as she puts it.

Cuthbertson's onstage versatility has her in demand, and she's relishing the opportunity to dance across the whole repertoire, from 19th-century classical pieces to the resolutely 21st-century work of Wayne McGregor, the Royal Ballet's resident choreographer – and the first to have have come to the Royal Opera House (p148) via a background in contemporary dance. 'You drop your tutu and get your hot pants on and run to the next rehearsal room, run to the next one and put the tiara on... then I'm buzzing,' she grins.

As ballet choreography goes, McGregor is extreme, full of hyperactive and hyperextended bodies slicing and dicing the air. The choreographic process can be mindbendingly complex and hugely demanding for the dancers. But it's not simply a technical feat. 'He doesn't want just moves. He wants his moves to happen because two people are talking or bickering or having fun. Like you're having a conversation.

'Every time you go into the studio with him it's like you go in there naked and let everything out, and see what you come out with. Then you forget the technicalities and you just dance.'
■ www.roh.org.uk

glory in 2004 as part of an £80m restoration. All the resident English National Opera (ENO) needs is for artistic director Edward Gardner to develop an impressive programme to match the setting; the English National Ballet (www.ballet.org.uk) also makes its home here. Unlike the Royal Opera House (below), all works here are performed in English.

Donmar Warehouse

41 Earlham Street, WC2H 9LX (0870 060 6624/www.donmarwarehouse. com). Covent Garden or Leicester Square tube. **Map** p131 E2 ③⓪
The Donmar is less a warehouse than an intimate chamber. Artistic director Michael Grandage has kept the venue on a fresh, intelligent path – helped by regular celebrity casting scoops (Ewan McGregor, Gillian Anderson) – and productions are excellent. ⓪

Novello Theatre

Aldwych, WC2B 4LD (0870 040 0046). Covent Garden or Holborn tube. **Map** p131 F3 ③①
The US musical adaptation of Frank Wedekind's proto-Expressionist masterpiece *Spring Awakening* could be subtitled 'Emo – The Musical'. In between authentically German-angsty scenes tackling physical abuse, abortion and suicide, the put-upon 'kids' produce aerial microphones and belt out their woes with contemporary-American brashness. Something special. Production subject to change.

Playhouse Theatre

NEW *Northumberland Avenue, WC2N 5DE (0844 579 1940/www.lacage london.com). Embankment tube/Charing Cross tube/rail.* **Map** p131 E5 ③②
There's no better way to chase away recession blues. Jerry Herman and Harvey Fierstien's musical *La Cage aux Folles* is a celebration of homosexuality in which it is the most unappealing character who stands up for family values. Production subject to change.

Royal Opera House

Bow Street, WC2E 9DD (7304 4000/ www.royaloperahouse.org). Covent Garden tube. **Open** 10am-3pm Mon-Sat. **Admission** free. *Tours* £9; £7-£8 reductions. **Map** p131 E2 ③③
The Royal Opera House was founded in 1732 by John Rich on the profits of his production of John Gay's *Beggar's Opera*. The current massive eight-floor building is the third on the site; book ahead for an organised tour that will explain the disasters that befell the previous two incarnations (mainly fires and riots over ticket prices). Some of the building is open to the general public, including the glass-roofed Floral Hall, the Crush Bar and the Amphitheatre Café Bar, with its terrace overlooking the Piazza. The operas themselves are exquisite, with the resident Royal Ballet on hand to add some extra balance and poise.

Shaftesbury Theatre

210 Shaftesbury Avenue, WC2H 8DP (7379 5399/www.hairspraythemusical. co.uk). Tottenham Court Road tube. **Map** p131 D1 ③④
Hairspray is brainless, but its heart is triumphantly in the right place. Its butt's in the right place too: the choreography is glorious. Chubby heroine Tracy Turnblad teams up with black kids from Special Ed to overthrow 1960s racial prejudice and fulfil her dreams. Production subject to change.

Theatre Royal Drury Lane

NEW *Catherine Street, WC2B 5JF (0844 412 2955/www.oliverthe musical.com). Covent Garden tube.* **Map** p131 F2 ③⑤
Despite the fact that Dickens's grim novel about poverty and Lionel Bart's chirpy tunes are hardly a good match, this musical version of *Oliver Twist* has proved enduringly popular. Rupert Goold and Matthew Bourne's revival has already taken £15 million at the box office, helped by a TV show that selected Jodie Prenger as Nancy.

Tower Bridge p163

The City

Holborn to Clerkenwell

The City of London collides with the West End in Holborn and Clerkenwell. Be-wigged barristers inhabit the picturesque **Inns of Court**, while left-leaning City boys pull on their trainers to journey from loft conversion to the latest gastropub or restaurant in one of London's foodiest areas. Although the future of its splendid Victorian wrought-iron structure remains at issue, **Smithfield Market** still has butchers hauling fresh and frozen meat around at the crack of dawn – to the consternation of bug-eyed clubbers weaving their way unsteadily home from **Fabric**.

Sights & museums

Courtauld Gallery

Strand, WC2R 1LA (7848 2526/www. courtauld.ac.uk/gallery). Embankment or Temple tube/Charing Cross tube/rail. **Open** 10am-6pm daily. **Admission** £5; free-£4 reductions. Free 10am-2pm Mon. **Map** p150 A4 ❶

In the north wing of Somerset House (p153), the Courtauld's select collection of paintings contains several works of world importance. Although there are outstanding works from earlier periods (don't miss Lucas Cranach's wonderful *Adam & Eve*), the collection's strongest suit is its holdings of Impressionist and post-Impressionist paintings, such as Manet's astonishing *A Bar at the Folies-Bergère* and numerous works by Cézanne. Hidden downstairs, the sweet gallery café is too often overlooked.

Dr Johnson's House

17 Gough Square, off Fleet Street, EC4A 3DE (7353 3745/www.dr johnsonshouse.org). Chancery Lane or Temple tube/Blackfriars rail. **Open** *May-Sept* 11am-5.30pm Mon-Sat. *Oct-Apr* 11am-5pm Mon-Sat. **Admission** £4.50; free-£3.50 reductions; £10 family. No credit cards. **Map** p150 B4 ❷

The City

1	Sights & museums
1	Eating & drinking
1	Shopping
1	Nightlife
1	Arts & leisure

THE WEST END
pp98-148

River Thames

0 — 300 m
0 — 300 yds

© Copyright Time Out Group 2009

THE SOUTH BANK
pp58-73

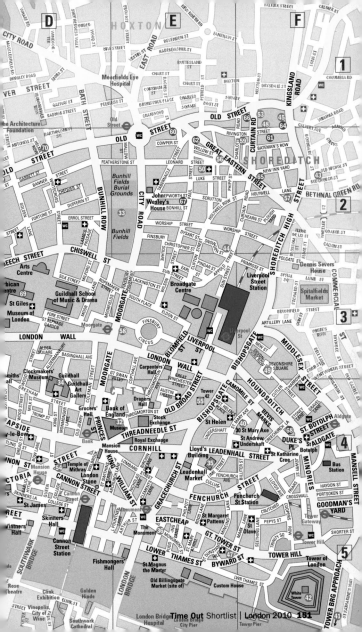

Inns of Court p155

ing away once Rupert Murdoch had won his bitter war with the print unions in the 1980s; the last of the news agencies, Reuters, followed suit in 2005. Interesting relics of the industry include the Portland-stone Reuters building (no.85), the Egyptian-influenced Daily Telegraph building (no.135) and the sleek, black, art deco Daily Express building (nos.121-128).

Hunterian Museum

Royal College of Surgeons, 35-43 Lincoln's Inn Fields, WC2A 3PE (7869 6560/www.rcseng.ac.uk/museums). Holborn tube. **Open** 10am-5pm Tue-Sat. **Admission** free. **Map** p150 A4 ❹
John Hunter (1728-93) was a pioneering surgeon and anatomist, and physician to King George III. His huge collection of medical specimens can be viewed in this two-floor museum. The sparkling glass cabinets belie the goriness of many of the exhibits – these include various bodily mutations, the brain of 19th-century mathematician Charles Babbage, and Churchill's dentures.

Museum & Library of the Order of St John

St John's Gate, St John's Lane, EC1M 4DA (7324 4005/www.sja.org.uk/ museum). Farringdon tube/rail. **Open** 10am-5pm Mon-Fri; 10am-4pm Sat. *Tours* 11am, 2.30pm Tue, Fri, Sat. **Admission** free; suggested donation £5, £4 reductions. **Map** p150 C2 ❺
A collection of artefacts (illuminated manuscripts, armour, Islamic items) related to the Order of Hospitaller Knights, from Jerusalem, Malta and the Ottoman Empire, is on display here. A separate collection relates specifically to the evolution of the modern ambulance service. The museum closes for major refurbishments in autumn 2009, but it's unlikely to affect the archive and tours; phone for more details.

St Bartholomew-the-Great

West Smithfield, EC1A 9DS (7606 5171/www.greatstbarts.com). Barbican

Famed as the author of one of the first, surely the most significant and beyond doubt the wittiest dictionary of the English language, Dr Samuel Johnson (1709-84) also wrote poems, a novel and one of the earliest travelogues. You can tour the stately Georgian townhouse off Fleet Street where Johnson came up with his inspired definitions – 'to make dictionaries is dull work,' was his definition of the word 'dull'.

Fleet Street

Chancery Lane or Temple tube. **Map** p150 B4 ❸
The first printing press on this legendary street of newspapers was installed behind St Bride's Church (p153) in 1500 by William Caxton's assistant, Wynkyn de Worde, but it wasn't until 1702 that London's first daily newspaper, the *Daily Courant*, rolled off the presses. By the end of World War II, half a dozen newspaper offices were churning out scoops and scandals between the Strand and Farringdon Road, gradually all mov-

tube/Farringdon tube/rail. **Open** 8.30am-5pm Mon-Fri (until 4pm Nov-Feb); 10.30am-4pm Sat; 2.30-6.30pm Sun. **Admission** £4; £3 reductions; £10 family. **Map** p150 C3 ⑥

This atmospheric medieval church was chopped about during Henry VIII's reign: the interior is now firmly Elizabethan, although it also contains donated works of modern art and an ancient font. You may recognise the main hall from the movies *Shakespeare in Love* and *Four Weddings & a Funeral*. Just around the corner, the Museum of St Bartholomew's Hospital (7601 8152, www.bartsandthelondon. nhs.uk/museums), in the hospital's North Wing, explains the history of medicine, taking you back to the days when surgery and carpentry were kindred occupations.

Event highlights Guided tour of the church and the hospital's Great Hall, with its Hogarth paintings (2pm Fri, £5; book ahead on 7837 0546).

St Bride's Church

Fleet Street, EC4Y 8AU (7427 0133/ www.stbrides.com). Temple tube/ Blackfriars rail. **Open** 8am-6pm Mon-Fri; 11am-3pm Sat; 10am-1pm, 5-7.30pm Sun. Times vary Mon-Sat, so phone ahead. **Admission** free. **Map** p150 B4 ⑦

St Bride's, still popularly known as the journalists' church, contains a shrine to journos killed in action. The interior was rebuilt after being bombed out in the Blitz. Down in the crypt, a quietly excellent museum displays fragments of the churches that have existed on this site since the sixth century and tells the story of the newspapers on Fleet Street. According to local legend, the Wren-designed spire was the inspiration behind the traditional tiered wedding cake.

Sir John Soane's Museum

13 Lincoln's Inn Fields, WC2A 3BP (7405 2107/www.soane.org). Holborn tube. **Open** 10am-5pm Tue-Sat; 10am-

Smithfield Market p149

5pm, 6-9pm 1st Tue of mth. *Tours* 11am Sat. **Admission** free; donations appreciated. *Tours* free-£5. **Map** p150 A3 ⑧

A leading architect of his day, Sir John Soane (1753-1837) was an obsessive collector of art, furniture and architectural ornamentation, partly for enjoyment and partly for research. In the early 19th century, he turned his house into a museum to which 'amateurs and students' should have access. Much of the museum's appeal derives from the domestic setting, but the real wow is the Monument Court. At its lowest level is a 3,000-year-old sarcophagus of alabaster so fine that it's almost translucent, as well as the cell of Soane's fictional monk Don Giovanni.

Event highlights Monthly candlelit tours – book in advance.

Somerset House & the Embankment Galleries

NEW *Strand, WC2R 1LA (7845 4600/ www.somersethouse.org.uk). Temple or Embankment tube/Charing Cross tube/*

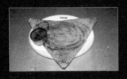

rail. **Open** 10am-6pm daily. **Admission** *Courtyard & terrace* free. *Embankment Galleries* £8; free-£6 reductions. **Map** p150 A5 **9**

Architect Sir William Chambers spent the last 20 years of his life from 1775 working on this neoclassical edifice overlooking the Thames. Effectively the first purpose-built office block in the world, it was built to accommodate learned societies such as the Royal Academy, and also the Inland Revenue. The taxmen are still here, but the rest of the building is open to the public. It houses the wonderful Courtauld Collection (p149), and boasts a beautiful courtyard with choreographed fountains, a terraced café and classy restaurant, as well as the new Embankment Galleries, which explore connections between art, architecture and design through temporary exhibitions.

Temple Church & Middle Temple

King's Bench Walk, EC4Y 7BB (7353 8559/www.templechurch.com). Temple tube. **Open** 1-4pm Mon-Wed; phone or check website for details Thur-Sun. **Admission** free. **Map** p150 B4 **10**

The quadrangles of Middle Temple (7427 4800, www.middletemple.org.uk) and Inner Temple (7797 8183, www.innertemple.org.uk) have been lodgings for training lawyers since medieval times, with Temple Church – the private chapel of the mystical Knights Templar, its structure inspired by Jerusalem's Church of the Holy Sepulchre – serving the religious requirements of both. Its rounded apse contains the worn gravestones of several Crusader knights, but the church was eventually completely refurbished by Wren and the Victorians, and few original features survived the Blitz. Tours of Inner Temple can be arranged (min five people, £10 each; book on 7797 8241).

Event highlights Organ recitals in Temple Church (Wed lunchtimes).

Eating & drinking

Ambassador

55 Exmouth Market, EC1R 4QL (7837 0009/www.theambassadorcafe.co.uk). Farringdon tube/rail/19, 38, 341 bus. **Open** 8.30am-2.30pm, 6-10.15pm Mon-Fri; 11am-4pm, 6-10.15pm Sat; 11am-4pm Sun. **££**. **Modern European**. **Map** p150 B1 **11**

Who needs diplomatic relations with France when the Ambassador creates so well the food we hope to find there? A proper all-day café, with wide-open doors and tables outside, it is run with real commitment and close attention to detail. Don't go expecting an all-Gallic menu: Yorkshire tea and a bacon sandwich on proper, thick-sliced, crusty white bread also come at keen prices.

Clerkenwell Kitchen

NEW *27-31 Clerkenwell Close, EC1R 0AT (7101 9959/www.theclerkenwell kitchen.co.uk). Angel tube/Farringdon*

Temple Church

tube/rail. **Open** 8am-5pm Mon-Fri. **££**.
Eco-restaurant. Map p150 B2 **⑫**
First winner of Best Sustainable
Restaurant in our Eating & Drinking
Awards, this new restaurant serves
delicious, fresh, seasonal food at fair
prices. The furnishings are simple:
plenty of wood, windows and white
walls, with architectural seating and an
open kitchen. Excellent.

Le Comptoir Gascon

*61-63 Charterhouse Street, EC1M 6HJ
(7608 0851/www.comptoirgascon.com).
Farringdon tube/rail*. **Open** noon-2pm,
7-10pm Tue, Wed; noon-2pm, 7-
10.30pm Thur, Fri; 10.30am-2.30pm,
7-10pm Sun. **££**. **French**.
Map p150 C3 **⑬**
Comptoir is the modern rustic cousin
(dainty velour chairs, exposed pipes,
open brickwork, pottery dishes) of the
more famous and high-falutin' Club
Gascon (57 West Smithfield, 7796 0600,
www.clubgascon.com), but it exudes
as much class and confidence as its
forebear in the presentation of delec-
table regional specialities of Gascony.
The posh café vibe is enhanced by
capable and amiable French staff.

Eagle

*159 Farringdon Road, EC1R 3AL
(7837 1353). Farringdon tube/rail*.
Open noon-11pm Mon-Sat; noon-5pm
Sun. **££**. **Gastropub**. Map p150 B2 **⑭**
Widely credited with being the first
gastropub (it opened in 1991), this is
still recognisable as a pub that serves
quality food: noisy, often crowded,
with no-frills service and dominated by
a giant open range where T-shirted
cooks toss earthy grills in theatrical
bursts of flame. The chalked-up,
Mediterranean-influenced menu has
stayed true to 'big flavours'.

Eastside Inn

NEW *38-42 St John Street, EC1M
4AY. Barbican or Farringdon tube/rail*.
£££/££££. **Bistro**. Map p150 C2 **⑮**
See box p158.

Hix Oyster & Chop House

*36-37 Greenhill Rents, EC1M 6BN
(7017 1930/www.hixoysterandchop
house.co.uk). Farringdon tube/rail*.
Open noon-3pm, 6-11pm Mon-Fri;
6-11pm Sat; noon-5pm Sun. **£££**.
British. Map p150 C3 **⑯**
Renowned for innovative updates of
British food, Mark Hix's menu is a roll-
call of local, seasonal produce, the farmers and growers duly name-checked.
His food is set against simple, pared-
down decor that recalls postwar village
halls. Service can be a bit clumsy, but
otherwise it's a professional operation.

Jerusalem Tavern

*55 Britton Street, EC1M 5UQ (7490
4281/www.stpetersbrewery.co.uk).
Farringdon tube/rail*. **Open** 11am-
11pm Mon-Fri. **Pub**. Map p150 C3 **⑰**
Tilting, creaking and uneven, the tatty
Jerusalem serves sought-after ales from
Suffolk's St Peter's brewery. A rag-tag
and loyal crowd muses over the *Evening
Standard* crossword and, in winter, a
homely fireplace smell encourages the
desire for warm sustenance. Fantastic
haddock and salmon fishcakes and various sausages fit the bill nicely.

Lobby Bar

*One Aldwych, the Strand, WC2B 4RH
(7300 1070/www.onealdwych.com).
Covent Garden or Temple tube*. **Open**
8am-11.30pm Mon-Sat; 8am-10.30pm
Sun. **Bar**. Map p150 A4 **⑱**
The signature bar of the upmarket
urban hotel One Aldwych is known for
the range and quality of its cocktails
and for a sculpture of a bemused rower.
Various sandwiches (£9) and working
lunch plates (beef carpaccio, £11.95)
make classy accompaniments to pricey
and excellently confected cocktails.

Modern Pantry

NEW *47-48 St John's Square, EC1V
4JJ (7250 0833/www.themodernpantry.
co.uk). Farringdon tube/rail*. **Open**
11am-11pm daily. **££**. **Brasserie**.
Map p150 C2 **⑲**

Hix Oyster & Chop House

Inside a handsome, Grade II-listed Georgian building that used to be townhouse and steel foundry, this good-looking café space has lots of natural light, silvery-grey walls and beautiful detailing. The style of cooking is a genre-bending fusion of ingredients and styles from around the world.

Moro

34-36 Exmouth Market, EC1R 4QE (7833 8336/www.moro.co.uk). Farringdon tube/rail/19, 38 bus. **Open** 12.30-11.45pm Mon-Sat (last entry 10.30pm). **£££. Spanish-North African**. Map p150 B2 ⑳
Moro has an enduring popularity that seems unassailable. It's fully booked night after night, so phone at least 48 hours ahead if you want to sample the secret of its success: high-quality cooking and a convivial dining space on Exmouth Market (p159). The inventive menu is Moorish – Spanish accents to essentially North African food.

St John

26 St John Street, EC1M 4AY (7251 0848/4998/www.stjohnrestaurant.com). Barbican tube/Farringdon tube/rail. **Open** noon-5pm, 6pm-midnight Mon-Fri; 6pm-midnight Sat. **£££. British**. Map p150 C2 ㉑
The leading light of the modern British cooking revival, St John is an austere-looking place, opened in the shell of a smokehouse by architect and chef-patron Fergus Henderson in 1995. Its spirit hasn't changed. The focus is entirely on seasonal and unusual British ingredients, simply cooked and presented. Less expensive is the short menu at the boisterous no-reservations bar.

Seven Stars

53 Carey Street, WC2A 2JB (7242 8521). Chancery Lane or Holborn tube. **Open** 11am-11pm Mon-Fri; noon-11pm Sat; noon-10.30pm Sun. **££.**
Gastropub. Map p150 A4 ㉒
Landlady Roxy Beaujolais' flagship pub is great. It's a fantastic social hub for London characters, from eccentric lawyers to burlesque babes. If you can squeeze into the small but perfectly proportioned interior, you'll get a slice of low-rent, bohemian London. It's one of the city's few pubs where you'll be happy to pay £6 for a large burgundy – you know you're not being ripped off.

Return of the bistro

Will Eastside Inn revive the art of day-and-night dining?

Bjorn van der Horst

When we visited the van der Horsts, they were picking their way through rubble in a boarded-up building next to St John (p157) and opposite Vinoteca (p159). Bjorn van der Horst's wife and future maitre d', Justine, showed us round. 'The show kitchen will be there, in the middle,' she explained, waving her hand at an exposed-brick wall. 'We do lots of dinner parties at home, and everyone always ends up in the kitchen. So we thought, let's build the restaurant around the kitchen.'

Van der Horst was nominated one of London's up-and-coming chefs by *Time Out* in 2006, just as he was about to open Gordon Ramsay's La Noisette – and win some Michelin stars. Two years later he parted company with Ramsay and went looking for his own place. This is it.

The Eastside Inn (p156), which should now be open, will be a bistro on one side, fine dining on the other, and crucially has a late licence that will allow them to wheel out jazz musicians at about 11pm. 'We've got a licence until 2am, 3am on weekends – we're going to be tired!' he says cheerily.

He'll need this can-do attitude, opening a restaurant near so much well-loved competition. And it's his first solo venture. And there's a recession on. But van der Horst, who has been in the trade since he was expelled from school at 15, has more sinew than his obliging manner might suggest: after all, he's survived working with Joël Robuchon, Alain Ducasse, Gordon Ramsay, even a mad but talented Corsican in Toulouse who would 'fall asleep in the wine cellar at about 7pm, then at 3am he'd be knocking on my door yelling that we were going truffle hunting, or morel hunting. I'd just finished cleaning the floors!'.

Van der Horst's combination of much-loved ingredients – steamed plaice, salt marsh lamb – and inventive weirdness is certainly exciting; how many top cooks want their fine-dining establishment to resemble dinner round the kitchen table? And on the recession? 'If necessary, we'll serve lentil soup and meatballs!' he grins.

Three Kings of Clerkenwell

7 Clerkenwell Close, EC1R 0DY (7253 0483). Farringdon tube/rail. **Open** noon-11pm Mon-Fri; 5.30-11pm Sat. No credit cards. **Pub**. **Map** p150 B2 ㉓

Rhino heads, Egyptian felines and Dennis Bergkamp provide the decorative backdrop against which a regular bunch of discerning bohos glug Old Speckled Hen, London Pride, Scrumpy Jack cider or Beck's Vier, and tap the well-worn tables to the Cramps and other gems from an excellent jukebox.

Vinoteca

7 St John Street, EC1M 4AA (7253 8786/www.vinoteca.co.uk). Farringdon tube/rail. **Open** noon-11pm Mon-Sat. **Wine bar**. **Map** p150 C3 ㉔

Inspired by the Italian *enoteca* (a blend of off-licence and wine bar, with bar snacks thrown in), Vinoteca is in fact more of a gastropub in spirit. But even if you want no more than a plate of bread and olive oil, come here for the impressive 200-bottle wine list, of which a range of 19 are available by the glass.

Ye Old Mitre

1 Ely Court, at the side of 8 Hatton Gardens, EC1N 6SJ (7405 4751). Chancery Lane tube/Farringdon tube/rail. **Open** 11am-11pm Mon-Fri. **Pub**. **Map** p150 B3 ㉕

The secluded location requires you to slink down an alleyway just off Hatton Garden, where you'll be transported to a parallel pub universe where the clientele are disconcertingly friendly and the staff (in pristine black and white uniforms) briskly efficient. A Monday-to-Friday joint, it's a pint-sized pub that's earned its top-notch reputation.

Shopping

Exmouth Market

Angel tube/Farringdon tube/rail/19, 38 bus. **Map** p150 B1 ㉖

Exmouth Market is a terrific collection of eateries and shops, scattered along a short pedestrianised street. Pop into Brill (no.27, 7833 9757, www.music coffeebagels.com), a small CD shop-cum-café with an excellently curated selection; ec one (no.41, 7713 6185, www. econe.co.uk), a showcase of jewellery from more than 50 designers; and Marco Araldi and Keng Wai Lee's colourful bags and accessories, made on the premises at Bagman & Robin (no.47, 7833 8780, www.bagmanand robin.com). Chic eats at Ambassador (p155) or Moro (p157) are balanced by beer and foosball in cheery Café Kick (no.43, 7837 8077, www.cafekick.co.uk).

Magma

117-119 Clerkenwell Road, EC1R 5BY (7242 9503/www.magmabooks.com). Chancery Lane tube/Farringdon tube/rail. **Open** 10am-7pm Mon-Sat. **Map** p150 B2 ㉗

If you can visualise it, this art and design specialist has probably got a book about it. Magazines, DVDs, trendy toys, T-shirts and a series of commissioned limited-edition posters and cards are also sold.

Old Curiosity Shop

13-14 Portsmouth Street, WC2A 2ES (7405 9891/www.curiosityuk.com). Holborn tube. **Open** 10.30am-7pm Mon-Fri; 11am-6pm Sat. **Map** p150 A4 ㉘

Apparently London's oldest shop and the inspiration for the Dickens novel, this is a place with wonderful, off-kilter charm. The stock is by Japanese designer Daita Kimura, whose avant-garde, unisex styles are mostly made by hand in the workshop downstairs.

Pure Groove Records

6-7 West Smithfield, EC1A 9JX (7778 9278/www.puregroove.co.uk). Farringdon tube/rail. **Open** 11am-7pm Mon-Fri. **Map** p150 C3 ㉙

A stylish, multimedia treasure trove of vinyl, poster art and CD gems, covering all things indie, alternative and cutting edge in guitar and electronic music. The rear, housing T-shirts, bags and posters, doubles as a stage for the regular live sets and film screenings.

Nightlife

Fabric

77A Charterhouse Street, EC1M 3HN (7336 8898/advance tickets 0870 902 0001/www.fabriclondon.com). Farringdon tube/rail. **Open** 10pm-6am Fri; 11pm-8am Sat. **Map** p150 C3 ③⓪
Fabric is the club most party people come to see in London: the main room has the stomach-wobbling Bodysonic dancefloor, the second is a rave-style warehouse, the third is where the cool stuff happens. Fridays belong to the bass: highlights include DJ Hype, who takes over all three rooms once a month for his drum 'n' bass and dub-step night Playaz. Saturdays rock to techy, minimal, deep house sounds.

Volupté

7-9 Norwich Street, EC4A 1EJ (7831 1622/1677/www.volupte-lounge.com). Chancery Lane tube. **Open** from 11.30am Tue-Fri; from 7.30pm Sat. **Map** p150 B3 ③①
Expect to suffer extreme wallpaper envy as you enter the ground-floor bar then descend to the club proper. Punters enjoy some of the best cabaret talent in town from tables set beneath absinthe-inspired vines. Wednesday nights are Cabaret Salon and once a month the Black Cotton Club turns back the clock to the 1920s.

The City

The City means business. Fewer than 10,000 souls live within the Square Mile (1.21 square miles, in fact), but every working day the population increases tenfold, as bankers, brokers, lawyers and traders storm into their towering office blocks to mash up billions of other people's money. The City still holds to the boundaries marked by

the 2nd-century walls of Roman Londinium (a few sections of which remain), although it then had six times more residents than now. Apart from the two big crowd-pullers – **St Paul's** and the **Tower of London** – the City might not immediately appear to have much to offer casual visitors, but dive into the throng of office workers and you'll find that the streets are full of historic gems.

For nightlife, head north-east of the City proper, where the pleasure zones of Shoreditch soak up bankers' loose change. The area's edginess and artiness have begun to follow cheaper rents further east, but the bars and clubs are still lively – on a Friday and Saturday night, often unpleasantly so.

Sights & museums

The art gallery on the third floor of the Barbican Centre (£8, £4-£6 reductions; p169) has good shows on design, architecture and pop culture, while the free Curve exhibition space shows commissioned work. Of the City's three classic modern skyscrapers – Lloyd's (p161), the Gherkin (30 St Mary Axe, p163) and the NatWest Tower (Tower 42) – only Tower 42's bar, Vertigo 42 (p166), is open to the public.

Bank of England Museum

Entrance on Bartholomew Lane, EC2R 8AH (7601 5545/www.bankofengland. co.uk/museum). Bank tube/DLR. **Open** 10am-5pm Mon-Fri. **Admission** free. **Map** p151 E4 ③②
Housed in the former Stock Offices of the Bank of England, this engaging museum explores the history of the national bank and offers a rare chance to handle a real 13kg gold bar. A new exhibit looks at the life of Kenneth Grahame: the author of *The Wind in the Willows* was a long-term employee of the bank.

Exmouth Market p159

Bunhill Fields

Old Street tube/rail. **Admission** free.
Map p151 E2 ③③
An important non-conformist burial ground until the 19th century, Bunhill contains memorials to John Bunyan, Daniel Defoe and William Blake. It's a rather moving little place, not least because it is now hemmed in by walls. Opposite, the former home and chapel of John Wesley are now a museum of Methodism (49 City Road, 7253 2262, www.wesleyschapel.org.uk).

Guildhall Art Gallery & Clockmakers' Museum

Guildhall Yard, off Gresham Street, EC2P 2EJ (7332 3700/www.guildhall-art-gallery.org.uk). Mansion House or St Paul's tube/Bank tube/DLR/Moorgate tube/rail. **Open** 10am-5pm Mon-Sat; noon-4pm Sun. **Admission** £2.50; free-£1 reductions. Free to all from 3.30pm daily, all day Fri.
Map p151 D4 ③④
The City of London's gallery contains numerous dull portraits of royalty and long-gone mayors, but also some wonderful surprises, including a brilliant Constable, some high-camp Pre-Raphaelites and a number of absorbing paintings of London through the ages. A sub-basement has the scant remains of a 6,000-seater Roman amphitheatre, built around AD 70. The single-room Clockmakers' Museum (www.clock-makers.org, closed Sun) is filled with ticking, chiming clocks and watches.

Lloyd's of London

1 Lime Street, EC3M 7HA (www.lloyds.com). Monument tube.
Map p151 E4 ③⑤
Lord Rogers' high-tech building has all its mechanical services (ducts, stairwells, lift shafts and even loos) on the outside, making it look like a disassembled washing machine. It still seems impressively modern, 20 years after completion. The original Lloyd's Register of Shipping, decorated with bas-reliefs of sea monsters and nautical scenes, is around the corner on Fenchurch Street. No public access.

Monument

NEW *Monument Street, EC3R 8AH (7626 2717/www.themonument.info). Monument tube.* **Open** 9.30am-5pm daily. **Admission** £2; £1 reductions; free under-5s. No credit cards. **Map** p151 E5 ❸❺

Reopened after a £4.5m refurbishment, the world's tallest free-standing stone column was designed by Sir Christopher Wren and his (often overlooked) associate Robert Hooke as a memorial to the Great Fire of London. It measures 202ft from the ground to the tip of the golden flame on the orb at its top, exactly the distance east to Farriner's bakery in Pudding Lane, where the fire is supposed to have begun on 2 September 1666. You can climb up the inside for fine City views.

Museum of London

NEW *150 London Wall, EC2Y 5HN (0870 444 3851/www.museumoflondon. org.uk). Barbican or St Paul's tube.* **Open** 10am-5.50pm Mon-Sat; noon-5.50pm Sun. **Admission** free; suggested donation £2. **Map** p151 D3 ❸❼

Nearing the end of what should be an impressive refurbishment, this expansive museum – set in the middle of a roundabout – shares the job of recreating London's history with the Museum of London Docklands (p178). The chronological displays include 'London Before London' – fossils and flint axes – and 'Roman London', its impressive reconstructed dining room complete with mosaic floor. Sound effects and audio-visual displays illustrate the medieval city, with clothes, shoes and armour on display. From Elizabethan and Jacobean London comes the jewellery of the Cheapside Hoard. The £20.5 million lavished on the downstairs galleries should see them reopen for Easter 2010: a huge window through ground-floor brickwork will parade the Lord Mayor's Coach to passersby, and new displays – 'wow' objects are to include an unexploded bomb – will take the collection into the 20th century.

Postman's Park

Barbican or St Paul's tube. **Map** p151 C3 ❸❽

This peaceful, fern-filled park contains the Watts Memorial to Heroic Sacrifice: a wall of Victorian ceramic plaques, each of which commemorates an heroic but fatal act of bravery.

St Paul's Cathedral

Ludgate Hill, EC4M 8AD (7236 4128/ www.stpauls.co.uk). St Paul's tube. **Open** 8.30am-4pm Mon-Sat. *Galleries, crypt & ambulatory* 8.30am-3.45pm Mon-Sat. **Admission** £10; free-£8.50 reductions; £23.50 family. *Tours* £3; £1-£2.50 reductions. **Map** p150 C4 ❸❾

The passing of three centuries has done nothing to diminish the magnificence of St Paul's. A £40m restoration project has left the main façade looking as brilliant as it must have when the first Mass was celebrated here in 1710. The vast open spaces of the interior contain memorials to national heroes such as Wellington and Lawrence of Arabia, as well as superb mosaics and gilt added by the Victorians. The Whispering Gallery, inside the dome, is reached by 259 steps from the main hall (the acoustics are so good a whisper can be clearly heard across the dome). Stairs continue up to first the Stone Gallery (119 steps), with its high external balustrades, then outside to the Golden Gallery (152 steps), with its giddying views. Head down to the crypt to see Nelson's grand tomb and the small tombstone of Sir Christopher Wren himself, inscribed: 'Reader, if you seek a monument, look around you'.

30 St Mary Axe

www.30stmaryaxe.com. Liverpool Street tube/rail. **Map** p151 F4 ❹

Completed only in 2004, Lord Foster's skyscraper has already become a cherished icon of modern London. The appropriateness of its 'Erotic Gherkin' nickname is immediately apparent – but only the resident officeworkers get to enjoy the views from inside.

Tower Bridge Exhibition

Tower Bridge, SE1 2UP (7403 3761/ www.towerbridge.org.uk). Tower Hill tube//Tower Gateway DLR. **Open** *Apr-Sept* 10am-6.30pm daily. *Oct-Mar* 9.30am-6pm daily. **Admission** £6; free-£4.50 reductions; £14 family. **Map** p151 F5 ④

Opened in 1894, this is the 'London Bridge' that wasn't sold to America. Originally powered by steam, the drawbridge is now opened by electric rams when big ships need to venture this far upstream (you can check when the bridge is next due to be raised on the website). An entertaining exhibition on the history of the bridge is displayed in the old steamrooms and the west walkway, which provides a crow's-nest view along the Thames.

Tower of London

Tower Hill, EC3N 4AB (0870 950 4466/www.hrp.org.uk). Tower Hill tube//Tower Gateway DLR/Fenchurch Street rail. **Open** *Mar-Oct* 10am-6pm Mon, Sun; 9am-6pm Tue-Sat. *Nov-Feb* 10am-5pm Mon, Sun; 9am-5pm Tue-Sat. **Admission** £16.50; free-£14 reductions; £46 family. **Map** p151 F5 ④

Despite the exhausting crowds and long climbs up narrow stairways, this is one of Britain's finest historical attractions. Who wouldn't be fascinated by a close-up look at the crown of Queen Victoria or the armour (and prodigious codpiece) of King Henry VIII? The buildings of the Tower span 900 years of history and the bastions and battlements house a series of interactive displays on the lives of British monarchs – and excruciatingly painful deaths of traitors. The highlight has to be the Crown Jewels, viewed from a slow-moving travelator, but the other big draw is the Royal Armoury in the White Tower, four floors of swords, armour, pole-axes, halberds and other gruesome tools for chopping up human beings. Executions of noble prisoners were carried out on the green in front of the Tower – the site is marked by a glass pillow, sculpted by poet and artist Brian Catling in 2006.

Tickets are sold in the kiosk just to the west of the palace and visitors enter

Old Curiosity Shop p159

through the Middle Tower, but there's also a free audio-visual display in the Welcome Centre outside the walls. There's plenty here to fill a whole day, but you can skip to the highlights using the audio tour, or by joining one of the highly recommended and entertaining free tours led by the Yeoman Warders (Beefeaters), who also care for the Tower's ravens.

Event highlights 'Henry VIII: Dressed to Kill' (until 17 Jan 2010).

Eating & drinking

Albion at the Boundary Project

NEW *2-4 Boundary Street, E2 7DD (7729 1051/www.albioncaff.co.uk).* **Open** noon-2pm, 6.30-10.30pm Mon-Fri; 6.30-10.30pm Sat; noon-4pm Sun. **£. British. Map** p151 F2 ⓭

Boundary Project is an astonishingly professional operation in otherwise dishevelled-looking Shoreditch. Albion is the ground-floor 'caff' (their description), food shop and bakery; Boundary is the smarter French restaurant in the basement, while a rooftop bar-grill and hotel rooms top off the operation. Everything served from Albion's British nostalgia-revival menu tastes delicious, from a little appetiser of perfect crackling to a proper Irish stew.

L'Anima

NEW *1 Snowden Street, EC2A 2DQ (7422 7000/www.lanima.co.uk). Liverpool Street tube/rail.* **Open** 11am-midnight Mon-Fri; 5.30-11pm Sat. **££££. Italian. Map** p151 E2 ⓮

The minimalist interior here – all clean lines, floor-to-ceiling glass, stark white linen and modernist leather chairs – is the setting for a seriously priced pan-Italian menu, which is served throughout the day for City suits.

Bar Kick

127 Shoreditch High Street, E1 6JE (7739 8700/www.cafekick.co.uk). Liverpool Street or Old Street tube/

30 St Mary Axe p162

rail. **Open** noon-11pm Mon-Wed, Sun; noon-midnight Thur-Sat. **Table football bar. Map** p151 F1 ⓯

A big square room with a bar, open kitchen, flags of all nations tacked to the ceiling and foosball tables under TVs that silently screen international football. Cool and excellently boisterous, Kick takes enough of a hint from European cafés (quality food, a curated selection of drinks) to draw in nearly as many women as men. The busy staff remain calm and friendly under the onslaught of twirl-crazed party groups.

Black Friar

174 Queen Victoria Street, EC4V 4EG (7236 5474). Mansion House tube/ Blackfriars rail. **Open** 11am-11pm Mon-Wed, Sat; 11am-11.30pm Thur, Fri; noon-10.30pm Sun. **Pub. Map** p150 C4 ⓰

This curiously wedge-shaped pub at the north end of Blackfriars Bridge offers a handful of real ales, a dozen or so wines by the glass, the standard lagers, and pub nosh (from steak pie to goat's cheese tart) that's more than adequate. But, if you can manage to push your way inside, it's the extraordinary interior, resplendent with wooden carvings of Dominican monks, that delights the most. Loopy, but it works.

Bodean's

16 Byward Street, EC3R 5BA (7488 3883/www.bodeansbbq.com). Tower Hill tube. **Open** noon-11pm Mon-Fri; 6-10.30pm Sat. **££. North American.** Map p151 E5 **47**

Across Bodean's five branches – Soho, Westbourne Grove, Fulham, Clapham and, handily, here – the schtick remains unchanged: Kansas City barbecue, with a small informal upstairs and bigger, smarter downstairs with US sport on TV. The food is decent, generously portioned and very meaty.

Callooh Callay

NEW *65 Rivington Street, EC2A 3AY (7739 4781). Liverpool Street or Old Street tube/rail.* **Open** 5-11pm Tue-Wed; noon-11pm Thur; noon-1am Fri; 6pm-1am Sat; 6-11pm Sun. **Bar.** Map p151 F1 **48**

All warm and whimsical, the neo-Victorian decor here is as eclectic as *Jabberwocky*, the Lewis Carroll nonsense poem from which the bar gets its name. The quirkiest touch is the hoodwinking oak Narnia wardrobe, through which you'll find a lounge, mirrored bar and loos tiled in old cassettes. The 'Mad Hatter Tiki Punchbowl' is served up in a gramophone speaker trumpet.

Cinnamon Kitchen

NEW *9 Devonshire Square, EC2M 4YL (7626 5000/www.cinnamonkitchen.co. uk). Liverpool Street tube/rail.* **Open** 7am-midnight Mon-Fri; 6pm-midnight Sat. **££££. Modern Indian** Map p151 F3 **49**

Westminster's acclaimed Cinnamon Club has a new sibling: Cinnamon Kitchen. It clearly hopes that regional Indian spice combinations with Western-style presentation will attract those City diners who've managed to hang on to upscale salaries. The decor combines, slightly oddly, industrial piping and grey interiors with warm wood tables and ethnic flourishes, but the elegantly appointed outdoor terrace should be a hit in summer. The cooking is at its best when expanding on traditional, home flavours.

Eyre Brothers

70 Leonard Street, EC2A 4QX (7613 5346/www.eyrebrothers.co.uk). Old Street tube/rail. **Open** noon-3pm, 6.30-10.45pm Mon-Fri; 6.30-10.45pm Sat. **££. Mediterranean.** Map p151 E2 **50**

News has got around: Eyre Brothers does everything exceptionally well. Hence, it can be hard to book a table. It's a labour of love for brothers David and Robert, who evidently spend as much time crafting the changing menu as fashioning the clean-lined, sophisticated decor – chic leather furniture, designer lamps and divided dining areas. Authentic Portuguese dishes reflect the brothers' upbringing in Mozambique, while Spanish and French flavours add range and luxury.

Fish Central

149-155 Central Street, EC1V 8AP (7253 4970). Old Street tube/rail/55 bus. **Open** 11am-2.30pm Mon-Sat; 5-10.30pm Mon-Thur; 5-11pm Fri, Sat. **£. Fish & chips.** Map p151 D1 **51**

This area was hardly residential in 1968, when Fish Central took a unit in the shopping precinct. Now it spans four units – rather stylishly, with etched glass and pale white and mint tones – but still serves simple fish to enthusiastic locals.

Northbank

One Paul's Walk, EC4V 3QH (7329 9299/www.northbankrestaurant.com).

St Paul's tube/Blackfriars tube.
Open noon-3pm, 6-11pm Mon-Sat;
11am-5pm, 6-11pm Sun. **££**. **British**.
Map p150 C5 52

On the brink of the Thames,
Northbank feels like a place for a special occasion. There's a terrace outside
where you can sip cocktails, and picture windows in the dining room frame
the South Bank. The menu is short,
straightforward and mainly modern
British.

Saf

NEW *152-154 Curtain Road, EC2A
3AT (7613 0007/www.safrestaurant.
co.uk). Old Street tube/rail.* **Open** 11am-
midnight. **££**. **Vegetarian**. **Map** p151
F1 53

Saf sets new standards for vegan and
raw food restaurants. It's almost a
shame to eat meals this pretty; and it's
remarkable when you realise their
vivid colours, variety of textures and
unusual flavours are created almost
entirely from uncooked fruit and veg (a
few ingredients are cooked, at low temperatures). A must-visit if you're a vegetarian bored of eating mushroom
risotto every time you eat out.

Sweetings

*39 Queen Victoria Street, EC4N 4SA
(7248 3062). Mansion House tube.*
Open 11.30am-3pm Mon-Fri. **£££**.
Fish. **Map** p151 D4 54

In these days of makeovers and global
menus, Sweetings is that rare thing –
a traditional British restaurant that
clings to its traditions as if the Empire
depended on it. It opens only for lunch,
takes no bookings, and is full soon after
noon, so order a silver pewter mug of
Guinness and enjoy the wait.

Vertigo 42

*Tower 42, 25 Old Broad Street, EC2N
1HQ (7877 7842/www.vertigo42.co.uk).
Bank tube/DLR/Liverpool Street tube/
rail.* **Open** noon-3pm, 5-11pm Mon-Fri.
££££. **Champagne bar**. **Map** p151
E4 55

Short of introducing iris-recognition
scanning, the process of going for a
drink in Tower 42 (book in advance,
then get X-rayed and metal-detected on
arrival) could scarcely be more MI5.
But it's worth it: the 42nd floor location
delivers stupendous views. There are
nibbles and the champagne list offers
eight labels by the flute (from £11.50).

Shopping

Bordello

*55 Great Eastern Street, EC2A 3HP
(7503 3334/www.bordello-london.com).
Old Street tube/rail.* **Open** 12.30-
7.30pm Tue, Wed, Fri, Sat; 12.30-
9.30pm Thur. **Map** p151 E2 56

Seductive yet welcoming, Bordello
stocks luxurious lingerie by Damaris,
Mimi Holliday, Myla, Buttress &
Snatch and Pussy Glamore, and
swimwear by Jemma Jube and
Flamingo Sands. The edgy vibe
appeals to East End glamazons, first-
daters and off-duty burlesque stars.

A Child of the Jago

NEW *10 Great Eastern Street, EC2A
3NT (7377 8694/www.childofthejago.
blogspot.com). Liverpool Street or Old
Street tube/rail.* **Open** 11am-7pm Mon-
Sat. **Map** p151 F2 57

Joe Corre (Viv Westwood's son and co-
founder of Agent Provocateur) and
designer Simon 'Barnzley' Armitage's
boutique is just about as far from the
high street as you can get: eclectic, com-
bining modern and vintage, and there's
Westwood's World's End collection
upstairs. Barnzley's cashmere hooded
tops are handmade in Scotland.

F Flittner

*86 Moorgate, EC2M 6SE (7606 4750/
www.fflittner.com). Moorgate tube/rail.*
Open 8am-6pm Mon-Wed, Fri; 8am-
6.30pm Thur. **Map** p151 E3 58

In business since 1904, Flittner seems
not to have noticed the 21st century has
begun. Hidden behind beautifully
frosted doors (marked 'Saloon') is a

simple, handsome room, done out with an array of classic barber's furniture that's older than your gran. Within these hushed yet welcoming confines, black-coated barbers skilfully deliver straightforward haircuts and shaves.

Three Threads

47-49 Charlotte Road, EC2A 3QT (7749 0503/www.thethreethreads.com). Old Street tube/rail. **Open** 11am-7pm Mon-Sat; noon-5pm Sun. **Map** p151 F2 ⑲

Free beer, a jukebox well stocked with dad rock and conveniently placed bar stools around the till... the Three Threads tempts even the most shop-phobic male. Exclusive, cult labels such as Japan's Tenderloin, Fjall Raven, Danish label Won Hundred and New York's Built by Wendy are here, but the vibe is more like a pal's house. It now also stocks womenswear from Carhartt and YMC, and bags from Mimi.

Nightlife

Aquarium

256 & 260 Old Street, EC1V 9DD (7251 6136/www.clubaquarium.co.uk). Old Street tube/rail. **Open** 10pm-11am Fri, Sat; 10pm-4am Sun. **Admission** £7-£15. **Map** p151 E2 ⑳

There's not much cool about this ever-popular club – except the wildly dressed clientele at Sunday's trendy minimal rave-up Wet Yourself! – but the queues of out-of-town girls know to pack bikinis for the long-running Saturday disco Carwash... there's a swimming pool and jacuzzi inside.

Comedy Café

66-68 Rivington Street, EC2A 3AY (7739 5706/www.comedycafe.co.uk). Liverpool Street or Old Street tube/rail. **Map** p151 F2 ㉑

Comedy Café is a purpose-built club, set up by comedian Noel Faulkner. He mainly keeps to the back room now but, with the emphasis on inviting bills and satisfied punters, his influence can

Starchitect shopping

The City's on a mission to make you shop.

The City is no longer a ghost town out of working hours. Bars and cafés stay open in the evenings and at weekends, with Paternoster Square (beside St Paul's Cathedral, p162) busy all week. Hotels have increased from two to ten this decade alone. Visitors now pour across the Millennium Bridge all week – and the City authorities are keen to make sure there's plenty for them to do when they get here.

Due to open in 2010, just opposite the cathedral on the corner of New Change and Cheapside, the biggest of many projects is **One New Change**, the first major building in London by 64-year-old French modernist starchitect Jean Nouvel (www. jeannouvel.com). Designer of the Arab World Institute in Paris and the Lyon Opera House, he is creating a 'ground scraper' (a building of monumental scale that isn't all that tall) that responds to the historic route of Watling Street. One New Change will frame dramatic views of St Paul's with its most distinctive feature: a kind of fissure driven through to the atrium at the heart of the building. It will house leisure facilities, some 70 high-end shops, roof gardens and a rooftop restaurant providing views at about the same level as the cathedral's Stone Gallery, as well as offices for 3,500.
■ www.onenewchange.com

Three Threads p167

still be felt. The atmosphere is fun, food is an integral part of the experience, and admission is free on Wednesday.

East Village

89 Great Eastern Street, EC2A 3HX (7739 5173/www.eastvillageclub.com). Old Street tube/rail. **Open** 5pm-1am Mon, Tue; 5pm-3am Wed-Sun. **Map** p151 E2 ⑫

Local lad Stuart Patterson, promoter of all-day house-music parties across London since 1999, took over the Medicine Bar in 2008, transforming it into this two-floor, 'real house' bar-club. Funky techno heads DDD's bi-monthly residency jumps, as does the NYC-styled disco punk night Sweatshop.

Ghetto

NEW *58 Old Street, EC1V 9AJ (7287 3726/www.ghetto-london.co.uk). Barbican or Old Street tube/rail.* **Map** p151 D2 ⑬

The Soho gay clubbing institution has found a new home in East London,

where most of the artier elements of London's gay life now reside. The new venue has kept the red New York basement feel of its old home, but with better, seating, lighting and sound.

Last Days of Decadence

NEW *145 Shoreditch High Street, E1 6JE (7729 2896/www.thelastdaysof decadence.com). Old Street tube/rail.* **Map** p151 F1 ⑭

Shoreditch High Street isn't going to win awards for being pretty, but it's pleasing to see boarded-up venues getting a new lease of life. The people behind Last Days completely remodelled this two-floor bar, bringing in a bit of art deco glamour. Despite cocktails drolly served in teacups, this isn't just a retro club: electro DJs jostle burlesque performers, and hip drag queen Jodie Harsh hosts a Circus party every week.

Old Blue Last

38 Great Eastern Street, EC2A 3ES (7739 7033/www.theoldbluelast.com).

Liverpool Street or Old Street tube/rail.
Open noon-midnight Mon-Wed; noon-12.30am Thur, Sun; noon-1.30am Fri, Sat. **Map** p151 F2 **65**

This shabby two-floor Victorian boozer was transformed by hipster handbook *Vice* in 2004. Klaxons, Amy Winehouse, Arctic Monkeys and Lily Allen have all played secret shows in the sauna-like upper room, but its high-fashion rock 'n' rollers also dig regular club nights from girlie indie DJ troupe My Ex Boyfriend's Records and Sean McLusky's scuzzy electro rock nights.

Plastic People

147-149 Curtain Road, EC2A 3QE (7739 6471/www.plasticpeople.co.uk). Old Street tube/rail. **Open** 9pm-2am 2nd Thur of mth; 10pm-4am Fri, Sat; 8-11.30pm Sun. **Admission** £5-£10. **Map** p151 F1 **66**

Plastic People subscribes to the old-school line that all you need for a kicking party is a dark basement and a quality sound system (the rig here embarrasses those in many larger clubs). Some of London's most progressive club nights here include dubstep and grime at Sunday's pioneering FWD.

Platinum Bar

23-25 Paul Street, EC2A 4JU (7638 4601). Old Street tube/rail. **Map** p151 E2 **67**

City boy strip-club by day, cool clubbing haunt by night. The three very small floors – reds, velvets, dim lights – are put to excellent use by a wide mix of canny promoters: El Nino's sleazy retro fest Lady Luck does well here, but so do minimal electronic nights. The ceiling of the top floor is often covered in decadent, swishy drapes; the ground floor has a small DJ booth, cocktail bar and recline-and-pose seating; and bands squeeze into a corner of the basement.

T Bar

NEW *32-38 Dukes Place, EC3A 7LP (http://tbarlondon.blogspot.com). Aldgate tube.* **Map** p151 F4 **68**

When the first T Bar opened on Shoreditch High Street, many said it was too far from Old Street to be a success. And every night, no matter which superstar DJs were playing, it was free to get in. Cue queues up the street every Thursday to Saturday night, some Sunday daytimes too. They've just reopened in this spanking new venue. It can stay open (legally) later than ever, and keeps its 'free-for-all' ethos.

Arts & leisure

Barbican Centre

Silk Street, EC2Y 8DS (7638 4141/box office 0845 020 7550/www.barbican. org.uk). Barbican tube/Moorgate tube/ rail. **Map** p151 D3 **69**

The Barbican is a prime example of 1970s brutalism, softened by rectangular ponds of friendly resident ducks. The complex houses a cinema, theatre, concert hall and art galleries, a labyrinthine array of spaces that isn't all that easy to navigate. The programming, however, is first class. At the core of the classical music roster, performing 90 concerts a year, is the brilliant London Symphony Orchestra (LSO), supplemented by top jazz, world-music and rock gigs. The annual BITE season cherry-picks exciting theatre and dance from around the globe, and the cinema shows art-house, mainstream and international films. **Event highlights** 'Radical Nature: Art & Architecture for a Changing Planet, 1969-2009' (until 18 Oct 2009); André Previn & BBC Symphony Orchestra (Apr 2010).

LSO St Luke's

161 Old Street, EC1V 9NG (7490 3939/Barbican box office 7638 8891/ www.lso.co.uk/lsostlukes). Old Street tube/rail. **Map** p151 D2 **70**

The London Symphony Orchestra's conversion of this decaying Hawksmoor-designed church into a rehearsal room, education centre and 370-seat concert hall cost £20m, but it was worth every penny.

Hampstead Heath

Neighbourhood London

Like many a modern metropolis, London is really two different cities. The centre is for work, play and lucky tourists, with most locals living where the rent is cheaper. This means restaurants and bars are often more vital – and exciting scenes more apt to develop – on the city's periphery. In **Greenwich**, the **Royal Botanic Gardens** at Kew and **Hampton Court**, however, neighbourhood London has tourist attractions that could easily fill a sightseeing day each on their own.

North London

The key destinations in north London are Islington and Camden. The gentrification of **Islington's** Georgian squares and Victorian terraces has attracted boutiques and cafés, with arterial Upper Street drawing a steady stream of visitors. **Camden** – famous for its market and situated beside London Zoo – is one of London's liveliest nightlife areas and is beginning to welcome classy eateries and bars. West of Camden, snooty **St John's Wood** is the spiritual home of cricket, while further to the north, **Hampstead** and **Highgate** are prettily leafy, well-off villages either side of the lovely heath.

Sights & museums

Hampstead Heath
Hampstead tube/Hampstead Heath rail.
It's always a delicious surprise to find oneself in among the trees or grassy hills of the heath, a surprisingly wild patch of the metropolis. Aside from the pleasure of walking, sitting and even swimming in the ponds, you can visit

Kenwood House/Iveagh Bequest (Hampstead Lane, 8348 1286, www.english-heritage.org.uk), every inch the stately pile. Built in 1616, the house was purchased by brewing magnate Edward Guinness, who donated his brilliant art collection to the nation in 1927. Highlights include Vermeer's *The Guitar Player* and one of Rembrandt's finest self-portraits.

Jewish Museum

NEW *Raymond Burton House, 129-131 Albert Street, Camden, NW1 7NB (8371 7373/www.jewishmuseum.org. uk). Camden Town tube.* **Open/ admission** check website for details. Due to reopen after a major expansion at the end of 2009, the Jewish Museum illustrates Jewish life over three and a half centuries, using oil paintings, artefacts from a tailor's sweatshop, silver and chinaware, photographs and passports, as well as a terrific collection of ceremonial art that includes a 17th-century Venetian synagogue ark.

Keats House

NEW *Keats Grove, Hampstead, NW3 2RR (7332 2820/www.cityoflondon.gov. uk/keats). Hampstead tube/Hampstead Heath rail/24, 46, 168 bus.* **Open/ admission** check website for details. Recently reopened – and doubtless expecting a surge of interest on the release of Jane Campion's biopic *Bright Star* – this was the home of the Romantic poet from 1818-20, when he left for Rome in the doomed hope of alleviating his TB. There are events, talks and poetry readings, as well as a display on Keats's 'bright star', his sweetheart and neighbour Fanny Brawne.

London Zoo

Regent's Park, Camden, NW1 4RY (7722 3333/www.zsl.org/london-zoo). Baker Street or Camden Town tube then 274, C2 bus. **Open** *Late Oct-mid Mar* 10am-4pm daily. *Mid Mar-late Oct* 10am-5.30pm daily. **Admission** £15.40; free-£13.90 reductions; £49.10 family.

London Zoo has been open in one form or another since 1826. Spread over 36 acres and containing more than 600 species, it cares for many of the endangered variety – as well as your nippers at the new children's zoo. The emphasis throughout is on upbeat education. Exhibits are entertaining – we especially like the recreation of a kitchen overrun with large cockroaches. The 'Meet the Monkeys' attraction allows visitors to walk through an enclosure that recreates the natural habitat of black-capped Bolivian squirrel monkeys. Bring a picnic and you can easily spend a day here.

Lord's Tour & MCC Museum

St John's Wood Road, NW8 8QN (7616 8595/www.lords.org). St John's Wood tube. **Tours** *Nov-Mar* noon, 2pm daily. *Apr-Oct* 10am, noon, 2pm daily. **Admission** £12; £6-£7 reductions; £31 family; free under-5s.
Lord's is more than just a famous cricket ground – as the headquarters of the Marylebone Cricket Club (MCC), it is official guardian of the rules of cricket. As well as staging test matches and internationals, the ground is also home to the Middlesex County Cricket Club (MCCC). Visitors can take an organised tour round the futuristic, pod-like NatWest Media Centre and august, portrait-bedecked Long Room.

Eating & drinking

In Camden, Proud (p177) is great for rock 'n' roll boozing, while the first Haché (24 Inverness Street, 7485 9100, www.hacheburgers.com; see also p95) can soak up the damage.

Bull & Last

NEW *168 Highgate Road, Kentish Town, NW5 1QS (7267 3641). Kentish Town tube/rail then 214, C1, C2, C11 bus/Gospel Oak rail.* **Open** 11am-11pm Mon-Sat; 11am-10.30pm Sun. **££**. **Gastropub**.

Seriously good, yet informal, cooking happens here: braised ox cheek with parsley risotto and roast marrow and cassoulet perhaps; or Cornish hake served with broad bean, shallot and potato salad. Even the bar snacks – sausage roll with black pudding, or a steak sandwich – are firmly in the gourmet bracket, and several real ales are on draught. Worth booking ahead.

Gilgamesh

Stables Market, Chalk Farm Road, Camden, NW1 8AH (7482 5757/ www.gilgameshbar.com). Camden Town tube. **Open** 6pm-2.30am Mon-Thur; noon-2.30am Fri-Sun. **Bar-restaurant**.
A Babylonian theme bar and restaurant so screamingly over the top that it makes Kubla Khan's palace look like a bouncy castle. The restaurant's retractable glass roof and inspired pan-Asian cuisine is similarly unexpected, although by the time you've weaved a path to the lapis lazuli bar you'll probably be prepared for the cocktail menu.

Market

NEW *43 Parkway, Camden, NW1 7PN (7267 9700). Camden Town tube.* **Open** noon-2.30pm, 6-10.30pm Mon-Sat; 1-3.30pm Sun. **££**. **British**.
Camden's other Market is a utilitarian but excellent British restaurant. Stripped-back hardly covers it: brick walls are ragged and raw; zinc-topped tables are scuffed; old-fashioned wooden chairs look like they were once used in a classroom. Food is similarly pared down, reliant on the flavours of high-quality seasonal produce.

Masala Zone

25 Parkway, Camden, NW1 7PG (7267 4422/www.masalazone.com). Camden Town tube. **Open** 12.30-3pm, 5.30-11pm Mon-Fri; 12.30-11pm Sat; 12.30-10.30pm Sun. **££**. **Indian**.
This addition to the Masala Zone chain is especially popular with hip youngsters who come for the buzzy vibe, reasonable prices and decent pan-Indian

food. The eye-catching decor is themed round colourful 1930s-style posters, retro artefacts and bright lampshades. The menu is notable for its earthy curries, thalis and zesty street snacks.

Old Queen's Head

44 Essex Road, Islington, N1 8LN (7354 9993/www.theoldqueenshead. com). Angel tube. **Open** noon-midnight Mon-Wed, Sun; noon-1am Thur; noon-2am Fri, Sat. **Pub**.
This 'superpub' has been packing them in since its 2006 relaunch, with Steve Blonde, formerly of Fabric (p160), bringing a new generation of all-day party promoters to its ace top floor. We're talking huge queues at the weekends and wall-to-wall skinny-jeaned hipsters, lured by the good DJ roster (Freestylers, Eno and Mr Thing). With two floors and outside seating front and back, there's plenty of room – though if you're hoping to bag a seat on a weekend night, you've missed the point entirely.

Ottolenghi

287 Upper Street, Islington, N1 2TZ (7288 1454/www.ottolenghi.co.uk). Angel tube/Highbury & Islington tube/rail. **Open** 8am-10.30pm Mon-Sat; 9am-7pm Sun. **££**. **Bakery-café**.
This is more than an inviting bakery. Behind the pastries piled in the window is a slightly prim deli counter with lush salads, available day and evening, eat-in or take away. As a stylish daytime café, Ottolenghi is brilliant, but the long canteen-style central table, slow-footed service and bright white decor are not really for special occasions.

Yum Cha

NEW *28 Chalk Farm Road, Camden, NW1 8AG (7482 2228). Chalk Farm tube.* **Open** noon-11pm Mon-Thur; noon-midnight Fri, Sat; noon-11pm Sun. **£**. **Dim sum**.
Within weeks of Yum Cha opening, local families and savvy Chinese stu-

Camden Lock

dents had laid claim to the tables here at prime dim sum time (12-2pm). Handsome wood detailing and a golden reclining Buddha statue distinguish the decor, but our highest praise has to go to the extraordinary mini egg custard tarts.

Shopping

Alfie's Antique Market

13-25 Church Street, Marylebone, NW8 8DT (7723 6066/www.alfies antiques.com). Edgware Road tube/Marylebone tube/rail. **Open** 10am-6pm Tue-Sat.
The far side of Regent's Park from Camden, Church Street is now probably London's most important area for antiques shops, with a cluster centred on the estimable Alfie's Antique Market. Alfie's has more than 100 dealers in vintage furniture and fashion, art, accessories, books, maps and quite a lot more. Look out for The Girl Can't Help It (7724 8984, www.thegirl-canthelpit.com), for example, a wonderful, sparkling cache of vintage Hollywood kitsch.

Camden Market

Camden Lock *Camden Lock Place, off Chalk Farm Road, NW1 8AF (www.camdenlockmarket.com).* **Open** 10am-6pm daily.
Camden Market *Camden High Street, at Buck Street, NW1 (www.camdenmarkets.org).* **Open** 9.30am-6pm daily.
Stables Market *off Chalk Farm Road, opposite Hartland Road, NW1 8AH (7485 5511/www.stablesmarket. com).* **Open** 10.30am-6pm Mon-Fri (reduced stalls); 10am-6pm Sat, Sun.
All *Camden Town or Chalk Farm tube.*
Camden Market is actually a series of markets spread out around Chalk Farm Road and the Regent's Canal. Camden Market (formerly Buck Street Market) is the place for fake sunglasses and cut-price interpretations of urban fashion. Further north, along the canal, Camden Lock Market has some good world food stands and vendors selling crafts and ethnic imports. North of the courtyard containing Gilgamesh (p172), the gentrified Stables Market offers more food stands, as well as vintage clothing and clubwear shops

Music, seen

The open mic uncovers another talented Londoner.

North London soul starlet Zarif Davidson is the latest product of London's stealthiest talent school – the open mic scene. These days she might be called on to duet with John Legend and support Chris Brown in a variety of enormodomes, but not too long ago Zarif was honing her chops alongside singer-songwriters in the same pubs and clubs – Camden's **Monkey Chews** (7267 6406, www.monkeychews.com), the **Pigalle** (p83), the legendary **Bedford in Balham** (8682 8940, www.thebedford.co.uk) – as her pop chart predecessors Amy Winehouse and Adele. It's just one of many great things Zarif says is unique to London.

'My music's quite eclectic because I've always been into loads of different music,' says the sunny 23-year-old. 'I'm not sure that would have been the case if I was brought up anywhere else. Whatever you want – a gig, a club, a record shop – it's all here. It's definitely part of me. I was always going to gigs at a young age. One day it would be metal, and the next hip hop.'

We can't say though that we could discern any thrash metal in her summery soul music, pitched somewhere between Lily Allen's chatty style and the vintage leanings of the mighty beehived one, but it has plenty of the jazz, funk and hip hop so readily available here. In fact it's almost like the sound of Camden's **Jazz Café** (p175), the venue for two of her favourite gigs: 'Rachelle Ferrell, who's a brilliant jazz singer, and Lewis Taylor. Those were two people who made me go, Wow, I really want to do that.'

And now she is. Beyoncé is taking her on a European tour and her debut album was due out in the summer. Just like her boundlessly energetic audio guide to London, the Inside Track, Zarif wants the album to evoke her own fun-filled experience of London, a place she moved to from Harrow at the earliest opportunity.

'When it's winter and raining, it's miserable. But in the summer I just want to go for a drink, go to a gig, you know? You want music in the background and London definitely has that. Even if you go to markets there's always stalls playing music. There's just this energy, all this stuff melting together. I love it.'

tucked into the rail arches. Antiques and contemporary designer furniture are sold at the north end of the market in the Horse Hospital area, where you'll also find the appealing Proud club-bar-gallery (p177).

Camden Passage

Off Upper Street, Islington, N1 (7359 0190/www.camdenpassageantiques. com). Angel tube.
Some of the quirky antiques dealers who first brought shoppers here remain, especially in characterful Pierrepont Arcade, but they have been joined by wonderful boutiques. Paul A Young Fine Chocolates (no.33, 7424 5750, www.payoung.net) is one gorgeous example, with almost everything made in the downstairs kitchen. Kirt Holmes (no.16, 7226 1080) does elegant handmade jewellery, Frost French (nos.22-26, 7354 0053) is full of wearable and desirable clothes, including cute knits, while Equa (no.28, 7359 0955) proves that eco-friendly clothes can be fashionable. Upper Street itself has throngs of independent shops, covering both fashion and design.

Nightlife

For great weekend vibes, get down to the Old Queen's Head (p172).

Barfly

49 Chalk Farm Road, Chalk Farm, NW1 8AN (0844 8472 424/box office 0870 907 0999/www.barflyclub.com). Chalk Farm tube. **Open** 5.30pm-1am Mon-Thur; 5.30pm-3am Fri, Sat; noon-midnight Sun. No credit cards.
This pokey, 200-capacity upstairs venue is a big part of the reason why guitar-meets-electro parties have been doing so well of late. Kill Em All Let God Sort It Out, held every other Saturday, stages bands guaranteed to get the crowd going; Adventures Close to Home (monthly) also packs out the dancefloor. And, naturally, our own monthly On the Up events are superb.

EGG

200 York Way, King's Cross, N7 9AP (7609 8364/www.egglondon.net). King's Cross tube/rail then free shuttle from York Way. **Open** 10pm-6am Fri; 10pm-2am Sat.
With its Mediterranean-styled three floors, garden and enormous terrace (complete with a small pool), EGG is big enough to lose yourself in but manages to retain an intimate atmosphere. The upstairs bar in red ostrich leather is rather elegant, but the main dancefloor downstairs has a warehouse rave feel.

Jazz Café

5 Parkway, Camden, NW1 7PG (box office 7485 6834/0870 060 3777/ www.jazzcafe.co.uk). Camden Town tube.
There's some jazz on the schedule here, but this two-floor club deals more in soul, R&B and hip hop these days, and has become the first port of call for soon-to-be-huge US acts (Mary J Blige, John Legend and the Roots all played their first European dates here).

KOKO

1A Camden High Street, Camden, NW1 7JE (0870 432 5527/box office 0870 145 1115/www.koko.uk.com). Mornington Crescent tube.
Opened in 1900 as a music hall, the former Camden Palace scrubbed up nicely during a 2004 refit and has built up a roster of events to match. The 1,500-capacity auditorium stages a fair few club nights (among them Friday's Club NME) alongside indie-heavy gigs.

Luminaire

311 Kilburn High Road, Kilburn, NW6 7JR (7372 8668/www.theluminaire. co.uk). Kilburn tube/Brondesbury rail. **Open** 6pm-2am daily.
The booking policy here is fantastically broad, taking in everything from the Young Gods to Scritti Politti via Acoustic Ladyland. The sound system is up to scratch, the decor is stylish, the drinks are fairly priced and the staff are approachable.

Get the local experience

Over 50 of the world's top destinations available.

Proud

Horse Hospital, Stables Market, Chalk Farm Road, Camden, NW1 8AH (7482 3867/www.proudcamden.com). Chalk Farm tube. **Open** 7.30pm-1am Mon-Wed; 7.30pm-2am Thur, Fri, Sat; 7.30pm-midnight Sun.

North London guitar slingers do rockstar debauchery at this former Horse Hospital, whether draping themselves – cocktail in hand – over the luxurious textiles in the individual stable-style booths, sinking into deck chairs on the outdoor terrace, or supping around in the main band room to trendonista electro, indie and other alternative sounds.

Roundhouse

Chalk Farm Road, Camden Town, NW1 8EH (information 7424 9991/ box office 0844 482 8008 /www. roundhouse.org.uk). Chalk Farm tube.

A one-time railway turntable shed, the Roundhouse was used for experimental theatre and hippie happenings in the 1960s before becoming a rock venue in the '70s. After years of dormancy, the venue reopened a few years ago, and now mixes arty rock gigs with dance, theatre and multimedia events. Sightlines can be poor, but acoustics are good.

Arts & leisure

Almeida

Almeida Street, Islington, N1 1TA (7359 4404/www.almeida.co.uk). Angel tube/Highbury & Islington tube/rail.

A well-groomed 325-seat venue with a funky bar attached and a classy restaurant opposite, the Almeida turns out thoughtfully crafted theatre for grown-ups. Under the reign of artistic director Michael Attenborough it has commanded loyalty from top directors.

Arsenal Football Club

Emirates Stadium, Ashburton Grove, Highbury, N7 7AF (7704 4040/ www.arsenal.com). Arsenal tube.

Although Arsenal seem unable to mount a serious challenge for the Premiership at the moment, the club's insistence on attractive passing football and bringing through exciting young players has many neutrals (and even some rivals) purring. The team's grand new stadium is one of the most attractive in the country, and you can check out the club's illustrious history at the museum (£6, £3 reductions).

Sadler's Wells

Rosebery Avenue, Islington, EC1R 4TN (box office 0870 737 7737/www. sadlerswells.com). Angel tube.

Purpose-built in 1998 on the site of the original 17th-century theatre of the same name, this dazzling complex is home to an impressive line-up of local and international performances.

Wembley Stadium

Stadium Way, Wembley, Middx HA9 0WS (8795 9000/www.wembley stadium.com). Wembley Park tube/Wembley Stadium rail.

Britain's most famous sporting venue finally reopened in early 2007, more than three years behind schedule – and by early 2009 there were major concerns about the state of the pitch, which seemed to be suffering from the range of sports held here. The 90,000-seat stadium, designed by Sir Norman Foster, is quite a sight though, its futuristic steel arch an imposing feature of the skyline.

East London

Right on the doorstep of the City, **Spitalfields** is known for its covered market, around which spread gourmet food shops, restaurants and bars. Just to the east, **Brick Lane** may be world-famous for its curries, but it is increasingly home to hip bars and new boutiques. Just north, **Hoxton** begins where the City overspill into Shoreditch comes to an end: the hip arts are moving east, but this is still your best bet for late drinking and clubbing. East of Shoreditch, **Bethnal Green** would be of scant interest to time-poor visitors were it not for the excellent Museum of Childhood, while unheralded **Dalston** has suddenly developed a cluster of music and arts venues. For a taste of a different kind of modern London – that of high finance – head to **Docklands**.

Sights & museums

Work is proceeding apace on the new **Olympic Stadium** buildings, but can for the moment only be observed from a distance.

Geffrye Museum

136 Kingsland Road, Hoxton, E2 8EA (7739 9893/recorded information 7739 8543/www.geffrye-museum.org.uk). Liverpool Street tube/rail then 149, 242 bus or Old Street tube/rail then 243 bus. **Open** *10am-5pm Tue-Sat; noon-5pm Sun.* **Admission** *free; donations appreciated.*

Housed in a set of 18th-century almshouses, the Geffrye Museum offers a vivid physical history of the English interior. Displaying original furniture, paintings, textiles and decorative arts, the museum recreates a sequence of typical middle-class living rooms from 1600 to the present – a fascinating take on domestic history.

Event highlights 'Eco Home' (13 Oct 2009-7 Feb 2010); 'A Garden Within Doors' (30 Mar-25 July 2010).

Museum of London Docklands

No.1 Warehouse, West India Quay, Hertsmere Road, Docklands, E14 4AL (recorded information 0870 444 3856/box office 0870 444 3857/www. museumindocklands.org.uk). West India Quay DLR/Canary Wharf tube. **Open** *10am-6pm daily.* **Admission** *£5; free-£3 reductions.*

Housed in a 19th-century warehouse (itself a Grade I-listed building), this huge sibling of the Museum of London (p162) explores the complex history of London's docklands and the river over two millennia. Displays spreading over three storeys take you from the arrival of the Romans all the way to the docks' 1980s closure and the area's subsequent redevelopment. A haunting new permanent exhibition sheds light on London's involvement in the transatlantic slave trade.

One Canada Square

Canary Wharf tube/DLR.

Cesar Pelli's dramatic office block, the country's tallest habitable building since 1991 (although shortly to be overtaken by numerous competitors), remains an icon of our last period of financial overconfidence. Instantly recognisable from all over London, it nowhere seems more impressive than gazing up forlornly from its foot.

Ragged School Museum

46-50 Copperfield Road, E3 4RR (8980 6405/www.raggedschoolmuseum.org.uk) Mile End tube. **Open** *10am-5pm Wed, Thur; 2-5pm 1st Sun of mth.* **Admission** *free; donations appreciated.*

Ragged schools were an early experiment in public education: they provided tuition, food and clothes for destitute children. This one was the largest in London, and Dr Barnardo himself taught here. It's now a sweet local museum with a complete mock-up of a classroom and an Edwardian kitchen.

V&A Museum of Childhood

Cambridge Heath Road, E2 9PA (8983 5200/recorded information 8983 5235/www.museumofchildhood.org.uk). Bethnal Green tube/rail/Cambridge Heath rail. **Open** *10am-5.45pm daily.* **Admission** *free; donations appreciated.*

Home to one of the world's finest collections of kids' toys, dolls' houses, games and costumes, the Museum of

Childhood shines brighter than ever after extensive refurbishment, which has given it an impressive entrance. Part of the Victoria & Albert (p88), the museum has been amassing child-related objects since 1872 and continues to do so, with *Incredibles* figures complementing Barbie Dolls and Victorian praxinoscopes. There are plenty of interactive exhibits and a decent café too.

Event highlights 'Make Do and Mend' (until 15 Nov 2009).

Whitechapel Art Gallery

NEW *77-82 Whitechapel High Street, E1 7QX (7522 7888/www.whitechapel gallery.org). Aldgate East tube.* **Open** 11am-6pm Tue, Wed, Fri-Sun; 11am-9pm Thur. **Admission** free.
See box right.

Event highlights 'Goshka Macuga: The Nature of the Beast' (until 18 Apr 2010); 'Social Sculpture' (ongoing).

Eating & drinking

Beside Old Spitalfields Market, **St John Bread & Wine** (94-96 Commercial Street, 7251 0848, www.stjohnbreadandwine.com) is the fine offshoot of St John (p157). **Charlie Wright's** (p184) is as much about late-night drinking as it is about jazz.

All Star Lanes

NEW *Old Truman Brewery, 87 Brick Lane, E1 6QR (7422 8370/www.allstar lanes.co.uk). Holborn tube.* **Open** noon-11.30pm Mon-Thur; noon-12.30am Fri-Sun. **£££. Bowling bar-restaurant.** Smart, diner-style seating, a comfortable bar with chilled glasses, classy furnishings and an unusual mix of bottled lagers (try the delicious Anchor Steam) complement the skittle action at this recently opened, much bigger brother of the popular Bloomsbury outfit (Victoria House, Bloomsbury Place, 7025 2676). Note that the lanes only open at 5pm Mon-Thur.

Whitechapel redux

The arty East End's key gallery reopens.

Nikolaus Pevsner described it as a 'wonderfully original and epoch-making building', but a century after it was built, the **Whitechapel Art Gallery** (left) – designed in an art nouveau style by Charles Harrison Townsend – needed to expand if it was to meet the needs of a flagship gallery in the heart of London's contemporary art quarter. The answer appeared when the adjacent Passmore Edwards library became vacant – a library, as luck would have it, where the Whitechapel Boys (London-based Jewish writers and artists who included early British modernists David Bomberg and Mark Gertler) used to meet.

Belgian architects Robbrecht en Daem, in association with London practice Witherford Watson Mann, adopted a low-key, intelligent approach. They've done a beautiful job, leaving each building with its own distinct personality.

Gallery space has grown by a whopping 78 per cent, and gallery director Iwona Blazwick has turned the Whitechapel's limitations into strengths. The Collections Gallery is a fine example. The Whitechapel itself has no permanent collection, so it is able to use this space for lengthy loans from British or international collections, public or private, that do not themselves have enough room to display their treasure.

Tayyabs

Bistrotheque

*23-27 Wadeson Street, Bethnal Green,
E2 9DR (8983 7900/www.bistrotheque.
com). Bethnal Green tube/rail/
Cambridge Heath rail/55 bus.* **Open**
6.30-10.30pm Mon-Thur; 6.30-11pm Fri;
11am-4pm, 6.30-11pm Sat; 11am-4pm,
6.30-10.30pm Sun. *Bar* 6pm-midnight
Mon-Sat; 1pm-midnight Sun. **£££**.

French.

An all-white warehouse space, with
louche cabaret and a classily funky little bar, Bistrotheque hits the area's new
demographic on the head with its blend
of sophistication and streetwise cool.
The relaxed clientele are happy with a
menu crafted to their whims: cocktails,
brunch, grazing, and a good prix fixe
(even at weekends).

Brick Lane Beigel Bake

*159 Brick Lane, E1 6SB (7729 0616).
Liverpool Street tube/rail/8 bus.* **Open**
24hrs daily. **£**. No credit cards.

Bagel bakery.

This charismatic little East End institution rolls out perfect bagels both
plain and filled (egg, cream cheese,
mountains of salt beef), superb bread
and moreish cakes. Even at 3am, fresh

baked goods are being pulled from the
ovens at the back; no wonder the queue
trails out the door when the innumerable local bars and clubs begin to close.

Chaat

NEW *36 Redchurch Street, Shoreditch,
E2 7DP (7739 9595). Liverpool Street
tube/rail.* **Open** noon-3pm, 6-11pm Tue-
Fri; 6pm-midnight Sat, Sun. **££**.

Bangladeshi.

Chaat, which means 'snack food', is a
welcoming, home-style Bangladeshi
kitchen just beyond the northern end
of London's most famous – and now
frankly over-egged – curry corridor.
Unpretentious, affordable comfort food
is served up here in sparsely decorated
but cheerful surroundings.

Commercial Tavern

*142 Commercial Street, Spitalfields, E1
6NU (7247 1888). Aldgate East
tube/Liverpool Street tube/rail.* **Open** 5-
11pm Mon-Fri; noon-11pm Sat; noon-
10.30pm Sun. **Pub**.

The inspired chaos of retro-eccentric
decor and warm, inclusive atmosphere make this landmark flatiron
corner pub very likeable. It seems to

have escaped the attentions of the necking-it after-work masses: perhaps because of the absence of wall-to-wall lager pumps. A great example of how a historic pub can be quite lit up with new life.

Dreambagsjaguarshoes

34-36 Kingsland Road, Hoxton, E2 8DA (7729 5830/www.dreambags jaguarshoes.com). Old Street tube/rail. **Open** 5pm-midnight Mon; noon-1am Tue-Fri; 5pm-1am Sat; noon-12.30am Sun. **Bar**.

Still as trendy as the day it first opened, this bar offers a fast-track education in what made (and continues to make) Shoreditch cool. Grungey but glam scruffs lounge on the battered sofas, surrounded by scrawled-on walls and lots of tatty art; staff look as though they're between modelling assignments; and the background music is self-consciously edgy.

E Pellicci

332 Bethnal Green Road, Bethnal Green, E2 0AG (7739 4873). Bethnal Green tube/rail/8, 253 bus. **Open** 7am-4.45pm Mon-Sat. **£**. No credit cards. **Café**.

Not just a caff, but a social club, taxi driver meeting room and unofficial matchmaking service, E Pellicci has been warmly welcoming customers since 1900. The heritage-listed marquetry-panelled interior is cramped and sharing tables for the trad English and Italian dishes is to be expected, nay relished.

Rosa's

NEW *12 Hanbury Street, Brick Lane, E1 6QR (7247 1093/www.rosaslondon. com). Aldgate East tube/Liverpool Street tube/rail.* **Open** 11am-11pm Mon-Thur; 11am-midnight Fri, Sat; 11am-11pm Sun. **££**. **Thai**.

Although the menu is mostly familiar, there is a freshness and honesty about the cooking here, and the carved vegetables and garnishes arrive in greater abundance than you might expect for dishes costing six or seven quid. Rosa's has a shared table set-up that rewards booking (or early arrival) if you're going to enjoy a meal here as a small group.

Royal China

30 Westferry Circus, Docklands, E14 8RR (7719 0888/www.royalchinagroup. co.uk). Canary Wharf tube/DLR. **Open** noon-11pm Mon-Thur; noon-11.30pm Fri, Sat; 11am-10pm Sun. **££**. **Dim sum**.

The Docklands branch of the fine Royal China chain has a broad riverside terrace and windows overlooking the river. We're particularly fond of the weekend dim sum lunches here, but you should expect to have to wait for a seat.

Sông Quê

134 Kingsland Road, Shoreditch, E2 8DY (7613 3222). Old Street tube/rail/ 26, 48, 55, 67, 149, 242, 243 bus. **Open** noon-3pm, 5.30-11pm Mon-Sat; noon-11pm Sun. **£**. **Vietnamese**.

North-east London still retains its monopoly on the capital's most authentic Vietnamese restaurants. And Sông Quê is still the benchmark. It's an efficient, canteen-like operation to which diners of all types are attracted – be prepared to share tables at busy times.

Tayyabs

83 Fieldgate Street, Whitechapel, E1 1JU (7247 9543/www.tayyabs.co.uk). Aldgate East or Whitechapel tube. **Open** noon-11.30pm daily. **£**. **Pakistani**.

Tayyabs is the East End equivalent of the caffs favoured by truckers in South Asia. It has been around since the 1970s, and although the interior has been extended, it's still a challenge to bag a table. Cooking is big, bold and sassy. The place gets noisy and crowded, but service is swift and prices low.

Shopping

On Sundays, the whole area from **Old Spitalfields Market** (p183) east to Brick Lane is a hectic shopper's paradise.

Agnès b

NEW *16 Lamb Street, Spitalfields, E1 6EA (7426 0014/www.agnesb.com). Liverpool Street tube/rail.* **Open** 11am-7pm Mon-Wed, Fri-Sun; 11am-8pm Sun.
Agnès Troublé opened her first boutique in an old Les Halles butcher's shop in 1975. More than three decades later, Troublé's Agnès b label has finally brought a little touch of oh-la-la to the East End. Her seventh UK store houses Agnès b's quietly quirky collections in an Old Spitalfields Market unit.

A Gold

42 Brushfield Street, Spitalfields, E1 6AG (7247 2487). Liverpool Street tube/rail. **Open** 9.30am-5.30pm Mon-Fri; 11am-6pm Sat; 10am-6pm Sun.
A Gold was flying the flag for British foods long before it became fashionable to do so. It resembles a village shop from a bygone era. The baked goods alone take customers on a whistlestop tour of Britain: Cornish saffron cakes, Dundee cakes, Welsh cakes and (of course) Lancashire Eccles cakes.

Brick Lane Thrift Store

NEW *68 Sclater Street, off Brick Lane, E1 6HR (7739 0242). Aldgate East tube/Liverpool Street tube/rail.* **Open** noon-7pm daily.
At this second-hand shop, almost everything is £10 or less. Across two levels is a refined collection of best-sellers and popular lines, such as checked Western shirts, from the East End warehouse. It's worth getting the tube along to Stepney Green too, for Brick Lane's predecessor the East End Thrift Store (Unit 1A, Watermans Building, Assembly Passage, 7423 9700).

Broadway Market

(www.broadwaymarket.co.uk). London Fields rail/236, 394 bus.
Ever since the Saturday farmers' market took off on the the street running south from London Fields to Regent's Canal, Broadway Market has seen a growing number of appealing boutiques take up residence. You can look after your feet with the shoes at Black Truffle (no.4, 79239450, www.blacktruffle.co.uk) and then your brain at Broadway Bookshop (no.6, 7241 1626, www.broadwaybookshophackney.com), before refuelling at the Cat & Mutton (no.76, 7254 5599, www.catandmutton.co.uk) or Dove (nos.24-28, 7275 7617, www.belgianbars.com). Just down the canal, Dog & Wardrobe (Unit 3B, Regent Studios, 8 Andrew's Road, www.thedogandwardrobe.com) is an excellent new design shop, open all day Saturday.

Cheshire Street

Aldgate East tube.
It doesn't look impressive, but this street off the northern section of Brick Lane is a haven for independent shops and vintage threads: artist Hackney and costume designer Jane Petrie's gift shop-cum-gallery Shelf (no.40, 7739 9444, www.helpyourshelf.co.uk); Labour & Wait (no.18, 7729 6253, www.labourandwait.co.uk), paying homage to timeless, unfaddy domestic goods that combine beauty with utility; and Beyond Retro (no.112, 7613 3636, www.beyondretro.com), an enormous bastion of second-hand clothing and accessories, give you a feel for the range on offer.

Columbia Road Market

Columbia Road, Bethnal Green, E2. Liverpool Street tube/rail, then 26, 48, bus/Old Street tube/rail then 55, 243 bus. **Open** 8am-2pm Sun.
On Sunday mornings, this unassuming East End street is transformed into a swathe of fabulous plant life and the air is fragrant with blooms. But it's not

Old Spitalfields Market

just about flora: alongside the market is a growing number of shops selling everything from pottery and Mexican glassware to cupcakes and perfume. Get there early for the pick of the crop, or around 2pm for the bargains; refuel at Jones Dairy (23 Ezra Street, 7739 5372, www.jonesdairy.co.uk).

Goodhood

NEW *41 Coronet Street, Hoxton, N1 6HD (7729 3600/www.goodhood.co. uk). Old Street tube/rail.* **Open** 11am-7pm Tue-Sat.
Stock here is selected by streetwear obsessives Kyle and Jo, and weighted towards Japanese independent labels. We particularly like the Gregory Japan rucksacks and Black Dollars Tees, both of them store exclusives.

Old Truman Brewery

91-95 Brick Lane, E1 6RF. Liverpool Street tube/rail.
The great brick buildings of this old brewery are home to a formidable array of funky retailers: Junky Styling (no.12, 7247 1883, www.junkystyling. co.uk) for innovative reworkings of second-hand clothes; Gloria's (no.6, 7770 6222) for retro and up-to-the-minute sneakers; or denim and brogues from understatedly cool A Butcher of Distinction (no.11, 7770 6111, www.butcherofdistinction.com). Despite the fading fortunes of many record shops, Rough Trade East (7392 7788, www.roughtrade.com) even chose to open a big, new, warehouse-style store, café and gig space here. Open only one day a week, the Sunday (Up)Market (7770 6100, www.sunday-upmarket.co.uk) is a buzzy collection of 140 stalls selling edgy fashion from fresh young designers, vintage gear, art and crafts, and well-priced jewellery. It's more relaxed, cheaper and all-round hipper than near neighbour Old Spitalfields Market.

Old Spitalfields Market

Commercial Street, between Lamb Street & Brushfield Street, E1 6AA (7247 8556/www.visitspitalfields.com). Liverpool Street tube/rail. **Open** 9.30am-5pm Thur, Fri, Sun. *Antiques* 8.30am-4.30pm Thur. *Food* 10am-5pm Wed, Fri, Sun. *Fashion* 9.30am-5pm Fri. *Records & books* 10am-4pm 1st & 3rd Fri of the mth.

LONDON BY AREA

Recent redevelopment has given a new lease of life to this East End stalwart. Spitalfields now consists of the refurbished 1887 covered market and an adjacent modern shopping precinct. Around the edge of Old Spitalfields Market, stands sell grub from around the world, while stalls sell crafts, clothes and records in the market itself. The busiest day is Sunday.

Store Rooms

NEW 43 Pitfield Street, Hoxton, N1 6DA (7608 1105/www.thestorerooms. com). Old Street tube/rail. **Open** 10am-7pm Mon-Fri; 11am-6pm Sat; 11am-5pm Sun.

A timely idea, this: a crisply styled sale shop where all items are discounted 35-70%, all the time. The stock changes constantly, but you might find Penfield gilets or Sibin Linnebjerg's 1960s-inspired cardigans among the bargains.

Nightlife

The cabaret room at Bistrotheque (p180) puts on exceptional, edgy drag shows, led by Jonny Woo.

Bardens Boudoir

36-44 Stoke Newington Road, N16 7XJ (7249 9557/www.bardensbar.co.uk). Dalston Kingsland rail/67, 76, 149, 243 bus. No credit cards.

Located in the heart of Turkish Dalston below a disused furniture store, the 300-capacity Boudoir is something of a shambles – but that doesn't bother the often out-there line-ups nor the hipsters that love them. Hungry? 19 Numara Bos Cirrik (next door at no.34) is one of the city's best Turkish restaurants.

Bethnal Green Working Men's Club

42-44 Pollard Row, Bethnal Green, E2 6NB (7739 2727/www.workers playtime.net). Bethnal Green tube.

The sticky red carpet and broken lampshades perfectly suit the programme of quirky lounge, retro rock 'n' roll and fancy-dress burlesque parties from spandex-lovin' dance husband-and-wife Duotard or Grind a Go Go. The mood is friendly, the playlist upbeat and the air always full of artful, playful mischief.

Charlie Wright's International Bar

45 Pitfield Street, Hoxton, N1 6DA (7490 8345/www.myspace.com/ charliewrights). Old Street/Liverpool Street tube/rail. **Open** noon-1am Sun-Wed; noon-2am Thur; noon-3am Fri, Sat.

Charlie Wright's ramshackle pub has hosted occasional gigs for years, but recently started staging an excellent regular jazz programme every night except Saturday. Expect US, African and Brazilian names alongside British players from the Jazz Warriors, Jazz Jamaica and the F-IRE Collective. Gigs don't usually start until 10pm but continue late on Thursday and Friday.

Star of Bethnal Green

359 Bethnal Green Road, Bethnal Green, E2 6LG (07932 869705/www. starofbethnalgreen.com). Bethnal Green tube/rail. **Open** 5pm-midnight Mon-Thur, Sun; 4pm-2am Fri, Sat.

Having been taken over and brilliantly refurbished by house and electro promoter Rob Star, this 'superpub' is indeed stellar. A bold red and silver star stamps the wall behind the stage in what is at once intimate boozer, space for low-key gigs from big bands and host to a funky fresh line-up of disco-indie-whatever nights.

Vortex Jazz Club

Dalston Culture House, 11 Gillet Street, Dalston, N16 8JN (7254 4097/www.vortexjazz.co.uk). Dalston Kingsland rail.

The Vortex is on the first floor of a handsome new building, with a restaurant on the ground floor. The space can feel a bit sterile but the programming is superb, packed with left-field talent from Britain, Europe and the US. London's most exciting jazz venue.

South London

South London's attractions are many, but not always immediately obvious. Due south you'll find buzzing residential districts such as boisterous **Brixton**, with its lively nightlife, and the excellent bars and restaurants of **Clapham** and **Battersea**. South-east is **Greenwich**, laden with centuries of royal and maritime heritage. South-west are further headline attractions: **Kew** and **Hampton Court Palace**.

Sights & museums

British Music Experience

NEW *O2 Bubble, Millennium Way, North Greenwich, SE10 0BB (8463 2000/www.britishmusicexperience.com). North Greenwich tube.* **Open** 10am-8pm (last entry 6.30pm) daily. **Admission** £15; free-£12 reductions; £40 family.

A permanent, high-tech, interactive music exhibition located in the O2 dome (p188), this pop and rock museum allows music lovers to retrace historic moments from the last 60 years of British pop music. Key pieces of music memorabilia include David Bowie's 'Ashes to Ashes' clown suit, Roger Daltrey's Woodstock outfit and an Amy Winehouse vintage dress. You can learn to play an instrument too.

Dulwich Picture Gallery

Gallery Road, Dulwich, SE21 7AD (8693 5254/www.dulwichpicturegallery. org.uk). North Dulwich or West Dulwich rail. **Open** 10am-5pm Tue-Fri; 11am-5pm Sat, Sun. **Admission** £5; free-£4 reductions.

This bijou gallery – the first to be purpose-built in the UK – was designed by Sir John Soane in 1811. It's a beautiful space that shows off Soane's ingenuity with and interest in lighting effects. The gallery displays a small but outstanding collection of work by Old Masters, offering a fine introduction to the baroque era through work by Rubens, Rembrandt and Poussin. **Event highlights** 'Drawing Attention: Tiepolo, Rembrandt, Van Gogh, Picasso' (21 Oct 2009-27 Jan 2010).

Hampton Court Palace

East Molesey, Surrey KT8 9AU (0870 751 5175/information 0844 482 7777/www.hrp.org.uk). Hampton Court rail/riverboat from Westminster or Richmond to Hampton Court Pier (Apr-Oct). **Open** Apr-Oct 10am-6pm daily. Nov-Mar 10am-4.30pm daily. **Admission** £13.30; free-£11.30 reductions; £37 family. *Maze only* £3.50; £2.50 reductions. *Gardens only* £4.60; £4 reductions (free Nov-Feb).

It's a half-hour train ride from central London, but this spectacular palace, once owned by Henry VIII, is well worth the trek. It was built in 1514 and for the next 200 years became a focal point of English history: Shakespeare gave his first performance to James I here in 1604; and, after the Civil War, Oliver Cromwell was so besotted by the building he ditched his puritanical principles and moved in. Centuries later, the rosy walls of the palace still dazzle. Its vast size can be daunting, so it's a good idea to take advantage of the costumed guided tours. The Tudor Kitchens are great fun, with their giant cauldrons, fake pies and blood-spattered walls. More spectacular sights await outside, where the exquisitely landscaped gardens contain superb topiary, peaceful Thames views and the famous Hampton Court maze. **Event highlights** 'Young Henry VIII' (until 31 Dec 2009).

National Maritime Museum

Romney Road, Greenwich, SE10 9NF (8858 4422/information 8312 6565/ tours 8312 6608/www.nmm.ac.uk). Cutty Sark DLR/Greenwich DLR/rail. **Open** 10am-5pm daily. **Admission** free; donations appreciated.

Royal Botanic Gardens

Old Royal Naval College

Greenwich, SE10 9LW (8269 4747/ www.oldroyalnavalcollege.org.uk). Cutty Sark DLR/Greenwich DLR/rail. **Open** 10am-5pm daily. **Admission** free.

Designed by Wren in 1694, with Hawksmoor and Vanbrugh helping to complete the project, this superb collection of buildings was originally a hospital for the support of seamen and their dependants. The public can visit the rococo chapel, where there are free organ recitals, and the Painted Hall, a tribute to William and Mary that took 19 years to complete. The Pepys building is in the process of becoming the £5.8m Discover Greenwich education centre: its exhibition on the history of Greenwich might detain you, but the revived brewery certainly will.

Royal Botanic Gardens (Kew Gardens)

Kew, Richmond, Surrey TW9 3AB (8332 5655/information 8940 1171/ www.kew.org). Kew Gardens tube/rail/ Kew Bridge rail/riverboat to Kew Pier. **Open** *Apr-Aug* 9.30am-6.30pm Mon-Fri; 9.30am-7.30pm Sat, Sun. *Sept, Oct* 9.30am-6pm daily. *Nov-Jan* 9.30am-4.15pm daily. *Feb-Mar* 9.30am-5.30pm daily. **Admission** £13; free-£12 reductions.

The unparalleled collection of plants at Kew was begun by Queen Caroline, wife of George II, with exotic plants brought back by voyaging botanists (Charles Darwin among them). In 1759, Lancelot 'Capability' Brown was employed by George III to improve on the work of his predecessors, setting the template for a garden that today attracts thousands of visitors every year. Head straight for the 19th-century greenhouses, filled to the roof with tropical plants, and next door the Waterlily House's quiet, gorgeous indoor pond (closed in winter). Brown's Rhododendron Dell is at its best in May, while the new Xstrata Treetop Walkway, almost 60ft above the ground, is terrific fun in autumn.

The National Maritime Museum, the world's largest maritime museum, has a huge store of creatively organised maritime art, cartography, models and regalia. Ground-level galleries include 'Passengers', a delightful exploration of the 20th-century fashion for cruise travel. 'Explorers' covers great sea expeditions, right back to medieval times, while 'Maritime London' concentrates on the city as a port. Upstairs, 'Your Ocean' uncovers our dependence on the health of the world's seas. From the museum a colonnaded walkway leads to the Queen's House (8312 6565), designed by Inigo Jones and holding art by the likes of Hogarth and Gainsborough. Up the hill in the park, the Royal Observatory and Planetarium (8312 6565, www.rog.nmm.ac.uk) are also part of the museum – here you can join the throngs straddling the Prime Meridian Line or take in a star show (£6, £4 reductions) in the Planetarium.

Wimbledon Lawn Tennis Museum

Museum Building, All England Lawn Tennis Club, Church Road, SW19 5AE (8946 6131/www.wimbledon.org/museum). Southfields tube/39, 493 bus. **Open** 10.30am-5pm daily; ticket holders only during championships. **Admission** £15.50; free-£13.75 reductions.

Highlights at this popular museum on the history of tennis include a 200° cinema screen that allows you to find out what it's like to play on Centre Court and a re-creation of a 1980s men's dressing room, complete with a 'ghost' of John McEnroe. Included in the ticket price is a behind-the-scenes tour. On Centre Court itself the big news is a retractable roof, which should allow for extended evening play – and will also bring those irritating rain delays to an end.

Eating & drinking

Franco Manca

NEW *4 Market Row, Electric Lane, Brixton, SW9 8LD (7738 3021/www.francomanca.co.uk). Brixton tube/rail.* **Open** noon-5pm Mon-Sat. **Pizza**.

Franco Manca is the sort of discreet place you might walk past while ogling the Afro-Caribbean goodies in the surrounding market. Don't. It uses well-sourced, quality ingredients (many organic), top-notch equipment and good sourdough bases, quickly baked at high temperatures in the Neopolitan manner to seal in all the flavours and locking in the moisture of the crust.

Greenwich Union

56 Royal Hill, Greenwich, SE10 8RT (8692 6258/www.greenwichunion.com). Greenwich rail/DLR. **Open** noon-11pm Mon-Fri; 11am-11pm Sat; 11.30am-10.30pm Sun. **Microbrewery pub.**

Alistair Hook's laudable Meantime Brewery flagship – you'll find his fine brews at good pubs across town – is based on the training and recipes he gleaned at age-old institutions in Germany. Throw in proper cheeses, steak and stout pies and it's no wonder the Union is reliably busy.

Inside

19 Greenwich South Street, Greenwich, SE10 8NW (8265 5060/www.inside restaurant.co.uk). Greenwich rail/DLR. **Open** noon-2.30pm, 6.30-11pm Tue-Fri; 6.30-11pm Sat; noon-3pm Sun. **£££**. **Modern European**.

That Inside is a local fine-dining fave is evident in the polite familiarity between owners and patrons. The interior is tasteful in white and dark brown, but the food is the real draw: based on classical Anglo-French traditions, dishes are cooked with flair and creativity, using freshest ingredients. The set-price dinner is excellent value (£16.95 two courses; £20.95 three).

Loft

NEW *67 Clapham High Street, SW4 7TG (7627 0792/www.theloft-clapham.co.uk). Clapham North tube.* **Open** 6pm-midnight Mon-Thur; 6pm-1.30am Fri; noon-1.30am Sat; noon-midnight Sun. **Bar**.

This glass-fronted space, courtesy of the folk behind Brixton's bar-club Plan B, takes its music, drinks and food seriously. And its minimal breeze block walls, low-slung leather chairs and smoky glass windows even make it just about possible to forget that you're sitting above Tesco. A huge DJ set-up is embedded into the high concrete bar.

Nightlife

Dogstar

389 Coldharbour Lane, Brixton, SW9 8LQ (7733 7515/www.antic-ltd.com/dogstar). Brixton tube/rail. **Open** 4pm-2am Mon-Thur; noon-4am Fri, Sat; noon-2am Sun.

A Brixton institution from back when Coldharbour Lane was somewhere people feared to go, Dogstar is a big street-corner pub exuding the urban authenticity loved by clubbers. The atmosphere can be intense, but it's never less than vibrant.

Fire/Lightbox
South Lambeth Road, Vauxhall, SW8 1UQ (www.fireclub.co.uk).
Craving clubs full of shirts-off muscle boys going at night-and-day techno? For a number of years the 'Vauxhall Village' has been destination of choice for hardcore gay clubbers, but key venues such as Fire are now also hosting mixed nights from the likes of Durr and Bugged Out. And there's the all-round LED sensation that is the Lightbox.

O2 Arena, IndigO2 & Matter
Millennium Way, North Greenwich, SE10 0BB (8463 2000/box office 0871 984 0002/www.theo2.co.uk). North Greenwich tube.
Since its launch in 2007, this conversion of the Millennium Dome has been a huge success. The O2 Arena – a state-of-the-art, 23,000-capacity enormodome with good acoustics and sightlines – hosts the headline rock and pop acts. Its little brother, Indigo2, isn't actually that little (capacity 2,350) but is a good fit for big soul, funk and pop-jazz acts (Roy Ayers, Stacey Kent), knackered old pop stars (Howard Jones, Gary Numan) and all points in-between. The newest addition to the nightlife portfolio, though is a mighty collaboration with superclub Fabric. The 2,600-capacity Matter (7549 6686, www.matterlondon.com) was designed by architect William Russell to operate as a concert venue, performing arts space or VIP club, and has good sightlines and magnificent sound. Thames Clippers (p214) operate half hourly boats back to central London.

RVT
Royal Vauxhall Tavern, 372 Kennington Lane, Vauxhall, SE11 5HY (7820 1222/www.rvt.org.uk). Vauxhall
tube/rail. **Open** 7pm-midnight Mon-Fri; 9pm-2am Sat; 2pm-midnight Sun.
Admission £5-£7.
If you're seeking a very London gay experience, this is where to start. The pub-turned-legendary-gay-venue operates an anything-goes booking policy. The most famous fixture is Saturday's queer performance night Duckie (www.duckie.co.uk), with Amy Lamé hosting turns at midnight that range from strip cabaret to porn puppets; Sunday's Dame Edna Experience drag show, from 5pm, is also absolutely essential, drawing quasi-religious devotees.

Up the Creek
302 Creek Road, Greenwich, SE10 9SW (8858 4581/www.up-the-creek. com). Greenwich DLR/rail.
Originally set up by the legendary Malcolm Hardee ('To say that he has no shame is to drastically exaggerate the amount of shame he has'), this extraordinary purpose-built club has been around since the 1990s, and is still one of the very best places in the capital to see comedy. It's renowned for its lively – some would say bear pit – atmosphere, but there's definitely a more chilled feel to the 'Sunday Special Club'.

Arts & leisure

BAC (Battersea Arts Centre)
Lavender Hill, Battersea, SW11 5TN (7223 2223/www.bac.org.uk). Clapham Common tube/Clapham Junction rail/77, 77A, 345 bus.
The superb, forward-thinking BAC, which inhabits the old Battersea Town Hall, plays alma mater to new writers and theatre companies – expect the very latest in quirky, fun and physical theatre as well as serious improv sessions. The venue has just secured a £500,000 grant which should save it from closing because of recent funding cuts.

West London

Notting Hill Gate, **Ladbroke Grove** and **Westbourne Park** tube stations form a triangle that contains lovely squares, grand houses and fine gardens, along with shops, bars and restaurants to serve the kind of bohemian who can afford to live here. Off Portobello Road are the boutiques of **Westbourne Grove** and **Ledbury Road**.

Sights & museums

Museum of Brands, Packaging & Advertising

Colville Mews, Lonsdale Road, Notting Hill, W11 2AR (7908 0880/www. museumofbrands.com). Notting Hill Gate tube. **Open** 10am-6pm Tue-Sat; 11am-5pm Sun. **Admission** £5.80; free-£3.50 reductions.

Robert Opie began collecting the things most of us throw away when he was 16. Over the years the collection has grown to include everything from milk bottles to vacuum cleaners and cereal packets. The emphasis is on British consumerism through the last century, though there are items as old as an Ancient Egyptian doll.

Eating & drinking

Le Café Anglais

8 Porchester Gardens, Bayswater, W2 4DB (7221 1415/www.lecafe anglais.co.uk). Bayswater tube. **Open** noon-3pm, 6.30-11.30pm Mon-Sat; noon-3pm, 6.30-10pm Sun. **£££.** **Modern European**.

Chef-proprietor Rowley Leigh's fine restaurant opened to great acclaim in 2007 and is still very popular. The white, art deco-style room is big, with floor-to-ceiling leaded windows on one side, the open kitchen, rotisserie grill and bar opposite. It's a see-and-be-seen place with a long menu that's a mix-and-match delight.

Kiasu

48 Queensway, Bayswater, W2 3RY (7727 8810). Bayswater or Queensway tube. **Open** noon-11pm daily. **£.** **Malaysian**.

A cheerful, cheap, all-day restaurant frequented by South-east Asians. Glass mugs of sweet teh tarik, Malaysia's favourite blend of tea and condensed milk, help to soothe the chilli heat of dishes such as soft-shell crab, served in the Singapore chilli crab style.

Ledbury

127 Ledbury Road, Westbourne Grove, W11 2AQ (7792 9090/www.theledbury. com). Westbourne Park tube. **Open** noon-2pm, 6.30-10.15pm Mon-Fri; noon-3pm, 6.30-10.15pm Sat, Sun. **£££.** **French**.

Notting Hillites flock to this elegant gastronomic masterpiece, where the food is as adventurous and accomplished as any, but less expensive than many. Aimed squarely at the palate,

Taqueria p191

Stores to explore

Step out of the West End for the best new boutiques.

Convenience Store

LONDON BY AREA

A string of local boutiques, pop-up shops and newly open studios have escaped high city-centre rents to mark out new shopping territories: true English eccentricity is to be found clustered alongside markets and in the backstreets of vogueish neighbourhoods.

Head out westwards to Westbourne Park to discover the newcomer **Convenience Store** (p191). Nearby, **Kokon to Zai II** (87 Golborne Road) is a new foothold of the legendary Soho shop, stocking the likes of Marjan Pejoski and Bernhard Willhelm. Award-winning Brit designer **Duro Olowu**'s must-see boutique is at 365 Portobello Road.

Tiny Columbia Road (p182) is now lined with one-offs and occasional stores (many only open at weekends). Although perfumier **Angela Flanders**' boudoir-like HQ has been at no.96 since 1985, look out for **Buddug** (hidden above vintage womenswear boutique Marcus & Trump at no.146) –

home to artists Jessie Chorley and Buddug Humphrey's handmade enamel jewellery – and cult homewares store **Treacle** (nos.110-112) – it sells the campest cupcakes in London. Fans of artist Rob Ryan are sated with **Ryantown** (no.126), a gallery-like store packed with his wonky, artless prints, tiles and mugs.

A trip to Broadway Market (p182) is as much about its homeware galleries and vintage stalls as locally sourced scrumpy and wild mushroom sandwiches. At no.4, the recently revamped **Black Truffle** is one of London's best stores for design-led shoes and accessories, while a short walk away, the **Dog & Wardrobe** (3B Regent Studios, 8 Andrew's Road, E8 4QN), a lock-up owned by local art directors Jane Money and Vishal Gohel, is a fresh and unique celebration of English oddness: you'll find antique Union Jacks, old anatomical models and even the odd stuffed weasel.

flavours are intense and delicate, often powerfully earthy. Spending only £20-£30 on wine is possible, but it's also worth pushing the boat out here.

River Café

Thames Wharf, Rainville Road, Hammersmith, W6 9HA (7386 4200/ www.rivercafe.co.uk). Hammersmith tube. **Open** 12.30-3pm, 7-9.30pm Mon-Sat; 12.30-3pm Sun. **££££**. **Italian**.
Following a kitchen fire, the legendary River Café added a private dining room-cum-cheese room, and now has an open kitchen and bar-counter dining. The produce-based menu still changes twice daily; the wine list (try a chilled red) and riverside setting remain flawless.

Taqueria

139-143 Westbourne Grove, Notting Hill, W11 2RS (7229 4734/www.cool chiletaqueria.co.uk). Notting Hill Gate tube. **Open** noon-11pm Mon-Thur; noon-11.30pm Fri; 10am-11.30pm Sat; noon-10.30pm Sun. **£**. **Mexican**.
With its tortilla-making machine from Guadalajara, this place shows what Mexican street food is about: masa (maize dough) is flattened into soft tortillas for tacos, fried crisp for tostadas and shaped into thick patties for griddled sopes. Masks, movie posters and gorgeous staff make the place easy on the eye as on the taste buds.

Westbourne House

65 Westbourne Grove, Westbourne Grove, W2 4UJ (7229 2233/www. westbournehouse.net). Bayswater or Royal Oak tube. **Open** 11am-11.30pm Mon-Thur; 11am-midnight Fri, Sat; noon-10.30pm Sun. **Cocktail bar**.
This big, handsome pub has swapped nicotine stains and pint glasses for shiny surfaces, gilding on the mirrors and faux-French furniture, made all the more twinkly by low lighting and candles. The cocktail list is the work of drinks supremo Mat Perovetz: there are seven 'proper' martinis, spirits are premium and the delivery is pristine.

Shopping

Convenience Store

NEW *1A Hazelwood Tower, Golborne Gardens, Notting Hill, W10 5DT (8968 9095). Westbourne Park tube.* **Open** 10am-6pm Mon-Sat.
The brainchild of designer and consultant Andrew Ibi, the store echoes Ernö Goldfinger's brutalist tower with severe styling (floor-to-ceiling concrete) and stocks limited numbers of pieces from some of today's most progressive womenswear designers, including Rick Owens, Hannah Marshall and Sophie Hulme. Clothes as wearable art.

Ledbury Road

Notting Hill Gate tube or Westbourne Park tube.
This strip of boutiques is shopping cat-nip for west London's yummy mummies. They flock to the likes of chi-chi French fashion store Paul & Joe (nos.39-41, 7243 5510, www.pauland-joe.com), designer jeweller's Ec one (no.56, 7243 8811, www.econe.co.uk) and master chocolatier Keith Hurdman's Melt (no.59, 7727 2348/ www.meltchocolates.com).

Portobello Road Market

Portobello Road, Notting Hill, W10 & W11 (www.rbkc.gov.uk/streettrading). Ladbroke Grove or Notting Hill Gate tube. **Open** 8am-6.30pm Mon-Wed, Fri, Sat; 8am-1pm Thur. *Antiques* 4am-4pm Fri, Sat.
Portobello is super-busy, but fun. Antiques start at the Notting Hill end, further down are food stalls, and emerging designer and vintage clothes congregate under the Westway and along the walkway to Ladbroke Grove on Fridays (usually marginally quieter) and Saturdays (invariably manic). Portobello also has fine shops, such as Honest Jon's 30-year-old record emporium (no.278, 8969 9822, www.honestjons.com) and Jasmine Guinness's hip kids' shop Honeyjam (no.267, 7243 0449, www.honeyjam.co.uk).

Rellik

8 Golborne Road, Ladbroke Grove,
W10 5NW (8962 0089/www.rellik
london.co.uk). Westbourne Park tube.
Open 10am-6pm Tue-Sat.
This celeb fave was set up in 2000 by
three Portobello market stallholders:
Fiona Stuart, Claire Stansfield and
Steven Philip. The trio have different
tastes, which means there's a mix of
pieces by the likes of Halston,
Vivienne Westwood, Bill Gibb,
Christian Dior and the ever-popular
Ossie Clark.

Westfield London

NEW *Shepherd's Bush, W12 7SL*
(www.westfield.com/london). White City
or Wood Lane tube/Shepherd's Bush
tube/rail. **Open** 9am-10pm Mon-Fri;
9am-8pm Sat; noon-6pm Sun.
Occupying 46 acres and nine different
postcodes (above we list the one for
the carpark), Westfield London
opened as Europe's largest urban
shopping centre in autumn 2008. The
impressive site – which held the 1908
Olympics – cost around £1.6bn to
build and houses approaching 300
shops, including popular labels that
have never had stand-alone stores
(Hollister, UGG). You'll also find luxury fashion from Louis Vuitton and
Armani, and innumerable eating and
entertainment options.

Nightlife

Notting Hill Arts Club

21 Notting Hill Gate, Notting Hill, W11
3JQ (7460 4459/www.nottinghillarts
club.com). Notting Hill Gate tube. **Open**
6pm-2am Mon-Fri; 4pm-2am Sat; 4pm-
1am Sun.
Cool west London folk are grateful for
this small, basement club. It isn't
much to look at, but somehow almost
single-handedly keeps this side of
town on the radar thanks to nights
like Thursday's YoYo – for fans of
eclectic crate-digging, from funk to
1980s boogie.

Paradise by Way of Kensal Green

NEW *19 Kilburn Lane, Kensal Green,*
W10 4AE (8969 0098/www.the
paradise.co.uk). Kensal Green tube.
Open noon-midnight Mon-Wed;
noon-1am Thur; noon-2am Fri, Sat;
noon-11.30pm Sun.
The sort of boozer everyone wishes
was on their doorstep. Perfectly decked
out in shabby-chic finds and religious
iconography, it has staff who really
know their way round a bar. The dining room is spacious and airy, with tea-
candles in china tea cups and a
top-notch seasonal British menu; elsewhere there's plenty of space to enjoy
DJ/producer Tayo's eclectic line-ups.

Shepherd's Bush Empire

Shepherd's Bush Green, W12 8TT
(8354 3300/box office 0870 771 2000/
www.shepherds-bush-empire.co.uk).
Shepherd's Bush Market tube/
Shepherd's Bush tube/rail.
This former BBC theatre is a great mid-
sized venue, holding 2,000 standing or
1,300 seated. The sound is decent (with
the exception of the alcove behind the
stalls bar) and the staff are lovely.
Bookings range from Steve Winwood
to the Ting Tings.

Arts & leisure

Lyric Hammersmith

King Street, Hammersmith, W6 0QL
(0871 221 1722/www.lyric.co.uk).
Hammersmith tube.
The Lyric has a knack for vibrant, offbeat scheduling. Outgoing artistic director David Farr's programme last year
ranged from a gala performance of
Pinter's *The Birthday Party* to celebrate
its 50th anniversary, to headphone-
assisted voyeuristic theatre which invit-
ed audience-members to spy on an
S&M-style murder in the tower block
across the square and innovative
theatrical adaptations of classic texts –
among them Tamasha's Bollywood
version of *Wuthering Heights*.

Essentials

York & Albany p209

Hotels

Given general gloom about the recession, London's hotel sector seems surprisingly buoyant. The West End has welcomed **Sanctum** and will soon greet **Dean Street Townhouse**, while redevelopment at Leicester Square promises Britain's first W Hotel (www.starwoodhotels.com) by late 2010. At the top end, huge refurbishment of the **Savoy** should be complete, and the St Pancras Marriott – in the amazing Victorian red-brick edifice that fronts the new Eurostar terminal – could well open in 2010. Mid-range business hotels also seem to be thriving: **Apex** is to have opened two more City hotels by winter 2010, while **Hotel Indigo** has plans for another three London venues by 2012.

The sheer amount of activity is pushing hoteliers into new parts of town – witness the **Bermondsey Square Hotel**, on a new square in a hitherto unfancied patch of south-east London – and driving pleasingly eccentric add-on treats at the likes of Bermondsey Square and Sanctum (see box p199). Pressure may even be beginning to build on prices: the stylish budget category, in which the **Hoxton** has had few credible competitors outside an Earl's Court cadre – **Base2Stay**, the **Mayflower** trio, **Stylotel** – may well be about to get a shake-up. Bermondsey Square's standard rooms start at £119 and we're told attic rooms at the much-anticipated Dean Street will be offered for £85.

One trend we've enjoyed in the last couple of years has been what you might call 'B&B deluxe'. Dean Street and Conran's **Boundary** look likely to become the new leaders of a field that already includes **York & Albany** and the **Fox & Anchor**.

Money matters

When visitors moan about London prices (you know you do), their case

ESSENTIALS

is strongest when it comes to hotels. The average room rate has dipped recently, but we still reckon any decent double averaging under £120 a night is good value: hence, **£** in the listings below represents a rack rate of £100 or less. Hotels do offer special deals, though, notably at weekends; check their websites or ask when you book, and also look at discount websites such as www.london-discount-hotel.com and www.alpharooms.com.

The South Bank

Bermondsey Square Hotel

NEW *Bermondsey Square, Tower Bridge Road, SE1 3UN (0870 111 2525/www.bespokehotels.com). Borough tube/London Bridge tube/rail.* **££**. See box p199.

Park Plaza County Hall

NEW *1 Addington Street, SE1 7RY (7021 1800/www.parkplaza.com). Lambeth North tube.* **££**.
From the tube the approach is rather grimy, but this enthusiastically – if somewhat haphazardly – run new-build is well located just behind County Hall. Each room has its own kitch-enette (microwave, sink), room sizes aren't bad (floor-to-ceiling windows help them feel bigger) and there's a handsomely vertiginous atrium, into which you peer down on the restaurant from infrequent glass lifts. The views from the penthouse terraces are great.

Premier Inn London County Hall

County Hall, Belvedere Road, SE1 7PB (0870 238 3300/www.premiertravelinn.com). Waterloo tube/rail. **£**.
This budget chain hotel is housed in the back of County Hall (p58), slap bang next to the London Eye. There may be queue-control barriers in the too-small lobby, but the somewhat dark rooms are as spacious (and acceptably kitted

SHORTLIST

Best new
- Bermondsey Square Hotel (left)
- Rough Luxe (p204)
- Sanctum (p204)
- York & Albany (p209)

Most exciting prospects
- Boundary (p207)
- Dean Street Townhouse & Dining Room (p203)
- Savoy (p206)

All-round winners
- Covent Garden Hotel (p203)
- One Aldwych (p204)

Best old London atmosphere
- Fox & Anchor (p207)
- Hazlitt's (p203)
- Rookery (p208)

Best bars
- Connaught at the Connaught (p202)
- Lobby Bar at One Aldwych (p204)

Best eats
- Albion at Boundary (p207)
- York & Albany (p209)

Best bargains
- Dean Street Townhouse & Dining Room (p203)
- Fox & Anchor (p207)
- Hoxton Hotel (p208)

Budget style
- B&B Belgravia (p198)
- Bermondsey Square Hotel (left)
- Hoxton Hotel (p208)
- Mayflower Hotel (p209)

Money the only object
- Clink Hostel (p202)
- EasyHotel (p197)

ESSENTIALS

ARRAN HOUSE HOTEL

77-79 Gower Street,
London WC1E 6HJ
tel: 020 7636 2186
fax: 020 7436 5328
email: arran@dircon.co.uk
www.london-hotel.co.uk

**This is a small family run hotel, owned by the same
family for more than 30 years.**
*Our warmth and hospitality has brought back the
same guests over and over again.*

*The building is a 200-year-old Georgian Town House
located in the heart of the Literary Bloomsbury - home
of the University of London. You are within walking distance
of the British Museum, Piccadilly Circus, and Oxford Street
shopping area, cinemas, restaurants and Theatre Land.
To make your stay pleasant and comfortable,
we provide the following:*

- *Full English breakfast • TV Lounge (24 hour, Cable
and Satellite) • Tea and Coffee making facilities*
- *Direct dial Telephones in all rooms • Laundry facilities*
- *Colour TV in all rooms • Rose garden (in the summer!)*
- *Reception opening hours every day 7:00a.m. - 23:00*
- *Kitchen Facilities open until 23:00*
- *Fridge facilities are available to guests*
- *24 Hour Internet facilities*
- *Taxi service • **Wireless Access**
(WiFi compliant) in all rooms*

The hotel is registered and approved by the LONDON TOURIST BOARD

"LET'S GO" – *The Arran House Hotel offers various precious detail
spotless bathrooms and lovely garden.*

out) as many more expensive places. A rolling refurbishment is planned over 2009, but Premier assures us it won't affect the running of the hotel.

Southwark Rose

47 Southwark Bridge Road, SE1 9HH (7015 1480/www.southwarkrosehotel. co.uk). London Bridge tube/rail. **££**.
The five-year-old Rose declares itself as sleekly modern with giant domed brushed aluminium lampshades and smart metal-framed cube chairs in a lobby hung with the work of Japanese photographer Mayumi. The rooms feature the dark woods, panelled headboards and crisp white linens of most 'contemporary' London hotels – but hey, who's knocking it? Fully wired up, there are even electric blackout blinds.

Westminster & St James's

City Inn Westminster

30 John Islip Street, Westminster, SW1P 4DD (7630 1000/www.cityinn. com). Pimlico tube. **££**.
There's nothing particularly flashy about this chain, but it is neatly designed, well run and obliging: the rooms have all the added extras you'd want (iMacs, CD/DVD library for your in-room player, free broadband, flatscreen TVs) and the floor-to-ceiling windows mean that river-facing suites on the 12th and 13th floors have superb night views – when the businessmen go home for the weekend you might grab one for £125.

EasyHotel

36-40 Belgrave Road, Westminster, SW1V 1RG (www.easyhotel.com). Pimlico tube/Victoria tube/rail. **£**.
The budget airline no-frills approach has been applied to this mini-chain of five London hotels. Rooms come in three sizes – small, really small and tiny – the last of which feels like it's the width of the bed. Rooms come with a bed and

pre-fab bathroom unit (toilet, sink and showerhead almost on top of the sink), with no wardrobe or breakfast. Want a window? Pay extra. TV? £5, please.

Haymarket Hotel

1 Suffolk Place, St James's, SW1Y 4BP (7470 4000/www.firmdale.com). Piccadilly Circus tube. **££££**.
This is the most recent London opening from Kit Kemp's exemplary Firmdale group. The block-size building was designed by John Nash, architect of Regency London, and it is a pleasure simply to inhabit spaces he created, one that Kemp's sinuous sculptures, fuschia paint and shiny sofas manage to enhance. Wow-factors are the bling basement swimming pool and bar (shiny sofas, twinkly roof) and couldn't-be-more central location. The well-equipped rooms are generously sized and there's plenty of attention from switched-on staff.

Trafalgar

2 Spring Gardens, Westminster, SW1A 2TS (7870 2900/www.thetrafalgar. com). Charing Cross tube/rail. **£££**.
In an imposing building, the Trafalgar is a Hilton – but you'd hardly notice. The mood is young and dynamic at what was the chain's first 'concept' hotel. To the right of the open reception is the cocktail bar, with DJs most nights, while breakfast downstairs is accompanied by gentle live music. The good-sized rooms (a few corner suites look into Trafalgar Square) have a masculine feel, with white walls and walnut furniture.

Windermere Hotel

142-144 Warwick Way, Westminster, SW1V 4JE (7834 5163/www. windermere-hotel.co.uk). Victoria tube/rail. **££**.
Heading into a procession of small hotels, the Windermere is a comfortable, traditionally decked-out London hotel with no aspirations to boutique status. The decor may be showing its age a bit

ESSENTIALS

Connaught p202

in the hall, but you'll receive a warm welcome and excellent service – there are over a dozen staff for just 20 rooms.

South Kensington & Chelsea

Aster House

3 Sumner Place, South Kensington, SW7 3EE (7581 5888/www.asterhouse. com). South Kensington tube. **££**.
On a swish, white-terraced street, the Aster triumphs through great attention to detail (impeccable housekeeping, the mobile phone guests can borrow) and the warmth of its managers, Leona and Simon Tan. It's all low-key, comfortably soothing creams with touches of dusty rose and muted green. Breakfast in a lovely plant-filled conservatory.

B+B Belgravia

64-66 Ebury Street, Belgravia, SW1W 9QD (7823 4928/www.bb-belgravia. com). Victoria tube/rail. **£**.

B+B Belgravia have taken the B&B experience to a new level, although you pay a bit more for the privilege of staying somewhere with a cosy lounge that's full of white and black contemporary furnishings. It's fresh and sophisticated without being hard-edged. And there are all kinds of goodies to make you feel at home: an espresso machine for 24/7 caffeine, an open fireplace, newspapers and DVDs.

Blakes

33 Roland Gardens, South Kensington, SW7 3PF (7370 6701/www.blakes hotels.com). South Kensington tube. **££££**.
As original as when Anouska Hempel opened it in 1983 – the scent of oranges and the twittering of lovebirds fill the dark, oriental lobby – Blakes and its maximalist decor have stood the test of time, a living casebook for interior design students. Each room is in a different style, with antiques from Italy, India, Turkey and China. Downstairs

ESSENTIALS

is the Eastern-influenced restaurant, complemented by a gym and wireless internet for a celebrity clientele enticed by the discreet, residential location.

Gore

190 Queen's Gate, South Kensington, SW7 5EX (7584 6601/www.gorehotel. com). South Kensington tube. **££££.**
This fin-de-siècle period piece was founded by descendants of Captain Cook in two grand Victorian town houses. The lobby and staircase are close hung with old paintings, and the bedrooms all have carved oak beds, sumptuous drapes and shelves of old books. The suites are spectacular: the Tudor Room has a huge stone-faced fireplace and a minstrels' gallery, while tragedy queens should plump for the Venus room and Judy Garland's old bed (and replica ruby slippers).

Halkin

Halkin Street, Belgravia, SW1X 7DJ (7333 1000/www.halkin.como.bz). Hyde Park Corner tube. **££££.**
Gracious and discreet behind a Georgian-style façade, Christina Ong's first hotel (sister to the more famous Metropolitan) was ahead of the East-meets-West design trend when it opened in 1991 and its subtle marriage of European luxury and oriental serenity looks more current than hotels half its age. Off curving black corridors, each room has a touchscreen bedside console to control everything from the 'do not disturb' sign to the air-con.

Lanesborough

1 Lanesborough Place, Knightsbridge, SW1X 7TA (7259 5599/www. lanesborough.com). Hyde Park Corner tube. **££££.**
Considered one of London's more historic luxury hotels, the Lanesborough was in fact impressively redeveloped only in the 1990s. Occupying an 1820s Greek Revival hospital building, its luxurious guest rooms are traditionally decorated (antique furniture, Carrera-

The rock 'n' roll years

If you want a new hotel to stand out, let it rock!

Has London been falling behind its quota for televisions thrown through hotel windows? That might be the thinking behind a pair of rock-flavoured spring 2009 hotel openings.
Bermondsey Square Hotel (p195) is a deliberately kitsch 79-room new-build on a newly developed square at the bottom of hip Bermondsey Street. Suites are named after the heroines of psychedelic rock classics (Lucy, Lily and so on) and there are classic discs on the walls. **Sanctum** (p204), in a former MI5 research building, is Soho club cool with its dark colours, bling room handles, deco lamps, handful of rotating beds, no-questions-asked policy and 24hr-means-24hr bar.

There some similarities – the multi-person jacuzzi (on the roof and open to all residents at Sanctum; with a great terrace view but only available to the occupants of the Lucy suite at Bermondsey Square), sex toys from reception, a Brit food restaurant-bar on the ground-floor, pretty staff who seem to enjoy their work – and a central perception is shared by both: hotels needn't be boring, they can be fun… and a bit naughty. Whether you want your guitar tuned at Sanctum, or just to kick your heels from the suspended Bubble Chair in Bermondsey Square, you'll surely appreciate their sense of humour.

ESSENTIALS

marble bathrooms) but with electronic keypads to change the air-conditioning or call on the superb 24hr room service. Rates include high-speed internet, movies and calls within the EU and to the USA; complimentary personalised business cards are offered that state you are resident here.

Meininger

Baden-Powell House, 65-67 Queen's Gate, South Kensington, SW7 5JS (7590 6910/www.meininger-hostels. com). Gloucester Road or South Kensington tube. **£**.

This German hostel chain now runs the accommodation part of the Scout Association's London HQ. It's a classy early 1960s building beside the Natural History Museum (p85). All the public spaces, bedrooms and dorms are spacious and light-filled, with en suite bathing facilities, individual reading lights, free wireless internet and flatscreen TVs in all rooms. Traffic noise might be a problem in some rooms.

Morgan House

120 Ebury Street, Belgravia, SW1W 9QQ (7730 2384/www.morganhouse. co.uk). Pimlico tube/Victoria tube/rail. **£**.

The Morgan has the understated charm of the old family home of a posh but unpretentious English friend: a pleasing mix of nice old wooden or traditional iron beds, pretty floral curtains and coverlets in subtle hues, the odd chandelier or big gilt mirror over original mantelpieces, padded wicker chairs and sinks in every bedroom. Though there's no guest lounge, guests can sit in the little patio garden.

Myhotel Chelsea

35 Ixworth Place, Chelsea, SW3 3QX (7225 7500/www.myhotels.com). South Kensington tube. **£££**.

The Chelsea Myhotel feels a world away from its sleekly modern Bloomsbury predecessor (11-13 Bayley Street, 7667 6000, www.myhotels.co.uk), its aesthetic softer and more feminine. Pink walls,

a floral sofa and a plate of scones in the lobby offer a posh English foil to the mini-chain's signature feng shui touches and aquarium. The modernised country farmhouse feel of the bar-restaurant works better for breakfast than for a boozy cocktail, but the conservatory-style library is wonderful.

Number Sixteen

16 Sumner Place, South Kensington, SW7 3EG (7589 5232/www.firmdale. com). South Kensington tube. **£££**.

This may be Firmdale's most affordable hotel, but there's no slacking in style – witness the fresh flowers and origami-ed birdbook decorations in the ultra-comfy drawing room. Bedrooms are generously sized, bright and very light, and carry the Kit Kemp trademark mix of bold and traditional. By the time you finish breakfast in the sweet conservatory, looking out on the delicious, large back garden with its central water feature, you'll have forgotten you're in the city.

Vicarage Hotel

10 Vicarage Gate, Kensington, W8 4AG (7229 4030/www.londonvicarage hotel.com). High Street Kensington or Notting Hill Gate tube. **£**.

Devotees return regularly to this tall Victorian town house, tucked in a leafy square by Kensington Gardens (p85). It's comfortable and resolutely old-fashioned. There's a grand entrance hall with red and gold striped wallpaper, a chandelier and a huge gilt mirror, as well as a sweeping staircase that ascends to an assortment of good-sized rooms furnished in pale florals and nice old pieces of furniture.

West End

Academy Hotel

21 Gower Street, Bloomsbury, WC1E 6HG (7631 4115/www.the etoncollection.com). Goodge Street tube. **£££**.

ESSENTIALS

Comprising five Georgian town houses, the Academy has a restrained country-house style – decor in most rooms is soft, summery florals and checks; the eight suites look more sophisticated. Guests are cocooned from the busy streets and those in the split-level doubles get plenty of breathing space at decent rates. The library and conservatory open on to walled gardens where drinks and breakfast are served in summer.

Arosfa

83 Gower Street, Bloomsbury, WC1E 6HJ (7636 2115/www.arosfalondon. com). Goodge Street tube. **£**.

A change of owner and the Arosfa's gone from spartan to Manhattan. Yes, those are Phillippe Starck Ghost chairs in the lounge, alongside the mirrored chests and black-and-white photo of New York. The rest of the hotel is more restrained: cappuccino-tinted walls hung with architectural engravings in the halls, neutrally decorated bedrooms. Bathroom units are a bit cramped.

Charlotte Street Hotel

15-17 Charlotte Street, Fitzrovia, W1T 1RJ (7806 2000/www.firmdale.com). Goodge Street or Tottenham Court Road tube. **££££**.

This gorgeous Firmdale hotel is a fine exponent of Kit Kemp's fusion of traditional and avant-garde – you won't believe it was once a dental hospital. Public rooms contain Bloomsbury Set paintings (Duncan Grant, Vanessa Bell), while the bedrooms mix English understatement with bold decorative flourishes. The huge beds and trademark polished granite bathrooms are suitably indulgent, and some rooms have unbelievably high ceilings. The bar-restaurant buzzes with media types, for whom the screening room must feel like a home comfort.

Claridge's

55 Brook Street, Mayfair, W1K 4HR (7629 8860/www.claridges.co.uk). Bond Street tube. **££££**.

Claridge's is sheer class and pure atmosphere, its signature art deco redesign still dazzling. Photographs of Churchill and sundry royals grace the grand foyer, as does an absurdly over-the-top Dale Chihuly chandelier. Without departing too far from the traditional, Claridge's bars and restaurant are actively fashionable – Gordon Ramsay is the in-house restaurateur, and the A-listers can gather for champers and sashimi in the bar. The rooms divide evenly between deco and Victorian style, with period touches balanced by high-tech bedside panels.

Clink Hostel

78 King's Cross Road, King's Cross, WC1X 9QG (7183 9400/www.clink hostel.com). King's Cross tube/rail. **£**.

In a former courthouse, the Clink sets the bar high for hosteldom. There's the setting: the original wood-panelled lobby and courtroom where the Clash stood before the beak (now filled with backpackers surfing the web). Then there's the urban chic ethos that permeates the enterprise, from the streamlined red reception counter to the dining area's chunky wooden tables and Japanese-style 'pod' beds. Clink's cosier elder sister, Ashlee House (261-265 Gray's Inn Road, 7833 9400, www.ashleehouse.co.uk) is nearby.

Connaught

Carlos Place, Mayfair, W1K 2AL (7499 7070/www.the-connaught.co.uk). Bond Street tube. **££££**.

The Connaught isn't the only London hotel to provide butlers, but there can't be many with 'a secured gun cabinet room' for hunting season. Too lazy to polish your shoes? The butlers are trained in shoe care by expert cobblers. This is traditional British hospitality for those who love 23-carat gold leaf and stern portraits in the halls, but all mod cons in their room. Both bars (p108) and the sumptuous Hélène Darroze restaurant are magnificent. A new wing should be open this year.

Covent Garden Hotel

*10 Monmouth Street, Covent Garden,
WC2H 9LF (7806 1000/www.firmdale.
com). Covent Garden or Leicester
Square tube.* **££££**.

On the ground floor, the 1920s Paris-style Brasserie Max and its retro zinc bar have been cunningly expanded – testament to the continuing popularity of Firmdale's snug and stylish 1996 establishment. Its location and tucked-away screening room ensure it continues to attract starry customers, and guests needing a bit of privacy can retreat upstairs to the lovely panelled private library. In the individually styled guest rooms, pinstriped wallpaper and floral upholstery are mixed with bold, contemporary elements.

Cumberland

*Great Cumberland Place, Marylebone,
W1H 7DL (0870 333 9280/www.
guoman.com). Marble Arch tube.* **££**.

Perfectly located (turn the right way out of Marble Arch tube and you're there in seconds), the Cumberland is a monster. There are 900 rooms, plus 119 in an annexe, and an echoing, chaotic lobby with dramatic modern art and a waterfall sculpture. The rather small rooms are minimalist and nicely designed (acid-etched headboards, neatly modern bathrooms, plasma TVs). Dine at exclusive Rhodes W1 (7616 5930, www.rhodesw1.com) or the bar-brasserie, or brave the late-night, trash-industrial-style DJ bar.

Dorchester

*53 Park Lane, Mayfair, W1K 1QA
(7629 8888/www.thedorchester.com).
Hyde Park Corner tube.* **££££**.

A Park Lane fixture since 1931: the view over Hyde Park from the expansive terrace is the same one Elizabeth Taylor would have seen when she took the call for *Cleopatra*. And the 49 other suites? Eisenhower planned the D-Day landings in one and Prince Philip held his stag do in another. This opulence is reflected in the grandest lobby in town,

with – yes – Liberace's piano. The rooms? Floral decor, antiques and lavish marble bathrooms. Service? Let's just say there are 90 full-time chefs.

Dean Street Townhouse & Dining Room

NEW *69 Dean Street, Soho, W1D 3SE
(www.sohohouse.com). Leicester Square
or Piccadilly Circus tube.* **££**.

Due to open in October 2009, Dean Street is the latest enterprise from the people behind Soho House members' club – and we're excited. Above a ground-floor dining room that will serve classic English food, four floors run from early Georgian panelling and reclaimed oak floors up to tiny half-panelled attic rooms. You can expect 24hr service and all modern comforts (rainforest showers, up-to-the-minute music systems and flatscreens); room prices starting from an eminently reasonable £85 are more of a surprise.

Harlingford Hotel

*61-63 Cartwright Gardens,
Bloomsbury, WC1H 9EL (7387 1551/
www.harlingfordhotel.com). Russell
Square tube/Euston tube/rail.* **££**.

It's very leafy, very Bloomsbury here, on a graceful Georgian crescent of B&Bs. Despite pretty reasonable room rates, the Harlingford has boutique hotel aspirations, leaving other contenders on the block far behind. A stylish redesign has produced light airy rooms with splashes of turquoise and purple – there's even a Harlingford logo. You can lob a tennis ball in the crescent's private garden or just dream under the trees on a summer's night.

Hazlitt's

*6 Frith Street, Soho, W1D 3JA
(7434 1771/www.hazlittshotel.com).
Tottenham Court Road tube.* **£££**.

Three Georgian town houses have become a charming hotel, named after William Hazlitt, a spirited 18th-century essayist who died in abject poverty here. The rooms have fireplaces, superb wooden four-posters and half-testers, free-standing bathtubs and cast-iron Shanks toilet cisterns, but air-conditioning, TVs in antique cupboards and triple-glazed windows are standard too. It gets creakier and more crooked the higher you go, culminating in enchanting garret single rooms.

Montagu Place

2 Montagu Place, Marylebone, W1H 2ER (7467 2777/www.montagu-place. co.uk). Baker Street tube. **£££**.
A stylish, small hotel in a pair of Grade II-listed Georgian town houses, catering primarily for the midweek business traveller. All rooms have pocket-sprung beds, as well as cafetières and flatscreen TVs (DVD players are available from reception). The look is boutique-hotel sharp, except for an uneasy overlap of bar and reception – though you can simply get a drink and retire to the graciously modern lounge.

Morgan

24 Bloomsbury Street, Bloomsbury, WC1B 3QJ (7636 3735/www.morgan hotel.co.uk). Tottenham Court Road tube. **£**.
Run by the same family since 1978, this comfortable budget hotel has guestrooms with a distinctly 1970s air – those nifty headboards with the built-in bedside tables and reading lamps, the gathered floral bedspreads. Still, they're well equipped, right down to wireless internet and voicemail. The cosy room where breakfast is served is a charmer with its wood panelling, London prints and china plates.

No.5 Maddox Street

5 Maddox Street, Mayfair, W1S 2QD (7647 0200/www.living-rooms.co.uk). Oxford Circus tube. **££££**.
A bit different, this: for your money, you get a chic, self-contained apartment. Shut the discreet brown front door, climb the stairs and flop into a well-furnished home from home with all mod cons, including new flatscreen

TVs. Each apartment has a fully equipped kitchen, but room service will shop for you in addition to the usual hotel services. The East-meets-West decor is classic 1990s minimalist, but bright and clean after refurbishment.

One Aldwych

The Strand, WC2B 4RH (7300 1000/ www.onealdwych.com). Covent Garden or Temple tube/Charing Cross tube/rail. **££££**.
You only have to push through the front door and enter the breathtaking Lobby Bar (p156) to know you're in for a treat. Despite weighty history – the 1907 building was designed by the men behind the Ritz – One Aldwych is thoroughly modern, from Frette linen through bathroom mini-TVs to environmentally friendly loo flushes. The location is perfect for Theatreland, but the cosy screening room and swimming pool may keep you indoors.

Piccadilly Backpackers

12 Sherwood Street, Soho, W1F 7BR (7434 9009/www.piccadillybackpackers. com). Piccadilly Circus tube. **£**.
Want to be at the centre of things? You couldn't be more so than at this enormous hostel plonked right behind Piccadilly Circus. The almost invisible entrance gives way to several floors of accommodation and facilities like a travel shop, laundry, internet café and TV lounge. Sure, it's basic, but it's relaxed, bright and airy. Try for the third floor – here's where you'll find dorms of pod beds quirkily decorated by graphic art students.

Rough Luxe

NEW *1 Birkenhead Street, King's Cross, WC1H 8BA (7837 5338/ www.roughluxe.co.uk). King's Cross tube/rail.* **£££**.
See box opposite.

Sanctum Hotel

NEW *20 Warwick Street, Soho, W1B 5NF (7292 6100/www.sanctumsoho.*

The rough and the smooth

A new concept in interior design.

We've seen the sleekly modern minimalists and grandly baroque maximalists, we've had an excess of East-meets-West fusion and are now facing as much Brit retro as London's second-hand shops can supply, but the latest in hotel design chic is – in the owners' words – **Rough Luxe** (opposite).

In an area choked with all the ratty B&Bs and cheap chains you'd expect near a train terminus as significant as King's Cross, Rough Luxe hotel is something new. This is a Grade II-listed property whose designer, Rabih Hage, has left walls distressed and wallpaper torn. He's even left up the sign for the hotel that preceded Rough Luxe: 'Number One Hotel'.

The style isn't quite unique – some will point to *Vanity Fair* editor-in-chief Graydon Carter's New York restaurant the Waverly Inn, others to the same city's ultra-hip Ace Hotel – but Rough Luxe is an interesting reversal of the hotel norm. The decor is

intended to signal that you are in someone's house, rather than impersonally bland or overstyled accommodation.

The nine rooms start from £155. Some have shared bathrooms, some rooms are without TVs – but then the owners are happy to entertain: 'If you are stuck for something to do in the evening, let us know and you can either eat with us or we can go out and grab a bite.' Each room has free wireless internet, but are otherwise very different: one has a free-standing copper tub, there are various pictures and works of art (including a Gilbert & George). Above all, great care has gone into preserving and revealing the character of previous incarnations of the house itself. If there are no room vacancies, book ahead on 7837 5338 for a luxury afternoon tea (3.30-5.30pm daily, £30) – and nibble cakes made 'just for you' while admiring the trompe l'oeil bookshelves and Daniel Baker's 'This is Shit' artwork.

Hoxton Hotel p208

com). Oxford Circus or Piccadilly Circus tube. **£££**.
See box p199.

Sanderson

50 Berners Street, Fitzrovia, W1T 3NG (7300 1400/www.morganshotelgroup. com). Oxford Circus tube. **££££**.
This Schrager/Starck statement creation takes clinical chic to new heights. The only touch of colour in our room was a naïve landscape painting nailed to the ceiling over the silver sleigh bed. Otherwise, it's all flowing white net drapes, glass cabinets and retractable screens. The residents-only Purple Bar sports a button-backed purple leather ceiling and fabulous cocktails; the 'billiard room' has a purple-topped pool table and weird tribal adaptations of classic dining room furniture.

Savoy

NEW *Strand, Covent Garden, WC2R 0EU (7836 4343/www.fairmont.com). Covent Garden or Embankment tube/ Charing Cross tube/rail.* **££££**.

Built in 1889, the Savoy is where Vivien Leigh met Laurence Olivier, Monet painted the Thames and Londoners learned to love the martini. Its discreet mix of neo-classical and art deco has undergone £100m of renovations; check www.savoy2009.com for the latest. An impressive £2.5m is being dropped on the fifth-floor Royal Suite, while the famous front entrance cul-de-sac gets new topiary and a Lalique crystal fountain. The Savoy Grill, American Bar and rooftop swimming pool return barely changed.

Sherlock Holmes Hotel

108 Baker Street, Marylebone, W1U 6LJ (7486 6161/www.sherlockholmes hotel.com). Baker Street tube. **££**.
Park Plaza transformed a dreary Hilton into this hip boutique hotel a few years back. Guests now mingle with local office workers in the casually chic bar (extending to a lounge in the style of a glossed-up gentlemen's club) and organic restaurant. The bedrooms resemble hip bachelor pads: beige and

brown colour scheme, leather head-boards and spiffy bathrooms. Split-level 'loft' suites take advantage of the first floor's double-height ceilings, and there's a gym with sauna.

22 York Street

22 York Street, Marylebone, W1U 6PX (7224 2990/www.22yorkstreet.co.uk). Baker Street tube. **£**.
Imagine one of those bohemian French country houses in *Elle Décoration* – all pale pink lime-washed walls, wooden floors and quirky antiques. That's the feel of this graceful, unpretentious bed and breakfast. There's no sign on the door and the sense of staying in a hospitable home continues when you're offered coffee in the spacious breakfast room-cum-kitchen with its curved communal table. Many of the rooms have en suite baths.

Weardowney Guesthouse

9 Ashbridge Street, Marylebone, NW8 8DH (7725 9694/www.weardowney. com). Marylebone tube/rail. **£**.
This 'artisan guesthouse' (thus named by its owners, knitwear designers Amy Wear and Gail Downey) is a charming place in a quiet backwater. It's just seven rooms above their corner boutique in an early Victorian house. Only three are en suite – but there are two bathrooms for the others to share. The decor is an appealing mix of handknit bedspreads, antiques, art and photos. There's also a pretty roof terrace.

The City

Andaz Liverpool Street

40 Liverpool Street, the City, EC2M 7QN (7961 1234/www.london.liverpool street.andaz.com). Liverpool Street tube/rail. **££££**.
A faded railway hotel until its £70m Conran overhaul in 2000, the Great Eastern became in 2007 the first of Hyatt's new Andaz portfolio. So it's out with closet-sized minibars and even the

lobby reception desk, and in with eco-friendliness and down-to-earth, well-informed service. The bedrooms still wear style-mag uniform – Eames chairs, Frette linens – but free services (breakfast, local calls, movies, internet, healthy minibar, laundry) and savvy efforts to connect with arty locals are appreciated. Check out the hotel's splendid little Freemasons' Temple too.

Apex City of London Hotel

1 Seething Lane, the City, EC3N 4AX (7702 2020/www.apexhotels.co.uk). Tower Hill tube. **££**.
Part of a small chain (with two new City outposts due over the coming year), this sleek, modern business hotel has built a sturdy reputation. The public areas, including a ground-floor restaurant down from the reception area at the front, are nothing special, but staff members are accommodating, room details are obliging (free Wi-Fi, pillow menu, rubber duck in the bathroom) and the location – right by the Tower of London – is terrific.

Boundary

NEW *2-4 Boundary Street, Shoreditch, E2 7JE (7729 1051/www.theboundary. co.uk). Liverpool Street tube/rail or 8, 26, 48 bus.* **£££**.
This is Sir Terence Conran's latest project, four individual businesses in a converted warehouse. The restaurants and café are already open (p164), with the 17 bedrooms due to follow shortly after we went to press. Each has a wet room and hand-made bed, but are otherwise individually designed and contain original art. We're already in the queue for the grand opening.

Fox & Anchor

115 Charterhouse Street, Clerkenwell, EC1M 6AA (0845 347 0100/www.fox andanchor.com). Barbican tube/ Farringdon tube/rail. **££**.
No more than a few atmospheric, well-appointed and luxurious rooms above a bustling, darkly panelled pub, this was

one of our most enjoyable stays of 2008. Each en suite room differs, but the high-spec facilities (big flatscreens, clawfoot bath, drench shower) and quirky attention to detail (bottles of ale in the mini-bar, 'Nursing hangover' signs to hang out if you want some privacy) are common throughout. Expect some clanking market noise in the early mornings.

Hoxton Hotel
81 Great Eastern Street, Shoreditch, EC2A 3HU (7550 1000/www.hoxton hotels.com). Old Street tube/rail. £.
Everything you've heard is true. First, there's the hip location. Then there are the great design values: the foyer is a sort of postmodern country lodge (with stag's head) and rooms that are small but well thought out and full of nice touches (Frette linens, free fresh milk in the mini-fridge). Above all, it's the budget-airline pricing system, by which early birds might even catch one of those publicity-garnering £1-a-night room.

Malmaison
Charterhouse Square, Clerkenwell, EC1M 6AH (7012 3700/www. malmaison.com). Barbican tube/ Farringdon tube/rail. £££.
It's part of a chain, but the Malmaison is a charming hotel, beautifully set in a cobblestone square near the lively restaurants and bars of Smithfield Market. The reception is stylish with its lilac and cream checked floor, exotic plants and petite champagne bar, while purples, dove-grey and black wood dominate the rooms, where there's free broadband and creative lighting. The gym and a subterranean brasserie complete the picture.

Rookery
12 Peter's Lane, Cowcross Street, Clerkenwell, EC1M 6DS (7336 0931/ www.rookeryhotel.com). Farringdon tube/rail. £££.
The front door of the Rookery is satisfyingly hard to find, especially when the streets are teeming with Fabric (p160)

devotees (the front rooms can be noisy on these nights). Once inside, guests enjoy a warren of creaky rooms, individually decorated in the style of a Georgian town house: clawfoot baths, elegant four-posters. The split-level Rook's Nest suite has views of St Paul's (p162).

Zetter
86-88 Clerkenwell Road, Clerkenwell, EC1M 5RJ (7324 4444/www.thezetter. com). Farringdon tube/rail. £££.
Zetter is a fun, laid-back, modern hotel. There's a refreshing lack of attitude – the polyglot staff clearly enjoy their job. The rooms, stacked up on five galleried storeys overlooking the intimate bar area, are sleek and functional, but cosied up with choice home comforts like hot-water bottles and old Penguin paperbacks. The picture windows in the restaurant make for good people-watching over breakfast, and top-floor suites have great rooftop views.

Neighbourhood London

Base2Stay
25 Courtfield Gardens, Earl's Court, SW5 0PG (0845 262 8000/www.base2 stay.com). Earl's Court tube. ££.
Base2Stay looks good, with modernist limestone and taupe tones, and keeps prices low by removing inessentials: no bar, no restaurant. Instead, there's a 'kitchenette' (microwave, sink, silent mini-fridge, kettle) in each room, with details properly attended to – proper cutlery, as well as a corkscrew and can opener. The rooms, en suite (with power showers) and air-conditioned, are carefully thought out, with desks, modem points and flatscreens, but the single/bunkbed rooms are small.

Hotel Indigo
NEW *16 London Street, Paddington, W2 1HL (7706 4444/www.hi paddington.com). Paddington tube/rail. ££.*

The first of four London boutique properties from the people behind Crowne Plaza and Holiday Inn has a relaxed all-day bar-restaurant, sharp-witted and friendly staff, and rooms with all mod cons (excellent walk-in showers rather than baths). But the decor is a bit try-hard: a clinical white foyer gives on to acid-bright striped carpets, wardrobe interiors are an assault by psychedelic swirl. Photos of Paddington past and ingenious ceiling strips of sky show how less could have been more. The smaller, cheaper attic rooms have most character.

Mayflower Hotel

26-28 Trebovir Road, Earl's Court, SW5 9NJ (7370 0991/www.mayflower-group.co.uk). Earl's Court tube. £.
The Mayflower Group – the other properties are New Linden (59 Leinster Square, Bayswater, 7221 4321, www.newlinden.co.uk) and Twenty Nevern (20 Nevern Square, Earl's Court, 7565 9555, www.twentynevernsquare.co.uk) – has been leading the budget style revolution for years, but here's where the lushly contemporary house style evolved, proving affordability can be opulently chic and perfectly equipped. Cream walls and sleek dark woods are an understated background for richly coloured fabrics and intricate wooden architectural fragments, like the lobby's imposing Jaipuri arch.

Pavilion

34-36 Sussex Gardens, Paddington, W2 1UL (7262 0905/www.pavilion hoteluk.com). Edgware Road tube/ Marylebone or Paddington tube/rail. £.
Behind a deceptively modest façade is what could be the city's funkiest, most original hotel. A voluptuously exotic paean to excess and paint effects, the Pavilion's madly colourful themed rooms ('Highland Fling', 'Afro Honky Tonk', 'Casablanca Nights') have become a celeb-magnet and are often used for fashion shoots. Not for lovers of minimalism and 'facilities' – though it's got most of the usual necessities.

Rockwell

181-183 Cromwell Road, Earl's Court, SW5 0SF (7244 2000/www.therockwell. com). Earl's Court tube. ££.
The Rockwell aims for relaxed contemporary elegance – and succeeds magnificently. There are no identikit rooms here: they're all individually designed with gleaming woods and glowing colours alongside creams and neutrals. Each has a power shower, Starck fittings and bespoke cabinets in the bathrooms. Garden rooms have tiny patios, complete with garden furniture.

Stylotel

160-162 Sussex Gardens, Paddington, W2 1UD (7723 1026/www.stylotel. com). Paddington tube/rail. £.
Stylotel is a retro-futurist dream: metal floors and panelling, lots of royal blue (the hall walls, the padded headboards) and pod bathrooms. But the real deal is its new bargain-priced studio and apartment (respectively, £120-£150 and £150-£200, including breakfast), designed – like the hotel – by the owner's son. These achieve real minimalist chic with sleek brushed steel or white glass wall panels and simply styled contemporary furniture upholstered in black or white.

York & Albany

NEW *127-129 Parkway, Camden, NW1 7PS (7387 5700/www.gordon ramsay.com). Camden Town tube. £££.*
Chef Gordon Ramsay has ventured into hotels – and has a success on his hands. Housed in a grand old John Nash building that was designed as a coaching house but spent the recent past as a pub, the York & Albany consists of a fine downstairs restaurant, bar and delicatessen, with ten handsome rooms, in pleasingly mellow shades, above. The decor is an effective mix of ancient and modern, sturdy and quietly charismatic furniture married to modern technology; if you're lucky, you'll have views of Regent's Park.

ESSENTIALS

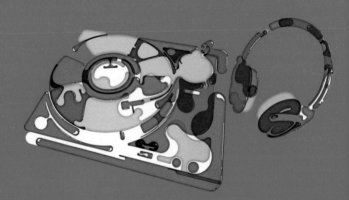

Ask New York City about New York City all night

nycgo.com

Getting Around

Airports

Gatwick Airport
0870 000 2468/www.gatwickairport.com. About 30 miles south of central London, off the M23.

The quickest rail link between Gatwick and London is the **Gatwick Express** (0845 850 1530, www.gatwickexpress.co.uk) to Victoria, which takes about 30mins and runs 3.30am-12.30am daily from London, 4.35am-1.35am daily from Gatwick. Tickets cost £16.90 single.

Southern (0845 127 2920, www.southernrailway.com) also runs a rail service between Gatwick and Victoria, with three trains an hour during the day and an hourly service through the night. It takes about 35mins, at £10.90 single, £9.20 day return (after 9.30am).

If you're staying near King's Cross, consider First Capital Connect's **Thameslink** service (0845 026 4700, www.firstcapitalconnect.co.uk) via London Bridge, Blackfriars, Farringdon and St Pancras International; journey times vary, but there are four trains an hour (an hourly service through the night). Tickets cost from £8.90 single.

Dot2Dot offers a shuttle bus service (0845 368 2368, www.dot2.com) for from £19 each way. A **taxi** costs about £100 and takes ages.

Heathrow Airport
0870 000 0123/www.heathrowairport.com. About 20 miles west of central London, off the M4.

The **Heathrow Express** (0845 600 1515, www.heathrowexpress.com) runs to Paddington every 15mins (5.10am-11.25pm daily), and takes 15-20mins. The train can be boarded at either of the airport's two tube stations. Tickets cost £16.50 single.

A longer (50-60mins) but cheaper journey is by **tube**. Tickets for the Piccadilly line ride into central London cost £4 one way. Trains run every few minutes, 5am-12.30am daily (7.30am-10.30pm Sun).

The **Heathrow Connect** (0845 678 6975, www.heathrowconnect.com) gives direct access to Heathrow Airport from various stations, including Ealing Broadway and Paddington. Trains run every half-hour, taking about 25mins. It serves Terminals 1, 2, 3 and 4, as well as direct from Paddington to the new Terminal 5. Ticket prices vary depending on which station you board at; a single from Paddington costs £6.90.

National Express (0870 574 7777, www.nationalexpress.com) runs daily coach services to London Victoria, leaving Heathrow Central bus terminal every 20mins. For a 35-60min journey to London, expect to pay £4.50 single.

As at Gatwick, **Dot2Dot** (above) offers an airport-to-hotel shuttle service. A **taxi** into town will cost roughly £100 and will take an hour or more.

London City Airport
7646 0088/www.londoncityairport.com. About seven miles east of the City.

The **Docklands Light Railway** (DLR) has a dedicated stop for City Airport. The journey to Bank takes 22mins, and trains run 5.28am-12.20am Mon-Fri or 7am-11.30pm Sun. A **taxi** costs around £30 to central London, less to the City or to Canary Wharf.

Luton Airport
01582 405100/www.london-luton.co.uk. About 30 miles north of central London, J10 off the M1.

Luton Airport Parkway Station is linked to the airport by a short shuttle-bus ride, costing £1 each way. The **Thameslink** (above) calls at many stations (London Bridge, Farringdon and City among them); journey time is from 35mins, leaving every 10mins and costing £11 one-way. **Trains**

from Luton to St Pancras International run hourly through the night, but with no service 1-3am. The Luton to Victoria journey takes 60-90mins by coach. **Green Line** (0870 608 7261, www. greenline. co.uk) runs a 24hr service every 30mins at peak times. A single is £13.50. A **taxi** costs £50 or more.

Stansted Airport

0870 000 0303/www.stanstedairport. com. About 35 miles north-east of central London, J8 off the M11.

The quickest way to get to London is the **Stansted Express** (0845 600 7245) to Liverpool Street; journey time is from 40mins, and trains leave every 15-45mins, 5.30am-12.30am. Tickets cost £17 single. **National Express East Anglia** (0845 600 7245, www. nationalexpresseastanglia.com) is one of several coach services. It runs to Victoria hourly off-peak, with no service on Sundays; a single costs around £10. A **taxi** will cost about £80.

Arriving by coach

National Express coaches (0871 781 8181, www.nationalexpress.com), the biggest coach company in the UK, arrive at **Victoria Coach Station** (164 Buckingham Palace Road, SW1W 9TP, 7730 3466, www.tfl.gov.uk).

Arriving by rail

Eurostar trains from mainland Europe (0870 518 6186, www.eurostar.com) arrive at **St Pancras International** (Pancras Road, King's Cross, NW1 2QP, www.stpancras.com).

Mainline stations

For information on train times and ticket prices, call 0845 748 4950 or go to www.nationalrail.co.uk. You can get timetable and price information, and buy tickets, for any train operator in the UK via www.thetrainline.com. All London's major rail stations are served by the tube.

Public transport

Transport for London (TfL) **Travel Information Call Centres** provide information about the tube, buses and Docklands Light (DLR; below). You can find them in Camden Town Hall, opposite St Pancras station (9am-5pm Mon-Fri), and in the stations below. Travel information and timetables are provided by Transport for London (7222 1234, www.tfl.gov.uk/journeyplanner).

Euston mainline rail station
7.15am-9.15pm Mon-Fri; 7.15am-6.15pm Sat; 8.15am-6.15pm Sun.
Heathrow Terminals 1, 2 & 3 tube station *6.30am-10pm daily.*
Liverpool Street & Piccadilly Circus tube stations, Victoria rail station *7.15am-9.15pm Mon-Sat; 8.15am-8.15pm Sun.*

London Underground

Delays are common. Escalators are often out of action. Some line or other is usually closed for engineering at weekends. It's hot, smelly and crowded at rush hour (8-9.30am, 4-7pm Mon-Fri). Nevertheless, 'the tube' is still the quickest way to get around London.

Using the Underground

A flat cash **fare** of £4 per journey applies across zones 1-6 on the tube; you can save up to £2.50 per journey with a pre-pay Oyster card (below). Anyone without a valid ticket or Oyster card is subject to a £25 on-the-spot fine (£50 if not paid within 21 days).

To enter and exit the tube using an Oyster card, simply touch it to the yellow reader, which opens the gates. Make sure you also touch the card to the reader when you exit the tube, otherwise you will be charged a penalty when you next use the card to enter any station.

To enter using a paper ticket, place it in the slot with the black magnetic strip facing down, then pull it out of the top to open the gates. Exiting at your destination is done in much the same way, though if you have a single journey ticket, it will be retained by the gate as you leave.

The 11 tube lines, plus the London Overground and DLR, are colour-coded on the **tube map** on the back flap.

Oyster cards

Oyster, a pre-paid travel smart-card, is the cheapest way of getting around on buses, tubes and DLR. There is a £3 refundable deposit payable for the card. Any tube journey in zone 1 using Oyster pay-as-you-go costs £1.60. A single tube journey within zones 1-2 is £2.20 (peak) or £1.60 (off-peak); in zones 1-6 it is £3.80 (peak) or £2.20 (off-peak). You can charge up at tube stations, London Travel Information Call Centres (see above), some national rail stations and at newsagents. For more details visit www.tfl.gov.uk/oyster or call 0870 849 9999.

Travelcards

Using Oyster pay-as-you-go will always be 50p cheaper than the equivalent Day Travelcard. Opt for a Day Travelcard, though, if you're also using National Rail services: Oyster may not be accepted. **Peak Day Travelcards** can be used all day, Monday to Friday. They cost from £7.20 (zones 1-2). All tickets remain valid for journeys begun before 4.30am the next day. The **Off-Peak Day Travelcard** meets most visitors' needs, allowing you to travel from 9.30am Mon-Fri, all day Sat, Sun and public holidays. It costs from £5.60 for zones 1-2. Zones 1-2 cover everything we list except for some venues in the Neighbourhood London chapter.

If you plan to spend a few days charging around town, it might be worth buying a **3-Day Travelcard**. The peak version can be used all day Mon-Fri, until 4.30am of the day after expiry; for zones 1-2, it would cost £17.40.

Travelling with children

Under-5s, accompanied by an adult with a valid ticket, travel free on any tube, bus, tram, DLR or London Overground service. **Under-11s** travel free on buses and trams, but on the tube, DLR and London Overground only if they have a 5-10 Oyster photocard. Children aged between **11 and 15** travel free on buses and trams only with an Oyster photocard, with which they must touch in and touch out or incur a penalty fare; the photocard also gives them travel on the tube, DLR and London Overground for only £1 a day. Visitors to the city can apply in advance for a **photocard**: visit www.tfl.gov.uk/photocard for details. For more information on all this, see www.tfl.gov.uk/fares or call 0845 330 9876. Photocards are not required for adult rate 7-Day Travelcards, Bus Passes or for any adult rate Travelcard or Bus Pass charged on an Oyster card.

Underground timetable

Tube trains run daily 5am-12.30am (except Sunday, when they start around 7.30am and finish at about 10.30pm), depending on the line. The only exceptions are Christmas Day, when there is no service, and New Year's Eve, when there is usually some kind of service all night. Generally, you shouldn't have to wait more than 10mins for a train, and during peak times services run every 2-3mins. Other than New Year's Eve, the only all-night public transport is by night bus (p214).

Docklands Light Railway

DLR trains (7363 9700, www.tfl.gov.uk/dlr) run from Bank or Tower Gateway, which is close to Tower Hill tube (Circle and District lines). At Westferry DLR the line splits east and south via Island Gardens to Greenwich and Lewisham; a change at Poplar can take you north to Stratford. The easterly branch forks after Canning Town to either Beckton or Woolwich Arsenal, the latter via London City Airport. Trains run 5.30am-12.30am daily.

With very few exceptions, the adult single **fares** on the DLR are the same as for the tube (pp212-3).

National Rail & London Overground services

Independently run commuter services coordinated by **National Rail** (0845 748 4950, www.nationalrail.co.uk) leave from the city's main rail stations. Visitors to south London or more remote neighbourhood destinations will need to use these overground services. Travelcards are valid on these services within the right zones, but not all routes accept Oyster pay-as-you-go; check before you travel.

Operated by Transport for London (so it does accept Oyster), the **London Overground** rail line runs a loop through north London from Stratford to Richmond. Trains run about every 20mins (every 30mins Sun).

Buses

All buses are now low-floor and accessible to wheelchair-users and passengers with buggies. The only exceptions are Heritage routes 9 and 15, which are served by the world-famous open-platform Routemaster buses. You must have a ticket or valid pass before getting on a bus in central London: inspectors patrol and board buses at random; they can fine you £25. You can buy a **ticket** (or 1-Day Bus Pass) from pavement machines but, frustratingly, they're often out of order or out of change. Better to travel armed with an Oyster card or other pass (p213).

Using pay-as-you-go on Oyster, the single **fare** is £1 a trip and the most you will pay a day will be £3. Paying with cash at the time of travel costs £2 for a single trip. Under-16s travel for free (using an Oyster photocard; p213).

A 1-Day Bus Pass gives unlimited bus and tram travel for £3.50.

Many buses run 24 hours a day, seven days a week. There are also some special **night buses** with an 'N' prefix to the route number, which operate 11pm-6am. Most night services run every 15-30mins, but many busier routes have a bus around every 10mins (they all feel a lot less frequent after a heavy night).

Water transport

Most river services operate every 20-60mins from 10.30am to 5pm; visit www.tfl.gov.uk for details. **Thames Clippers** (www.thamesclippers.com), which runs a reliable commuter-boat service, boarded at Embankment, Blackfriars, Bankside, London Bridge and Tower Pier, offers a third off fares with a Travelcard or, from November 2009, a pre-paid Oyster card (p213).

Taxis

If the orange 'For Hire' sign on a black taxi is switched on, it can be hailed. If a taxi stops, the cabbie must take you to your destination, if it's within seven miles. It can be hard to find a free cab, especially just after the pubs close or when it rains. Rates are higher after 8pm on weekdays and all weekend. You can book black cabs from the 24hr **Taxi One-Number** (0871 871 8710; a £2 booking fee applies, plus 12.5% on credit cards), **Radio Taxis** (7272 0272) and **Dial-a-Cab** (7253 5000; credit cards only, £2 booking fee).

Minicabs (saloon cars) are generally cheaper than black cabs, but only use licensed firms (look for the yellow disc in the front and rear windows) and avoid those who tout for business. They will be unlicensed, uninsured and possibly dangerous.

There are, fortunately, lots of trustworthy and licensed local minicab firms, including **Lady Cabs** (7272 3300), which employs only women drivers, and **Addison Lee** (7387 8888). To locate a licensed minicab firm, text HOME to 60835 – Transport for London will send you the phone numbers of the three nearest. Always ask the price when you book and confirm it with the driver.

Driving

Congestion charge

Drivers coming into central London 7am-6pm Mon-Fri have to pay £8; for the restricted area, see www.cclondon. com or watch out for signs and roads painted with a white C in a red circle. Expect a fine of £50 (rising to £100 if you delay further) if you fail to pay. Passes can be bought at garages, newsagents and NCP car parks; the scheme is enforced by CCTV cameras. You can pay any time during the day of entry. Payments are also accepted until midnight on the next charging day, although it's £2 more. For more information, phone 0845 900 1234 or go to www.cclondon.com.

Parking

Parking on a single or double yellow line, a red line or in residents' parking areas during the day is illegal, and you may end up being fined, clamped or towed. However, in the evening (from 6pm or 7pm in much of central London) and at various times at weekends, parking on single yellow lines is legal and free; if you find a clear spot, look for a sign giving the regulations for that area. Meters are also free at certain times during evenings and weekends. Parking on double yellow lines and red routes is illegal at all times.

NCP 24-hour **car parks** (0870 606 7050, www.ncp.co.uk) are numerous but pricey (£3-£12 for two hours). Central ones include Arlington House, Arlington Street, St James's, W1; Snowsfields, Southwark, SE1; and 4-5 Denman Street, Soho, W1.

Vehicle removal

If your car was parked legally and it's gone, chances are it's been stolen; if not, it's probably in a car pound. A release fee of £200 is levied for removal, plus £40 per day from the first midnight after removal. You'll probably also get a parking ticket of £60-£100 when you collect the car (£30-£50 if paid within 14 days). To find out how to retrieve your car, call 7747 4747.

Vehicle hire

Easycar (www.easycar.com) offers competitive rates, for luridly branded cars. Also try **Alamo** (0870 400 4508, www.alamo.com), **Budget** (0844 581 9999, www.budget.co.uk) or **Hertz** (0870 599 6699, www.hertz.co.uk).

Cycling

London isn't the friendliest of towns for cyclists, but **London Cycle Network** (www.londoncyclenetwork.org.uk) and **London Cycling Campaign** (7234 9310, www.lcc.org.uk) help make it better. Call **Transport for London** (7222 1234) or see www.tfl.gov.uk/cycling for free maps and route advice.

Cycle hire

London Bicycle Tour Company
1A Gabriel's Wharf, 56 Upper Ground, South Bank, SE1 9PP (7928 6838/ www.londonbicycle.com). Southwark tube. **Open** 10am-6pm daily. **Hire** £3/hr. **Deposit** £180 cash, £1 credit card.
OY Bike *0845 226 5751/www.oybike. com.* **Open** 24hrs daily. **Hire** £2/hr. To rent a bike 24/7 from OY Bike's 40 pick-up points, pre-register with £10 credit, then call to release the lock. Trips of under 30mins are free.
Velorution *18 Great Titchfield Street, Fitzrovia, W1W 8BD (7637 4004/ www.velorution.biz). Oxford Circus tube.* **Open** 9am-7pm Mon-Fri; 10.30am-6.30pm Sat. **Hire** £15/day.

A WILD PLACE TO SHOP AND EAT®

Rainforest Cafe is a unique venue bringing to life the sights and sounds of the rainforest.

Come and try our fantastic menu!
Includes gluten free,
dairy free and organic options for kids.

15% DISCOUNT
off your final food bill*

Offer valid seven days a week. Maximum party size of 6.

020 7434 3111

20 Shaftesbury Avenue, Piccadilly Circus, London W1D 7EU
www.therainforestcafe.co.uk

*Please present to your safari guide when seated.
Cannot be used in conjunction with any other offer.

Resources A-Z

Accident & emergency

In the event of a serious accident, fire or other incident, call **999** – free from any phone, including payphones – and ask for an ambulance, the fire service or police; the number from most mobile phones is **112**. If there is no current danger, call non-emergency number **0300 123 1212** instead. Each of the listed hospitals has a 24hr Accident & Emergency department.

Chelsea & Westminster *369 Fulham Road, Chelsea, SW10 9NH (8746 8000). South Kensington tube.*
Royal London *Whitechapel Road, E1 1BB (7377 7000). Whitechapel tube.*
St Mary's *Praed Street, Paddington, W2 1NY (7886 6666). Paddington tube/rail.*
St Thomas's *Lambeth Palace Road, SE1 7EH (7188 7188). Westminster tube/Waterloo tube/rail.*
University College *235 Grafton Road, Bloomsbury, NW1 2BU (0845 155 5000). Euston Square or Warren Street tube.*

Credit card loss

American Express *01273 696933.*
Diners Club *01252 513500.*
MasterCard/Eurocard *0800 964767.*
Switch *0870 600 0459.*
Visa/Connect *0800 895082.*

Customs

For allowances, see www.hmrc.gov.uk.

Dental emergency

Dental care is free for under-18s, resident students and people on benefits,

but all other patients must pay (NHS-eligible patients at a subsidised rate).

Disabled

London is a difficult place for disabled visitors, although legislation is slowly improving access and general facilities. The bus fleet is now low-floor for easier wheelchair access, but the tube remains escalator-dependent. The *Tube Access Guide* booklet is free; call the Travel Information (7222 1234) for more details.

Most major attractions and hotels have good accessibility, though provisions for the hearing- or sight-disabled are patchier. Enquire about facilities in advance. *Access in London* is an invaluable reference book for disabled travellers, available from Access Project (www.accessproject-phsp.org). Artsline (21 Pine Court, Wood Lodge Gardens, Bromley, Kent BR1 2WA, 7388 2227, www.artsline.org.uk; 9.30am-5.30pm Mon-Fri) has handy information on disabled access to arts and cultural events.

Electricity

The UK uses 220-240V, 50-cycle AC voltage and three-pin plugs.

Embassies & consulates

American Embassy *24 Grosvenor Square, Mayfair, W1A 1AE (7499 9000/http://london.usembassy.gov). Bond Street or Marble Arch tube.* **Open** 8.30am-5.30pm Mon-Fri.
Australian High Commission *Australia House, Strand, Holborn, WC2B 4LA (7379 4334/www.uk. embassy.gov.au). Holborn or Temple tube.* **Open** 9am-5pm Mon-Fri.

Canadian High Commission
*38 Grosvenor Street, Mayfair, W1K
4AA (7258 6600/www.canada.org.uk).
Bond Street or Oxford Circus tube.*
Open 8am-4pm Mon-Fri.
Embassy of Ireland *17 Grosvenor
Place, Belgravia, SW1X 7HR (7235
2171/passports & visas 7225 7700/
www.inis.ie). Hyde Park Corner tube.*
Open 9.30am-1pm, 2.30-5pm Mon-Fri.
New Zealand High Commission
*New Zealand House, 80 Haymarket,
St James's, SW1Y 4TQ (7930 8422/
www.nzembassy.com). Piccadilly Circus
tube.* **Open** 9am-5pm Mon-Fri.
South African High Commission
*South Africa House, Trafalgar Square,
St James's, WC2N 5DP (7451 7299/
www.southafricahouse.com). Charing
Cross tube/rail.* **Open** 9.45am-12.45pm
(by appointment), 3-4pm (collections)
Mon-Fri.

Internet

Most hotels have broadband and/or
wireless access, but there are plenty of
cybercafés dotted around town.

Left luggage

Security precautions have meant bus
and rail stations have left-luggage
desks rather than lockers; call 0845 748
4950 for details.

Gatwick Airport *South Terminal
01293 502014/North Terminal
01293 502013.*
Heathrow Airport *Terminal 1
8745 5301/Terminals 2-3 8759 3344/
Terminal 4 8897 6874/Terminal 5
8283 5073.*
London City Airport *7646 0162.*
Stansted Airport *01279 663213.*

Opening hours

Banks 9am-4.30pm (some close at
3.30pm, some 5.30pm) Mon-Fri;
sometimes also Saturday mornings.
Businesses 9am-5pm Mon-Fri.

Post offices 9am-5.30pm Mon-Fri;
9am-noon Sat.
Pubs & bars 11am-11pm Mon-Sat;
noon-10.30pm Sun.
Shops 10am-6pm Mon-Sat; some to
8pm. Many are also open on Sunday,
usually 11am-5pm or noon-6pm.

Pharmacies

Branches of Boots (www.boots.com)
and larger supermarkets have a phar-
macy, and there are independents on
most high streets. Staff can advise on
over-the-counter medicines. Most phar-
macies open 9am-6pm Mon-Sat.

Police

Look up 'Police' in the phone book or
call 118 118, 118 500 or 118 888 if none
of these police stations are convenient.

Belgravia *202-206 Buckingham
Palace Road, Pimlico, SW1W 9SX
(7730 1212). Victoria tube/rail.*
Charing Cross *Agar Street, Covent
Garden, WC2N 4JP (7240 1212).
Charing Cross tube/rail.*
Chelsea *2 Lucan Place, SW3 3PB
(7589 1212). South Kensington tube.*
West End Central *27 Savile Row,
Mayfair, W1X 2DU (7437 1212).
Piccadilly Circus tube.*

Post

For general enquiries, call 0845 722
3344 or consult www.postoffice.co.uk.
Post offices are usually open 9am-6pm
Mon-Fri and 9am-noon Sat, although
the **Trafalgar Square Post Office**
(24-28 William IV Street, WC2N 4DL,
0845 722 3344) opens 8.30am-6.30pm
Mon-Fri and 9am-5.30pm Sat.

Smoking

Smoking is banned in all enclosed public spaces, including pubs, bars, clubs,
restaurants, hotel foyers, shops and
public transport.

ESSENTIALS

Telephones

London's dialling code is 020; standard landlines have eight digits after that. If you're calling from outside the UK, dial your international access code, then the UK code, 44, then the full London number, omitting the first 0 from the code (Australia 61, Canada 1, New Zealand 64, Republic of Ireland 353, South Africa 27, USA 1).

US cellphone users will need a tri- or quad-band handset.

Public payphones take coins and/or credit cards. International calling cards (bargain minutes via a freephone number) are widely available.

Tickets

It is well worth booking ahead – even obscure acts can sell out and the high-profile gigs and sporting events do so in seconds. It is usually cheaper to bypass ticket agents and go direct to the box office – the former will charge booking fees that could top 20 per cent. Should you have to use them, booking agencies include **Ticketmaster** (0870 534 4444, www.ticketmaster.co.uk), **Stargreen** (7734 8932, www.stargreen.com), **Ticketweb** (0870 060 0100, www.ticketweb.co.uk), **See Tickets** (0871 220 0260, www.seetickets.com) and **Keith Prowse** (0870 840 1111, www.keithprowse.com); **tkts** (p140) sells reduced West End theatre tickets on the day of performance.

Time

London is on Greenwich Mean Time (GMT), five hours ahead of the US's Eastern Standard time. In autumn (25 Oct 2009, 31 Oct 2010) the clocks go back an hour to GMT; they go forward to British Summer Time on 28 Mar 2010.

Tipping

Tip in taxis, minicabs, restaurants (some waiting staff rely heavily on tips), hotels, hairdressers and some bars (not pubs). Ten per cent is normal, with some restaurants adding as much as 15%. Always check whether service has been included in your bill: some restaurants include a service charge, but also leave space for a tip on your credit card slip.

Tourist information

The new City of London Information Centre, which opened in 2008 beside St Paul's, offers tours with specialist City-trained guides as well as information.

City of London Information Centre *St Paul's Churchyard, EC4M 8BX (7332 1456/www.cityoflondon. gov.uk). St Paul's tube.* **Open** 9.30am-5.30pm Mon-Sat; 10am-4pm Sun.
London Information Centre *Leicester Square, WC2H 7BP (7292 2333/www.londontown.com). Leicester Square tube.* **Open** 8am-6pm Mon-Fri; 10am-6pm Sat, Sun. *Helpline* 8am-midnight Mon-Fri; 9am-10pm Sat, Sun.
Southwark Tourist Information Centre *Tate Modern: Level 2, South Bank, SE1 9TG (7401 5266/www.visit southwark.com). Southwark or St Paul's tube.* **Open** 10am-6pm daily.

Visas

Citizens of the EU don't require a visa to visit the UK; for limited tourist visits, citizens of the USA, Canada, Australia, New Zealand and South Africa can also enter the UK with only a passport. But *always* check the current situation at www.ukvisas.gov.uk well before you travel.

What's on

Time Out remains London's only quality listings magazine. Widely available in central London every Tuesday, it gives listings for the coming week from Wednesday. For gay listings, also look out for freesheets *Boyz* and *QX*.

Index

Eating & Drinking

ESSENTIALS

ESSENTIALS